Praise for *Toxic Grit*

"As a working mom who's constantly juggling ambition and bedtime, *Toxic Grit* was the mirror I didn't know I needed. Amanda Goetz gives language—and permission—to the many characters I play every day. This book is a permission slip to stop chasing balance and start embracing the beautiful, messy multiverse of motherhood, career, identity, and self-worth. It's honest, actionable, and deeply validating."

—Emily Calandrelli, NASA Astronaut, Emmy-nominated TV host, #1 *New York Times* bestselling author

"Amanda is a force, and the world needs her wisdom. For anyone with big goals and even bigger responsibilities, *Toxic Grit* is a powerful reminder that losing yourself isn't a prerequisite for success. Amanda delivers a candid, compelling roadmap for ambitious women who want to lead with impact and stay rooted in who they are."

—Tressie Lieberman, global chief brand officer at Starbucks, former CMO at Yahoo

"This book powerfully describes the internalized pressure so many women feel to do it all, perfectly. Amanda Goetz gives voice to the ambition-fatigue epidemic and offers a powerful, practical framework for letting go of guilt and reclaiming space for yourself. This book is a must-read for anyone ready to stop surviving life and start enjoying it."

—Eve Rodsky, *New York Times* bestselling author of *Fair Play* and *Find Your Unicorn Space*

"Amanda breaks down the ambition archetypes and programs we've been handed with clear, relatable language, lived experience, and research, and offers a new way for modern women to rewrite what success means uniquely to them in the workplace to create more sustainable lives and careers."

—Neha Ruch, *USA Today* bestselling author of *The Power Pause*

"This book will be a game-changer for so many women. Amanda has written a raw, honest, and deeply actionable guide for those of us juggling motherhood, ambition, and relationships—often all at once. *Toxic Grit* is a must-read for anyone ready to challenge the hustle culture narrative and create a life that actually feels good, not just looks good. I felt seen in these pages—and I know so many others will too."

—Whitney Port, designer, author, TV personality, and host of *With Whit* podcast

"*Toxic Grit* challenges what it means to be ambitious in today's society. Instead of framing a new guide to hustle, Goetz shows you how to reexamine your priorities and goals so you can truly thrive—not just get by—in every aspect of your life."

—Jason Tartick, host of *Trading Secrets* podcast & *Wall Street Journal* bestselling author of *The Restart Roadmap*

"*Toxic Grit* is an original take on personal growth, brilliantly explored through the lens of character theory. The belief that all women have ten inner characters competing within themselves at all times is universally relatable. You might think you're operating from your inner CEO when in reality, your Soloist is running the show. Amanda's expertise, gleaned from years of coaching high performers shines through on every page, but what makes this book so compelling is that she never stops being a student herself. Her insights are sharp, curious, and often disarmingly relatable. Reading this feels like hiring Amanda as your personal coach: you'll walk away with frameworks and tools that make you a better partner, teammate, manager, and friend. "

—Amy Shoenthal, *USA Today* bestselling author of *The Setback Cycle*

TOXIC GRIT

How to have it all

TOXIC

and (actually) love

GRIT

what you have

AMANDA GOETZ

sourcebooks

Copyright © 2025 by Amanda Goetz
Cover and internal design © 2025 by Sourcebooks
Jacket design by Jillian Rahn and Ellis Jones/Sourcebooks
Cover images © bosotochka/Getty Images, Sonja Lekovic/Stocksy Images
Cover art and lettering by Ellis Jones/Sourcebooks
Internal art by Lindsey Cleworth

Sourcebooks and the colophon are registered trademarks of Sourcebooks.

All rights reserved. No part of this book may be reproduced in any form or by any electronic or mechanical means including information storage and retrieval systems—except in the case of brief quotations embodied in critical articles or reviews—without permission in writing from its publisher, Sourcebooks.

No part of this book may be used or reproduced in any manner for the purpose of training artificial intelligence technologies or systems.

This publication is designed to provide accurate and authoritative information in regard to the subject matter covered. It is sold with the understanding that the publisher is not engaged in rendering legal, accounting, or other professional service. If legal advice or other expert assistance is required, the services of a competent professional person should be sought.—*From a Declaration of Principles Jointly Adopted by a Committee of the American Bar Association and a Committee of Publishers and Associations*

References to internet websites (URLs) were accurate at the time of writing. Neither the author nor Sourcebooks is responsible for URLs that may have expired or changed since the manuscript was prepared.

Published by Sourcebooks
1935 Brookdale RD, Naperville, IL 60563-2773
(630) 961-3900
sourcebooks.com

Cataloging-in-Publication Data is on file with the Library of Congress.

Printed and bound in the United States of America.
VP 10 9 8 7 6 5 4 3 2 1

To Hadley and Lincoln,
I hope you make space for all your characters
and write your own script.
I love you both so much.

To Greyson,
You were my reason to keep going
when many of my characters were lost.
I hope you continue to support and lift up the women around you.
I love you.

And lastly, to all the ambitious women
still wanting it all but struggling to carry it...
This book is for you.

Contents

Introduction   xiii

Part 1: Character Theory   1

Chapter 1.......How We Got Here   3

Chapter 2......Meet Your Characters   29

Chapter 3......Toxic Characters   55

Chapter 4......Character Compatibility   81

Part 2: Honor the Imbalance   91

Chapter 5.......Imbalanced. I'm Balanced.   93

Chapter 6......The Big 3   125

Chapter 7.......A Bigger Role   157

Chapter 8......The Spin Cycle   185

Chapter 9.......Lost and Found   215

Part 3: Master the Multiverse   241

Chapter 10.....Welcome to the Multiverse   243

Chapter 11......Character Collision   269

Chapter 12.....Supporting Cast   287

Chapter 13......Going Off Script   309

Conclusion: Seven Steps to Master the Middle   335

A Letter to the Reader   *343*

Acknowledgments   *345*

Notes   *349*

About the Author   *350*

Introduction

Every night my son gets to pull out three to seven (but almost always seven) books from my shoe-closet-turned-children's-library. One of my favorite books is called *Quick as a Cricket* by Audrey Wood. The incredible illustrations take you through a series of juxtapositions. "I'm as sad as a basset. I'm as happy as a lark. I'm as nice as a bunny. I'm as mean as a shark." After continuing through a series of oppositional descriptors, the final page says, "Put it all together, and you've got me." It is a particular favorite of mine because of the beautiful metaphor it creates, showing how none of us are any one thing. Giving us room to be and feel all that we are. As children, we are taught to embrace the multitudes that exist within us.

And then we grow up.

As adults, there are books about how to make money. How to be a CEO. There are books about how to find love. There are a lot of books on how to navigate parenting. But as I entered the world of single parenting as an entrepreneur looking for love and success, nothing equipped me to navigate the trade-offs and the push and pull between all of my ambitions, all of my multitudes. I was as hard as a hammer but as soft as a pillow. I wanted to break glass ceilings and curl up like a golden retriever. Yet the words I studied in pursuit of solutions felt more like siloed fiction than anything rooted in the realism of my unanswered Slack messages, piles of laundry, and swiping on Hinge after my kids' bedtime.

The problem, simply stated, is balance. Balance means everything is weighted equally. Yet in my experience, every time I tried to do it all, I felt like I was failing at everything. This is toxic grit: a feeling that we are supposed to handle it all and smile through the pain and suffering. I used to wear the word "grit" like a Girl Scout badge of honor. I'm a first-generation college grad from a small farm town in the Midwest. I've always believed I need to push harder to catch up. I was a single mom for seven years while still building my career. I had to carry it all and drop nothing because there was no safety net. But when does it go too far? When do we realize our push to have it all, all at once, is actually depriving us of joy and contentment and success itself? Toxic grit is the unrelenting pursuit of goals or achievements to the point where we cause harm to and detract from our other goals and achievements. If you climb the ladder and have no one around to celebrate with, that's not success. I know several people in retirement who poured everything into their careers with the goal of enjoying their lives in

Introduction

retirement only to be met with global pandemics, health issues, and the inability to travel and see the world. I know others who pour everything into their children only to wake up eighteen years later and no longer have a connection to their partner or passions. Toxic grit isn't just about losing yourself to career and monetary success. It's a lens through which we look at all the characters we play in our lives and determine where effort, resilience, and commitment end and where exhaustion, deprivation, and a loss of enthusiasm for the role itself begin.

Life is meant to be lived and enjoyed, yet so many of us are struggling right now with the definition of ambition and how to honor the competing feelings and goals within us. This book is a culmination of all the things I've learned along the way of building and selling companies, enjoying motherhood, building community, finding love, and enjoying it all along the way.

"Main character energy" is something we've all likely seen on social media. Having main character energy refers to a sense of confidence a person displays as they command attention and become the protagonist of their own story. But our internal movie doesn't have just one main character. I've coached and managed hundreds of women throughout my career, and writing this book helped illuminate the ten roles we all play; ten different characters fighting for the spotlight, each possessing their own values, goals, and plotlines. The pages in this book are meant to be a practical and actionable guide for navigating the various and competing plotlines in the movie of your life.

The first part of this book will help you meet the characters inside of you and give you the tools and frameworks to assess which ones have been taking over the spotlight and which ones have been left off the script. You will become an expert in toxic grit identification—knowing when a character's desire for more is coming at the expense of the others in the movie.

Once you understand each of your characters and their goals, we will use the second part of this book to write a new script for the movie of your life. As you write your new script, this book will equip you with the tools to transition between characters and ensure no one is dominating the spotlight for too long. When you sit in the director's seat of the movie of your life, you call the shots. You set the characters and the plotline and decide when it's time for a scene change.

Once we've met each of your characters and set the plot for the movie of your life, it's time to enter the multiverse. This is the whack-a-mole reality of life as a multihyphenate (someone juggling success in multiple areas of their life). When you attempt to focus on one goal and character at a time, chances are another character wants to pop up and distract you. Your boss texting you while you are on a date. Your friends blowing up your phone while you are at work. Your to-do list writing itself in your head while you are attempting to decompress on the couch. Character collision is a gateway drug to toxic grit. "Everyone needs me so I will overextend to be everything to everyone, all the time." We will study character collision more closely and give you permission to set boundaries

Introduction

on your time and energy and leave the third section of the book equipped to handle all life throws at you.

Ultimately, I want this book to create a new vision for life that is full of **and**. To be bold **and** soft. To be powerful **and** supported. To experience success **and** enjoyment. This book is like Marie Kondo for your *life*. Let's focus on the things that give our characters joy and move each of their plotlines forward, and embrace the beauty of imbalance, while we rid ourselves of the toxic grit/hustle culture narratives our generation has been handed.

Part 1

Character Theory

Chapter 1

How We Got Here

We are all told we have a role to play. Which role exactly? Well, that's kind of like doing your taxes in America. No one is going to tell you what's correct, but if you pick wrong, you'll certainly hear about it. So, we all pick a role and adjust our identity around it so society can place us neatly in a box of stereotypes. Many of us were exposed quite early to society's obsession with binary constructs and the difficulty in accepting an **AND** not **OR** in someone's personality. It reminds me of shopping for a Barbie for my daughters. Do you want to be an astronaut or a mom? Pick one. Vet or gymnast? Pick one.

Growing up in a small farm town in central Illinois, I felt a need to pick a singular, palatable identity for myself so people could quickly categorize me as if they were trying to add me to a Pinterest board. Even at a young age, I began to feel the tension of these binary constructs and slowly began to understand the diversity of characters within me, each with complex goals and desires. In high school, I was an all-state three-point shooter (basketball player), straight-A student, and class president, so naturally, that made me a "good girl" and an "athlete."

Sometimes I wanted to focus entirely on my basketball career or entirely on my academics. But other times I wanted to be with my boyfriend, forgetting all responsibility. Sometimes I wanted to forget it all and finally go to one of those drinking parties. And sometimes I wanted no one around, left alone to stare at the vast Illinois sky, daydreaming of my future that didn't include basketball...or always being the good girl...or even that boyfriend. I worried people would not understand the complexity or nuance of the diversity inside me, so I stuck to single-scoop identities that felt more appetizing, relatable, and categorical. I was stuck leading with the same good-girl character, afraid of what would happen if I presented myself any other way.

Going to college was the first identity shift...er, crisis? I no longer had sports to define me and started to get a glimpse of the freedom others allowed themselves to play with. But, instead, I created my next box to live inside and focused on being the "high achiever": a straight-A student with four jobs (I was paying for college myself). Phew. I had my script to follow. Study. Don't black out. Have a boyfriend. Be stable. Be responsible.

Oh wait... Graduation is coming... What persona do I need to adopt now? Wife. I'm nineteen and in the Midwest. That feels right. I'll get my degree in business with an MRS degree on top of it. I got engaged at nineteen—after just three months of dating—and married at twenty-one, thankful to have clearly defined roles and hierarchy laid out for my postgraduation era. Wife first. Career second.

I continued this clean, paint-by-numbers lifestyle throughout my twenties. Working at Big Four accounting firm Ernst & Young, writing tax white papers in Chicago and then New York. I climbed the ladder and colored inside the lines. Society sat on the sidelines and golf-clapped my way through life.

Fast-forward to thirty-two. All my boxes were shifting beneath me and breaking wide open. I was a mom of three going through a divorce at the height of my career, a time when society would like me to step inside the box of either "girlboss" or "stay-at-home mom" or even "single mom," pity faces sold separately. Oh, let's also throw in that I realized I was bisexual after my divorce, which came with a concoction of feelings that felt impossible to untangle amid everything else that was happening. **I was struggling to find what version of me was societally approved.** Professionally, I was the youngest VP of marketing, leading a team of fifty. Personally, I was exploring new boxes and characters within me, finding a freedom in life like I never had before. For the first time, I was able to explore roles that were just for me, not my work or family or society.

But now all those identities were in a WWE *Raw Is War* match deep within my soul. My newfound freedoms, family dynamics, growing career, ever-present mom guilt, and a new world of work responsibilities and sexual desires were all unfurling simultaneously. My burnout and overwhelm were coming from multiple characters trying to exist in one singular human. No Barbie purchase had prepared me for this.

They say we don't know who discovered water, but it probably wasn't a fish. When you are in something for so long, it just is. It took years of therapy, coaching, and then creating my own frameworks to help me see the tangled mess of toxic grit I was existing within. It took years to learn to navigate the push and pull between these entirely different characters within me and when one or more of them were crossing the threshold from ambitious to toxic.

Before we move forward to the core thesis of this book, the framework I created to solve this internal tug-of-war of characters within us, let's take a moment to zoom back out—so we can look at how we got here.

Our Parents' Software

In the 1950s and '60s (when most of our parents' generation was getting married), marriage and careers tended to mirror the lower levels of Maslow's hierarchy of needs. People were marrying and working for pragmatic reasons: for financial safety, to buy houses and other things at the bottom of the hierarchy. Yes, they wanted to love their partner and job, but conversations were mostly centered around stability first, emotions second.

SELF-ACTUALIZATION
Desire to accomplish everything that one can, to become the most that one can be

ESTEEM NEEDS
Self-confidence and independence, respect and acknowledgement from others

LOVE AND BELONGING
Friendships, family, social groups, community, intimacy

SAFETY NEEDS
Protection, stability and well-being, health and financial security

PHYSIOLOGICAL NEEDS
Food, water, breathing, homeostasis, sexual reproduction

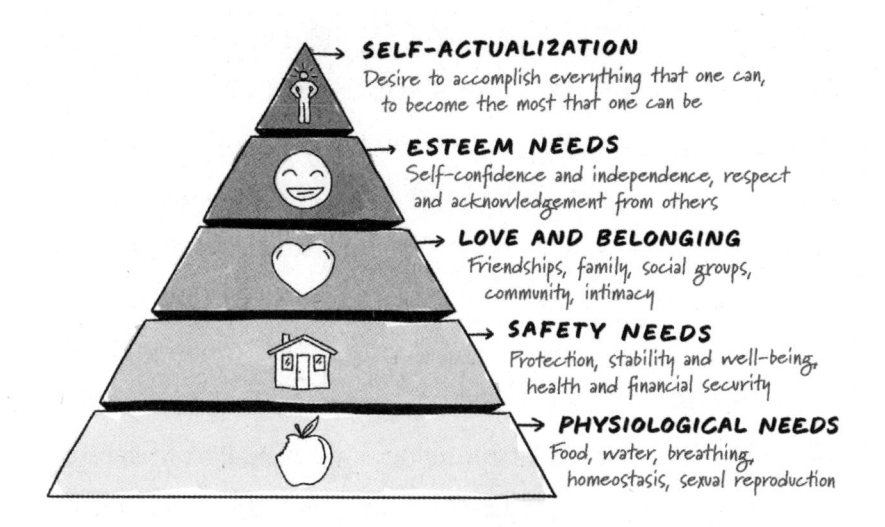

Maslow's Hierarchy of Needs

As someone who got married at twenty-one and divorced at thirty-two, I've spent a lot of time studying social psychology and understanding the evolution of marriage. In the book *The All-or-Nothing Marriage*, Eli Finkel describes America as having witnessed three major eras of marriage: pragmatic, love-based, and self-expressive (mirroring the moving up of Maslow's hierarchy of needs). The twentieth century made it possible for relationships, jobs, familial setup, and lifestyle to be a reflection of the person's journey of self-expression and self-actualization. But our parents likely didn't have the same circumstances. So our internal software was programmed by past generations with different needs, futures, and goals for their lives. We were programmed by the past, not for the future.

Some of us were raised in homes where traditional gender

roles were played. Mom took care of the kids and the house while Dad worked and provided for the family. That was my setup. So I worked hard to course correct and build my own career and independence, almost allergic to the idea of centering my entire life around my home and family. Fast-forward almost forty years, and I open up my phone today to see a tradwives movement on TikTok and Instagram with an undertone that career ambition is anti-feminine. Girlboss is out. Lazy girl era is in. We are now inundated with videos of moms making bread from scratch, Pinterest-perfect birthday parties, and matching kids' outfits with zero stains or wrinkles. It feels like those "traditional" gender norms are knocking on our door with a fresh apple pie. This book isn't about right or wrong. I'm not giving any prescriptions in these pages. This book is about the constant state of guilt and toxicity we find ourselves in as we try to navigate all the roles society wants us to play and the binary DNA baked into them (pie pun intended). If Maslow and gender norms created our parents' generation's software, let's continue exploring how *our* software was created.

The Binary BS

I'm writing this book because the war of competing internal characters and baked-in toxic grit and guilt is a topic of conversation I find myself in over and over among my circles of ambitious women. If you are reading this book, you may have found yourself struggling to navigate what I'm just going to go ahead and call the *post*-girlboss era. Not to throw shade at the era itself but to place a timeline in our minds: starting around 2014, when girlboss saw its first hashtag on Instagram. Whether you believe the girlboss era was good or bad is not the point. The reality is that this decade-plus of intense magnification of women in business, building companies and start-ups and side hustles, shaped us at some level, either consciously or subconsciously. For me personally, it was an era that showed me what was *possible*. It was the yellow brick road for me to follow and launch my second start-up, House of Wise, a luxury wellness business to empower women to take control of their sleep, sex, stress, and strength through originally formulated CBD products. With girlboss as my guide, I raised millions of dollars from venture capitalists, NBA players, and celebs while I built in public on social media. I followed society's paint-by-numbers yet again. Are you ambitious? Be a girlboss. Build a company.

Four years later, I found myself selling my company in a premature exit, personally burned to a crisp. I was ready to swing the pendulum as far away from girlboss as possible. In my eyes, I had failed all the women looking to me to succeed while juggling three kids, which brought immense feelings of guilt and shame…so I retreated from everyone.

That's the power of societal movements. If you are swimming with the stream, you feel empowered and on your way to your destination. Swimming against it? You feel like you are going to drown.

That's the power of societal movements. If you are swimming with the stream, you feel empowered and on your way to your destination. Swimming against it? You feel like you are going to drown.

Perhaps you've decided you no longer wish to win "at all costs" or "play the game" and, in fact, desire to live a life of softness and balance. But what the fuck does that actually mean? Does it mean giving up your career? Does it mean pouring everything into family or friends or travel? This book will help you better understand the difference between denouncing one part of yourself and, instead, giving other parts permission to take up space.

How We Got Here

Our *girlboss* programming was coded to break glass ceilings, have it all, be independent, build an empire, lean in...you get the picture. This is where the binary BS starts to truly reveal itself.

- *If I'm not leaning in, am I leaning out?*
- *If I'm not independent, am I dependent?*
- *If I'm not climbing, am I retreating?*

And here is where they left us. Smack in the middle of a girlboss-lazy girl Venn diagram.

I AM HERE.

Girlboss — Lazy Girl

We have been programmed with competing goals and values of two very different generations of women. No one is teaching us how to navigate a life of ANDs not ORs where we push and pull, ebb and flow. No one is teaching us what to do with all the guilt for stepping outside our societally appointed box and exploring the not-so-neatly-defined middle.

> **Sri Varre**
> @sri_varre
> We need something in between being a girlboss and a lazy girl. When someone comes up with it, please let @alexis__stovall and I know

Last Stop: Guilt Central Station

The definition of "guilt" in the *Oxford English Dictionary* states: *verb: make (someone) feel guilty, especially in order to induce them to do something.* Let's underline that last part: *to induce them to do something.* So when big movements come along telling us to be one thing, they have a natural tendency to conjure a feeling within us of guilt in order to get us to abide by them. Think about every major beauty and fashion trend and how marketers get you to succumb to them. As a marketer, I have studied all of these tricks. Humans have a herd mentality, so brands surround you with the influencers, content, and products to follow the trend and follow the herd.

> Clean girl is in. The no-makeup makeup look is everywhere.
> Now be a mob wife. The more lipstick and hairspray, the better.
> Now '90s baggy jeans and hippie, beachy vibes.
> Now it's Alix Earle Miami vibes. Grab your bodycon dress.
> Scratch that. It's all about being polished. Be Sofia Richie.

We listen. We buy. We follow. The same is happening for the roles we play in our lives. If we aren't girlbossing, we feel guilty. Why? Because we feel we are letting someone down, just like I did when I sold my company in an early exit. We feel responsible for forging the paths to make it easier for those behind us. We need to be doing our part to lift up the women around us. But then, on the flip side, if we aren't in our soft or lazy girl era, we also feel guilty. We are seen as too aggressive or hustling too hard. Setting unrealistic standards and expectations for women as we try to have it all, do it all. Not accessing our "natural feminine" energy…whatever that means.

It's so fucking exhausting. Our life is not meant to be a string of societal trends. Do I believe guilt is the originating motivator behind any of these movements? No. I do not. I've watched how the media tore down a series of women who forged the paths before me. Radical shifts are how progress is made. We purposely have to swing the pendulum far in one direction to wind up somewhere in the middle. The eras (and women) before us gave us the ability to create a new approach to life today. But now is the time for the pendulum to stop swinging so far in these dichotomous directions. I'm a girlboss AND a lazy girl.

"Balance" is a tricky word for me. I don't believe in it on a micro level. The reality for me is that the days I kill it at work are the days I phone it in as a friend, partner, or mom. And the days I kill it as a mom, I find my inbox goes unanswered, work piles up, or my partner is wondering when we are going to be intimate. I've been interviewed on hundreds of podcasts, and inevitably I'm asked, "How do you achieve work-life balance as a single mom of three building and selling companies?" And I, being the media-trained executive that I am, give the political answer: I focus on the task at hand and have ruthless prioritization of my time and energy.

But it's just you and me right now, and I want to write this book from a place of pure transparency. Balance is not something you will ever achieve at the **micro** level, at a singular moment or day. Balance is a **macro** goal over a longer time horizon. In fact, the core theme of this book, and antidote to toxic grit, is **intentional imbalance**. In part 2 of this book, I will teach you to honor the imbalance in your life and give you the tools to create intentionality around the trade-offs we make in the days and weeks and months of our lives.

Balance happens in the macro, not the micro.

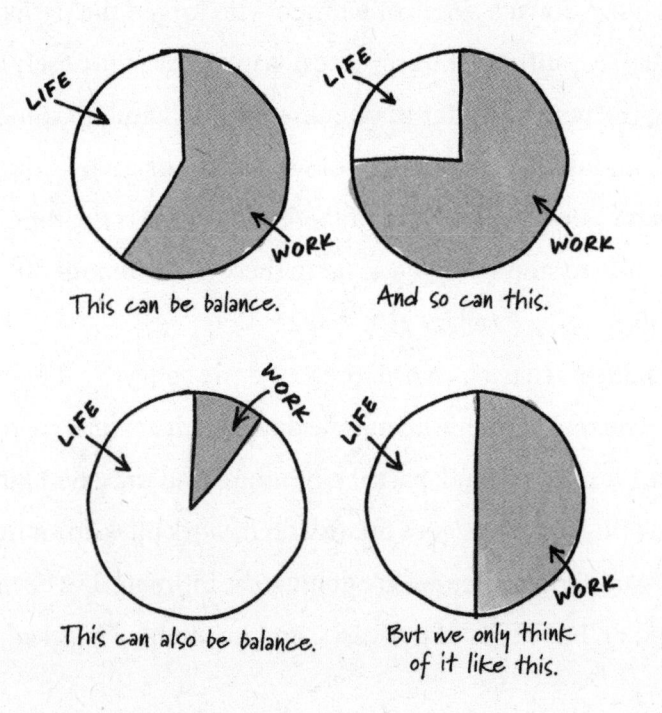

This can be balance.

And so can this.

This can also be balance.

But we only think of it like this.

My desk has a row of books on it as inspiration for my social content. As I sit at my desk surrounded by other authors, I notice many of the books tell me **what to be** but not **how** to achieve it, so I wanted to create the most practical guide for women on how to build a life of ambition without toxic grit and burnout. To ebb and flow between your boxes. **To not break the cycle of ambition but to redefine ambition altogether.** We will install new software updates to the way you think about success across your personal and professional lives and give you the tools and strategies to get back on track, rediscover your energy and passion, and start building toward your goals—for each character in your life.

Rather than creating yet another new buzzword for women, I'd like to take a different approach to help you navigate the ebbs and flows of your life that are inevitable. For some of you reading this, part of you may want to take on the world while another wants to imitate a house cat and curl up, unbothered, in the warm light of the sun. I'm here to tell you that's totally OK. Those are just two of the characters within you. Soon we will meet the other eight.

The Origin of Character Theory

Rewind to November 2017. It's a typical day in my NYC life leading the brand marketing team at The Knot and juggling three kids under the age of four. I wake up at the crack of dawn and get dressed in my couldn't-afford-it-if-my-life-depended-on-it Rent the Runway dress. Shower? LOL. Good one. Once a week, I ask my babysitter to come early so I can get a Drybar blowout on the way to work so I don't have to wash or dry my hair for the rest of the week.

After dropping my oldest child at her Upper West Side preschool (the other two stay home with my sitter), I sprint to the subway, gulping my ordered-ahead venti iced latte. I arrive at my office in the financial district, where I spend the day bouncing between the tiny closet-turned-lactation-room to meetings with engineers, product managers, and the marketing and editorial teams. I make sure we're moving the roadmap forward while also simultaneously collecting the only source of nourishment for my chubby ginger baby waiting for me at home. I finish pumping and go straight into a meeting with our lead male designer, laughing to myself that I was sitting tits out just a few seconds prior and now have to talk seriously about user journey maps.

I leave work at 5:00 p.m. to ensure I make it home for bedtime routine. My husband is, once again, on a business trip, so it's on me to keep the three tiny humans alive, clean, fed, and put to sleep. It is now 6:00 p.m. Sitter gone. Alone with a four-year-old, two-year-old, and five-month-old baby. I glance at the clock and realize I've got forty-five minutes before my home turns into a messy Bravo reality TV reunion where all humans involved are screaming, crying, or both (myself included).

Bathtime has begun. My brain is flooding with a list of to-dos from work, groceries that I need to order, and wondering when I'm going to drop off my Rent the Runway dresses, and then I'm snapped back to the present moment as my toddler starts shaking their naked butt at me. I laugh because that's exactly what my toddler expects me to do, but I can't help but wonder when we move from butt-shaking pride to sarongs and shame. A new thought starts to enter my brain: *Will I ever be that happy naked again?* The bathroom starts to fill with splashes of water, and it's time to get the kids out of the tub and ready for bed. Little did I know growing up in a farm town where the activity at the 4-H fair was attempting to catch greased baby pigs would prepare me for this stage of mom life. After jammies, I wipe the sweat from the cleavage of my nursing bra and find myself snuggled on a beanbag reading *Goodnight Moon* to the six eyes beside me.

I put the two larger and more mobile babies in their cribs, sound machine on, lights off, and venture to my bedroom to rock and nurse the baby to sleep. By now, I'm delirious. I can hear the older ones crying, which sends a feeling of pure adrenaline into my body, yet I must sit and rock and nurse. Thirty minutes later, it's finally quiet. I debate putting the sleeping baby in the crib, but he's giving an almost weighted blanket level of tranquility to my soul, so I remain there and open the notes app on my phone.

You.

Can.

Have.

It.

All.

I type the five words in staccato sentences as if I'm starting a prolific haiku. I stare at the words, wondering where the friction is coming from.

You.

Which *you*? The high achiever inside of me doesn't want to give up her career and leave every meeting ten minutes early to go stick her boob in a plastic funnel to be milked. She's killing it, finally feeling confident in her skills and abilities to make an impact on the organization. The passionate lover of sex and party girl inside of me has many other things she'd rather be doing with her boob. But the mother inside me just wants to sit and rock the baby all night and forget every corporate and social responsibility given to her.

"You" feels like too many people for three little letters.

Who can have it all?

Which version?

For once I could clearly see the various characters I was playing throughout my day and realized the more I tried to merge them into a singular human, the more chaos and guilt I felt inside.

The more I tried to merge them into a singular human, the more chaos and guilt I felt inside.

Alignment felt like a fool's errand. Each character has its own needs and goals. "Have it all" would be a great, synonymous tagline for toxic grit because each of our characters wants something different, and it's impossible to have all of it all at once. There are different things that drive them and light them up. Different things that make them feel fulfilled. So I stopped trying to fit them into one neat human and started to extract them into singular characters in the movie of my life. Honoring them and their individuality. Finally, it started to click.

I think we can all agree on this: Success is no longer one-dimensional. We all have multiple characters inside of us at any given time, each with their own definition of success, and we have to allow the space for each to exist and thrive. Having all the money in the world won't equate to strong relationships and longevity. Raising amazing kids won't guarantee a lasting marriage. Having the busiest social life doesn't mean you will feel supported and connected. Sticking to a strict wellness routine won't guarantee partnership or financial success.

After more than a two-decade career and working with hundreds of people, I have identified ten common characters within all of us. In this book, we will use my version of character theory to explain the relationship between these ten characters. We will learn to identify the characters, prioritize certain characters in a defined period of time, set their goals, transition between them, and assess when a character has been in the spotlight for too long.

Character theory will help us navigate the push-and-pull cycles between our various characters and achieve the life we want without burning out. Before we dive into character theory and how it works, it's important to outline the five laws of character theory.

The Five Laws of Character Theory

Law #1: You write the script.
Taking ownership of your characters and their success is the first law of character theory. The quicker you realize you are the writer of the script, the faster you will help each character get what they want.

Law #2: Characters vary by person.
There are ten characters we all have within us. But which characters you choose to prioritize will be different from what your friends, family, and society choose. And that's OK. We are not subscribing to the trends of the moment but rather learning which character is leading for a season and then communicating it to the people in your life so they can play a supporting role. This book is not a directive on becoming a parent, although we will touch on your caregiver character. This book is not a directive on making your career the most important thing, although we will talk about how to set up that character for success if that is the case for you. This book is about variance and allowing the movie of your life to evolve and shift based on your selected character's goals and needs.

Law #3: Characters vary by season.
The prominence of certain characters will change throughout different seasons of your life. We will walk through an evaluation and transition process for when and how to bring new characters forward and send others back.

Law #4: Characters evolve.
The goal of life is character development. How boring would it be to watch a character in a movie make the same mistakes over and over again, never learning, never growing? Growth is the goal. Your characters can and should evolve. Their goals, values, and needs will change over time. Character theory will give you the tools to stay curious, aware, and pushing for these evolutions.

Law #5: Not all characters are created equal.
Some people give space to five or six main characters in their lives while others may have two or three characters remain as the leads. Character theory will help you define a leading cast of prominent characters and will make sure your supporting characters still get their needs met without taking over or derailing the plot.

Character Theory 101

Historically, character theory has been used to classify the relationship between characters in a narrative. One commonly studied character theory is Propp's character theory. Named after folklorist researcher Vladimir Propp, Propp's character theory argues that all stories are character-driven and plots develop from the decisions and actions of characters and how they function in a story. After studying one hundred fairy tales in tremendous detail, he claimed characters could be classified into seven certain roles that progress a story: the villain, the donor, the helper, the princess, the false hero, the dispatcher, and the hero. I'm not sure what a false hero is, unless he studied my dating history.

Let's look a bit more closely at **Vladimir Propp's seven archetypal character roles** commonly found in folktales:

1. **The Hero**: The central character who embarks on a quest or journey, facing challenges and adversaries along the way.
2. **The Villain**: The antagonist who opposes the hero, creating conflict and obstacles for them to overcome.
3. **The Donor**: A character who provides the hero with magical objects, knowledge, or assistance to aid them in their quest.
4. **The Helper**: A supportive character who aids the hero on their journey, offering guidance, advice, or physical assistance.
5. **The Princess (or Seeker)**: The character who is sought after or rescued by the hero, often serving as a reward or motivation for their quest.
6. **The False Hero**: A deceptive character who initially appears to be a hero but ultimately reveals their true villainous nature. Oh yes, he definitely studied my dating history.
7. **The Dispatcher**: A character who sends the hero on their quest, often providing the initial impetus or reason for their journey.

Unlike Propp's theory, this book is about the *internal* characters inside of us and is based on hundreds of not-so-fairy-tale hours of coaching sessions I've done with women at various stages of their careers.

Character theory is also rooted in the present moment rather than some utopian future where we all have amazing and empathetic bosses and partners and ample time for fun and hobbies and health. This book is written to be practical and actionable. Over my lengthy career in tech and e-commerce, I've attended and spoken at a lot of women's events. Something that always struck me as equal parts comforting and frustrating: A large part of the conversation was outlining all the headwinds we faced, commiserating over the cards stacked against us. And unlike Vladimir Propp's fairy tales, I can assure you we don't have a white knight hero on a horse waiting to rescue us from our towers filled with two weeks of laundry and eighty-five unread Slack notifications. Yes, women are pulled in a lot of directions, but I needed a framework to help me navigate my life *now*—not some utopic future state that I can't bank on existing anytime soon. My version of character theory is designed to put you in the pilot seat of your life to navigate the inevitably turbulent skies. The mindset transition from one of despair and frustration to one of agency and control was something that likely saved my life. And I promise you I don't say that lightly or with hyperbole. Juggling a thriving career, social life, being a caregiver, and figuring out what I wanted for my marriage were too many balls for one person to handle. So, I needed to rethink how I was doing the juggling.

I've created ten character archetypes we are all pulled between. Whether you are still in college, starting your career, choosing a partner, deciding whether to add pets or babies to your life, or amid a big life transition, these ten characters encapsulate the push and pull within all of us. For each character, I've provided some prompts to help you get to know this character within you. Grab a journal and a coffee. Let's explore your characters.

A quick note: Not everyone will connect with each of the ten as they read through the descriptions. Characters will come in and out of your life at various seasons, and we will explore these transitional moments in later chapters. Remember, this is about the movie of your life, and, like all movies, you don't see every single character in every single scene. Sometimes a character's storyline needs more camera time to develop the plot and further that character's development while others are off chilling in their trailers, waiting for their next scene.

Before you meet the ten character archetypes, please remember:

Adjectives sold separately.
Characters should be met and analyzed based on their goal and what drives them. *How* they show up in your life and the emotions or adjectives you choose to describe them are completely up to you. We do not assign positive or negative emotions to the character itself but rather to how that character is showing up in your life. There is a part of you that's ambitious. A part of you that's less so. A part of you that craves solitude. Another part that craves

companionship. Those are facts. How you prioritize those characters and assess their roles in your life is up to you and may stir up feelings. Toxic grit comes to light when we start assigning shame and guilt—or even disgust—to characters.

Seasons change, and so do characters.
You may be in a season where some of these characters have not been written into your script or they have taken a supporting role for this season. The importance or impact of a character in your life will evolve. You will also experience things in life that change how you feel toward a character. This book will give you the tools and frameworks to analyze those feelings and identify those shifts.

Pause and notice the subconscious.
Our subconscious can subtly influence how much we prioritize certain characters. This is what I referred to earlier as your programming. As you read through the following characters, take notice of how you feel about them as part of your life. If you were dropped on this earth today without any childhood, cultural or media imprinting, or adult experiences, do you think you would still feel the way you do about the character? Pausing and noticing is the first step. Getting curious is the second.

This book will be your guide to creating a life of intentional imbalance. We will give you the tools to navigate the transitions and goals for each of your separate and, oftentimes, contradictory characters.

Guilt will no longer be an everyday accessory given to us by society.

Each chapter of this book is designed for introspection and reflection. I will provide journal prompts to get you thinking more deeply about your characters and the themes in each chapter.

As you begin this journey, here are a few programming questions to sit with:

→ *How were success and work modeled to you as a child?*
→ *How were relationships modeled to you as a child?*
→ *How were rest and fun modeled to you as a child?*
→ *How was love shown to you as a child?*

A Bit about Me and My Characters

A mantra I've picked up for myself over time is "I'll go first." I was in the first generation of my family to go to college. At twenty-one years old, I was the first of my friends to get married. I was the first of my friends to leave the Midwest when I moved to NYC at age twenty-three. I was the first of my friends to go through fertility struggles and treatment. First to have a miscarriage. First to start having children. First to make a million dollars. First to file for divorce. First to lose money in a divorce and have to start over. First to start a company. First of my friends to explore my sexuality outside of a heteronormative relationship. First to hit the reset button on my entire life. For me, personally, I have often found myself in a position of forging something new for myself that doesn't match what I see around me.

Because of this, I've found the easiest way to connect with others is through stories, and my life (especially the last decade) certainly has some growth-focused stories to share. I will share stories and walk you through a process of goal setting, transitioning, and evaluating which character gets the main stage at various points in your life. These stories are solely meant to underline and contextualize a lesson, but I recognize some of you are still evaluating which characters will be written into your story, and I fully support that. Character theory allows you to have the tools and frameworks to navigate any character you choose to give the main stage.

I am using my life examples because I hope you relate to them, but you may or may not. Luckily, you don't need to pick up my path or relate to my life verbatim to find your perfect character balance. As you read on, I want you to always remember that you (and you alone) are writing your script. Please use my script and my path as inspiration—not direction.

A Bit about You and Your Characters

This book is not about me; it's about **you**. It's designed to be like a stop at Home Depot to pick up the tools you need to navigate all life is throwing at you and return the toxic grit and guilt we've been handed. So grab what you need, and leave what you don't.

No matter where you are in life, this book is written to help you define what success means to you in this season with the understanding that it will grow and change. You will learn to create a life that works for you. Not what you think others want for you or what the latest societal buzzword tells you.

Ready to meet your ten characters? *Let's do this.*

Chapter 2

Meet Your Characters

All ten of these characters should feel familiar to you, albeit in varying degrees, given we all have more dominant roles and less dominant roles in accordance with our personalities and desires and goals for the current season of life. We'll explore each character more in-depth in the coming chapters, but for now, let's make some introductions!

The Ten Character Archetypes of Character Theory

Character #1: The CEO

Focused on impact, power, and **accomplishment**, this character loves setting and achieving career goals. Not everyone wants to be in the C-suite or be a literal boss, but this character is focused on success, power, and moving their career or aspirations forward.

This character also cares about money and financial security. They are checking your bank account and focusing on saving over spending. For high performers, our inner CEO tends to be the loudest character with a large role in the movie of our lives.

Here are some questions to ask yourself to get to know your inner **CEO** better:

- → *What drives you?*
- → *How do you envision success in your career?*
- → *How was work modeled for you as a child?*
- → *If your life were a movie, how much would the audience see this character?*
- → *What does your inner CEO need right now to feel like she's growing?*

Character #2: The Partner

This character is strong enough to do it alone but soft enough to not want to. The Partner character is focused on being surrounded with companionship and partnership. They value meaningful and deep relationships—not surface-level interactions. Your inner Partner navigates life's journey with a focus on shared experiences. This character values meaningful connection and derives their identity from those who contribute to the happiness and stability in their life. The Partner character is on a mission to find people she can be at peace around. To be fully accepted and loved as is. Dating, break-ups, situationships, committed relationships, and close friendships will all be a mirror for the Partner to look into to grow and evolve.

Some questions to get to know your inner **Partner** better:
- → *What does companionship mean to you?*
- → *How did your childhood and family dynamics influence your current views on love, companionship, and the importance of partnership?*
- → *What do you value in a close relationship?*
- → *How much of your time do you dedicate to this character?*
- → *Is it difficult for you to soften in a relationship? Why or why not?*
- → *If you were to grab coffee with your inner Partner, what do you think she would say she needs right now?*

Character #3: The Soloist

This character craves solitude and *personal* growth. They're independent and have their routines down—not wanting anything or anyone to rock them. This character tends to come in and out of seasons at various magnitudes, meaning they may require a lot of alone time in some episodes and very little in others. This character is focused on being self-reliant and values personal space and the freedom to navigate life on their terms. Understanding the significance of independence will guide you in creating a life that honors this character's need for space, self-discovery, and growth. The Soloist can be a gatekeeper to some of the other, harder-to-access characters.

Your Soloist character is one that can be misunderstood or shamed often. Let's get a deeper understanding of your inner **Soloist**:

→ *How does alone time contribute to your well-being, and in what ways do established routines empower you?*

→ *How did your childhood environment contribute to your preference or dislike for solitude and independence?*

→ *What experiences or seasons in life dictate how much time you can dedicate to the needs of this character?*

→ *What does your inner Soloist need right now?*

Character #4: The Caregiver

The Caregiver does a lot of mental gymnastics, ensuring everyone around them is OK. This character is the consummate nurturer and has a deep desire to feel useful and needed by others. Whether you are a human mom, puppy or cat mom, daughter, sister, partner, or friend, the Caregiver is focused on what they need to do to take care of those around them. Note there is some overlap between the Caregiver and the Partner (of course you care about your Partner), but the distinction comes from the flow of energy: The Partner gives *and* receives. The Caregiver gives. The Caregiver derives their identity from supporting others and helping them in reaching their goals. This character will always put others' needs before their own as they find purpose and identity in acts of caregiving and connection. The Caregiver loves planning things for others, celebrating their milestones, and taking care of them when they need help. This character's badge of pride is being the first text when something big happens to a person they care about.

The **Caregiver** may be overpowering in some people's movies

and harder to access in others, so let's look a little more closely at this character's origin story:
- → *How was caregiving modeled to you as a child? Was it seen as a burden, or did it come effortlessly?*
- → *In what ways do your childhood experiences with responsibility and empathy contribute to your current caregiving roles?*
- → *Think of the last time you did something to help someone else. How did it make you feel?*
- → *What does your inner Caregiver need right now?*

Character #5: The Goddess

This character wants to feel powerful, desired, and sexy. The Goddess is guided by the pursuit of pleasure (partner optional). This archetype seeks fulfillment through intimate connections and embraces passion and sensuality. When they are activated and on the set of your movie, you see the world through a flirtatious lens. They navigate relationships and experiences with a focus on emotional and physical satisfaction. The Goddess can be easily accessible in some seasons and harder to access in others.

The **Goddess** character can go through a lot of impactful and altering events. Let's get more familiar with yours:
- → *How have your experiences shaped your current relationship with intimacy and desire?*
- → *What emotions does this character evoke in you? Shame? Guilt? Excitement? Empowerment? Where do you think those come from?*

→ When was the last time you felt this character take over?
→ What makes you feel desired? What makes you feel sexy?
→ What does your inner Goddess need right now?

Character #6: The Lazy Girl

This character is on "do not disturb" mode. The Lazy Girl's goal is to decompress in college sweats and binge *New Girl*, and they have likely forgotten to put on deodorant...or a bra. In the pursuit of relaxation and decompression, the Lazy Girl character needs downtime and comfort. Unapologetically prioritizing cozy self-care, they find solace in moments of rest and majored in couch potato. Many women struggle to prioritize this character in their life, and it is the one we relegate to societally approved times like weekends and vacations. We will later dive into the importance of rest and how it actually fuels other characters' success to help you feel better about creating more space for the Lazy Girl in your life. They're maybe not the most glamorous character, but they're just as important as anyone else in the cast. The Soloist and Lazy Girl are great friends, but they share an important distinction. The Soloist desires independent growth, structure, and freedom. The Lazy Girl doesn't want to grow. She just wants to exist with no expectations of herself.

Get to know your inner **Lazy Girl** better:

→ How was rest and downtime modeled to you as a child?
→ How often do you let this character take over? Do you think it's too much, too little, or just enough?

- → When you let this character get some screen time, what do you feel? Guilt? Peace?
- → What does your inner Lazy Girl need right now?

Character #7: The Socialite

The Socialite's goal is to be around people. It's important to not confuse the Socialite character with the term "extrovert." The Socialite archetype thrives in social settings of various sizes, but the focus is on connection and the depth and richness of interactions with others. As humans, we have an ever-present urge to connect with people. Unlike the Partner character, the Socialite's badge of honor is their depth of connection with friends and a calendar of activities to look forward to. This character desires to be *included and connected*. Later in this book, we will spend an entire chapter auditing the cast of supporting characters in your life.

Get to know your inner **Socialite** better:

- → How were friendships and community modeled to you as a child?
- → What role do relationships play in your life, and how does community contribute to your sense of belonging?
- → How often do you connect with those important to you?
- → What is your screen time on social media? How is that impacted during times with more IRL social connection?
- → How often do you audit and prune the relationships in your life?
- → What does your inner Socialite need right now?

Character #8: The Creative

This character needs space for their creative outlets. Whether it's baking, painting, making music, writing, photography, home decor, gardening—or even just cultivating the perfect Instagram grid, writing a newsletter, making a TikTok, or composing a charcuterie board or capsule wardrobe—they are focused on *creation*. Sometimes the CEO character makes space and serves the needs of the Creative, and other times the CEO character starves the Creative. This combination must be analyzed often. Making space for this character fuels success for many other characters and sparks new neural connections in the brain. It's important to note that you don't have to be a quote, unquote, artist or creator to find the Creative inside of you, and this character seems to be a hard one to find for ambitious, goal-oriented women.

Get to know your inner **Creative** better:

→ *What was the last time you felt like you created something?*
→ *If you could take a class to learn a new skill, what would it be?*
→ *How did you play as a child? What brought you joy?*
→ *How was creative expression modeled for you as a child? Did your parents or role models include you in any creative pursuits?*
→ *What does your inner Creative need right now?*

Character #9: The Doctor

Think of this character as your "Inner Caregiver." They will do whatever it takes to make you feel your best. This character is driven by the goal of feeling good and healthy. They're focused on physical, mental, and emotional health. Sleep routines. Therapy. Protein intake. Supplement regimens. Blood work. Morning workouts. This is the character that pops up and says, "Did you drink water today?" Your Doctor character is saving workouts and possible meditation retreats on TikTok, but this is not a second-generation almond mom. We all have an inner Doctor that cares about us from a place of self-love, not self-hate.

Get to know your inner **Doctor** better:
- → *How was health and wellness modeled to you as a child?*
- → *What is your relationship with wellness?*
- → *What activities do you prioritize each week to help you feel your best physically, mentally, and emotionally?*
- → *What does your inner Doctor need right now?*

Character #10: The Explorer

Get this character off Zoom so they *can* zoom. The Explorer archetype is motivated by experiencing new things. These could be something as big as an international adventure or as small as a coffee shop tour of a city or even walking a new route in your neighborhood. They want to explore and are fueled by a passion for novelty and a readiness to see the world. The Explorer archetype is adventurous and curious. They desire to broaden their horizons, so they seek experiences beyond the familiar.

Get to know your inner **Explorer** better:
- → *In what ways do your childhood experiences with discovery and*

open-mindedness shape your current approach to broadening your horizons?
- → *How has this character shown up in your life so far?*
- → *Are you happy with the size of the role you have given them?*
- → *What does your inner Explorer need right now?*

Congrats! You've officially met the ten characters of character theory. Take a moment to pause here and reflect on a recent week in your life. Go through each day, start to finish. Now that you've met the ten character archetypes of character theory, which ones feel the most dominant in your movie? Which ones have yet to show up? Which ones do you feel pulled toward to give some more screen time? Not sure? Let's give you a tool to examine your current character setup.

Character Needs and Analysis

Now that we have a general understanding of the ten characters' goals and desires, it's important to look at what *your* characters need. Remember Law #2 of character theory: **Characters vary by person.** This book is about embracing variance and creating space for each of *your* specific versions of these characters to thrive and understand the spectrum of their needs.

Every person has a foundation of human needs in their life. These are important to understand and recall throughout this assessment because each character fulfills only *some* of these needs, not all. Now we are starting to understand why grit can become so toxic. When we push for success in one area, we are likely depriving the needs of another. We are starting to understand the foundation of character theory: the need to create space for multiple characters in order to meet our needs as a whole human.

The Seven Human Needs

Need #1: Energy
To thrive, humans require adequate energy (physical, mental, and emotional) to tackle daily challenges and pursue their passions. Some characters give us energy, and others take it away, depending on the person.

Need #2: Growth
Continuous personal and professional growth is essential for people to expand their capabilities, learn new skills, and fulfill their potential.

Need #3: Significance
Feeling valued and making a meaningful impact in our own lives and the lives of others provides humans with a sense of significance and purpose.

Need #4: Connection
Humans crave meaningful connections with others, fostering relationships that bring joy, support, and a sense of belonging.

Need #5: Stability
A stable foundation, encompassing financial security, emotional well-being, and a sense of predictability, is crucial for humans to navigate life's uncertainties with resilience.

Need #6: Fun
Engaging in enjoyable activities, hobbies, and experiences adds color to human existence, promoting happiness, relaxation, and overall well-being.

Need #7: Responsibility
Taking ownership of one's actions, obligations, and contributions to society cultivates a sense of accountability and integrity.

Some of us need a lot more stability than others. Some of us need more connection than others. These sliding scales affect each of your characters. It's important to identify the characters you are playing every day and how they show up in your life, as well as how they are contributing to the needs you have as a human. Not every character will contribute to each of the seven needs, but it's important that you balance the seven needs across your most visible characters. For example, if you spent the majority of last week in your CEO and Caregiver characters and neither of them fulfilled the need for fun, then your overall human needs will be in a deficit. If you spent the last week in your Socialite and Caregiver characters and neither of them has a need for significance or growth, then your overall needs will be in a deficit. If you spent the last week in your Soloist and CEO characters, then your need for connection may be in a deficit.

To assess if your overall needs are being met, you must look at the characters showing up in your life. Think about who is getting the majority of the screen time right now. Remember, characters vary from season to season (character theory Law #3). Which characters are leading during this season?

Each of those characters meets some, but not all, of the human needs. Now assess which of the seven human needs were not addressed by the main characters of your current season of life. When we proactively identify any unmet needs, we are also proactively avoiding the toxic grit pendulum swing from burned-out girlboss to lazy girl and instead find ourselves swaying in the happy middle of the Venn diagram.

Ask yourself:
- → *Which of the seven needs are you over-indexing?*
- → *Which needs have gone unmet?*
- → *What characters could you prioritize to better meet those needs?*

You have now started to apply character theory to your life. Character theory helped me feel less guilt when my inner Caregiver wanted to pull away from the world and rock my baby. I now understand that character requires less fun or energy but meets my human needs of connection and responsibility. Character theory helped me feel less guilty when I left my kids for a work trip. My

CEO character craves growth and significance. Using this lens, I'm now able to see when my basic human need for fun is being unmet, and I can start to pull other characters to the stage and go out dancing with girlfriends, guilt-free.

Something I think about often: An unhealthy relationship with ambition is actually a symptom of missing needs. Ambition is not a core need in and of itself but rather a result of our subconscious feelings and needs for growth, significance, connection, stability, or responsibility—or a mixture of all of the above. The CEO character is just *one* of the characters who can fulfill those missing needs. Most people push so hard at work because they haven't met the other characters and don't understand how else they can support the fulfillment of these needs. But now you've met nine other characters that can help rebalance your life and meet some of those needs if you find yourself bordering on the unhealthy side of ambition and feeling the effects of burnout and toxic grit. Awareness is a magical thing. Let's keep pulling back the layers of these characters and learn how they were shaped.

Who Wrote the Script?

I viewed my twenties as a check-the-box activity. Find a husband? Check. Grow career? Check. Have babies? Check. If I had viewed each of these characters on their own and really examined what they needed to be happy and thrive, I would have slowed down. I don't *need* a husband... I *want* someone who is my best friend and makes life fun, easier, and better. I don't *need* a C-suite title... I *want* to do work that lights me up and makes an impact while not taking over my life. I don't *need* to be the perfect mom with the perfect house... I *want* to be relaxed and present with my children. Instead, by following the American Dream Checklist, I found myself in my own version of a nightmare.

> **By following the American Dream Checklist, I found myself in my own version of a nightmare.**

I had allowed society and culture to shape and create my reality. My parents didn't get the chance to go to college. They met in high school and got married at eighteen and nineteen years old. It was normal in the Midwest to talk about marriage and babies before career goals and aspirations...so I followed the generational checklist that had been given to me.

This happens more often than we realize. Our storyline develops based on a script given to us, not one created by us. Let's examine the different dimensions that influence our characters' scripts and how we may be subconsciously programmed toward certain things, whether they're best for our character or not.

The characters within us and around us weren't created in a vacuum, nor do they exist in one. They were created and exist within five different dimensions of reality: societal, cultural, generational, others' experiences, and, ultimately, your experiences. These dimensions are the writers' room of our script and help us further understand Law #2 of character theory: **Characters vary by person.** Your inner Goddess was shaped differently than someone else's. You may feel more or less shame around accessing that character. Your inner CEO may feel more or less impostor syndrome than the person next to you in the meeting. Your inner Caregiver was greatly shaped by how the world around you—society, social media (culture), your family (generational)—viewed and respected the role of motherhood. Understanding these realities helped me to better navigate the world no matter which character I was playing and what scripts were being *given* to them, not written *for* them. It also helped me have more empathy and understanding for those around me. Their characters were also formed through these five realities.

The first step in gaining back control over your script is knowing what was given to you, not written for you.

The Five Dimensions of Character Reality

Let's look more closely at the five dimensions of reality that have shaped and continue to shape our characters.

```
     5        LEVEL 5
                Societal Reality
       4      LEVEL 4
                Cultural Reality
        3     LEVEL 3
                Generational Reality
         2    LEVEL 2
                Their Reality
          1   LEVEL 1
                Your Reality
```

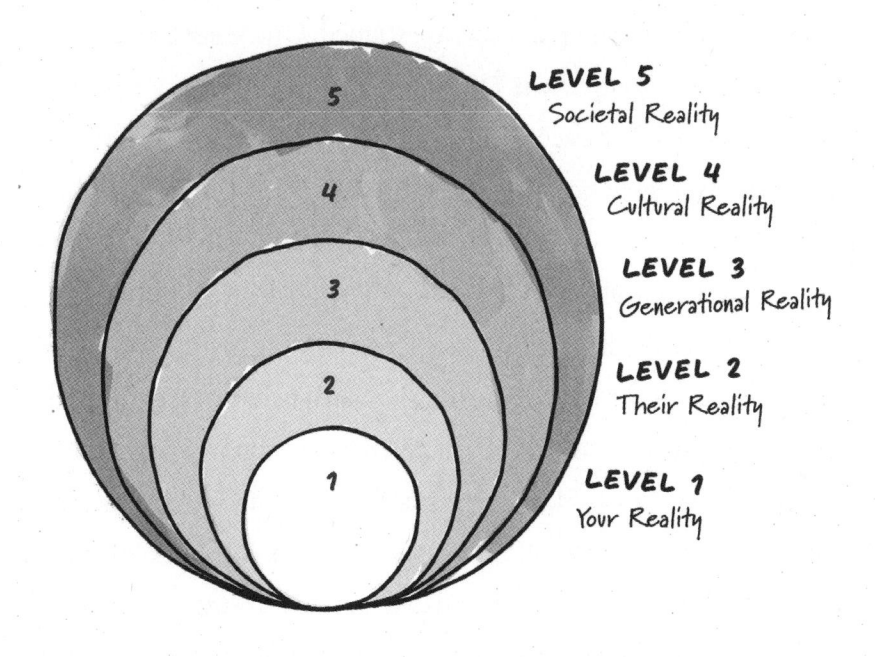

Level 5: Societal Reality

The macro landscape of the world we live in

Societal influence is how we're all affected by the people around us—our thoughts, feelings, and actions are shaped by our social environment. There is a human benefit to "going with the flow" or "following the crowd." Conformity leads us to stronger connection with others, a sense of belonging. For animals, that can help ensure survival and procreation. For humans, it can lead to both positive and negative implications and programming for our characters. Societal programming can hand us a script that we aren't sure we want to read.

It's worth recognizing that society moves in cycles, and these cycles affect how our characters are shaped. One book that illuminated these cycles for me is *The Fourth Turning* by William Strauss and Neil Howe. It dissects hundreds of years of history to reveal four cycles every generation goes through. First comes a High, a period of confident expansion. Next comes an Awakening, a time of spiritual exploration and rebellion. Then comes an Unraveling, in which individualism triumphs over crumbling institutions. Last comes a Crisis—the Fourth Turning—when society passes through a great and perilous season of war and destruction where we eventually find our way back to the restabilization and rebuilding, and the cycle restarts. It's kind of reassuring when you can look back and see this cycle repeat over and over again in history.

We've been living in a time of hyperindependence for women in the United States. For decades, society has been pushing women to be more, make more, and want more while simultaneously removing our freedom and autonomy. We see the cycle coming. More and more women are talking about softening and not subscribing to hustle culture while feeling the intense need to keep pushing for our freedom. These realities and cycles may be affecting how you feel when you are in Partner mode, which usually requires a more dependent and receiving state of mind than an independent, provider mode. Or perhaps it's causing your CEO character to feel guilt and shame. The same goes for your Caregiver. There have been many musings about what a parent "should do" in today's society that have affected how this character feels and evolves. Just the sheer creation of the Instagram mommy blogger telling me to be tot-schooling my toddler when I could barely figure out how to get home from work to complete dinner and bathtime before things unraveled was enough to make me want to put a scarlet letter B on my head for "bad mom." Macro societal trends greatly affect your characters.

Get to know your Level 5 inputs:
- → *What macro trends have affected how you view each of your characters today?*
- → *Go through them one by one and see what comes into your head when you think about how society views this character.*
- → *What characters have you given less space to because of this?*
- → *What characters have you given more space to because of this?*

Level 4: Cultural Reality
The world a culture exists within

Every culture has its own history and reality. Some cultures share histories of trauma and oppression. It's important to acknowledge this dimension as you navigate the world and your own characters. Understanding and working through your cultural reality is critical for setting up your characters for success.

Let's say you're from a culture that highly values collectivism, where the needs of the group outweigh those of the individual. In such a culture, you might prioritize family and community over personal achievement. Your worldview might emphasize cooperation and interdependence, leading you to see success as something achieved collectively rather than individually. In contrast, if you were raised in a culture that emphasizes individualism, you might focus more on personal goals and achievements, valuing independence and self-expression. So, your cultural background significantly influences how you navigate and perceive the world around you. You can quickly see how your Partner, CEO, and Caregiver characters would be greatly affected by the cultural reality in which you were brought up and whether or not you accepted those realities or rejected them.

A familiar example of cultural impact is the children of immigrant parents who share the common experience of the pressure to succeed, stemming from the sacrifices their parents made to provide them with better opportunities. These young individuals often feel a dual responsibility: to honor their parents' culture while attempting to assimilate into a new culture. I live in Miami, and many of my friends are from Latin cultures. We've had many talks about the guilt they feel about wanting (or needing) to move away from their families because, culturally, they've been programmed to stay near their parents and grandparents.

Let's look at how your cultural upbringing may have shaped your characters:

- → *How would you describe the culture in which you were raised?*
- → *What is your culture's relationship with love and relationships?*
- → *What is your culture's relationship with career and money?*
- → *Which characters have you given less space to because of this?*
- → *Which characters have you given more space to because of this?*

Level 3: Generational Reality
The reality of our family's past experiences

Every family has its own generational realities. *Generational trauma* refers to the emotional and psychological wounds passed down from one generation to the next. For example, if a family has experienced war, oppression, or persecution, the trauma from those experiences may linger and impact subsequent generations. On the other end of the spectrum, *generational resilience* refers to the capacity of families to overcome adversity and thrive despite historical or familial trauma. It involves the cultivation of strength, coping mechanisms, and supportive relationships.

Perhaps you are part of a family with years of abundance and success, and you feel the weight of carrying that lineage forward. Perhaps, like me, you hope to break through generations of limited resources and limited access to generational wealth and prosperity.

Perhaps your parents got divorced, and that experience greatly affected how you think about partnership. Perhaps your parents stayed married but didn't work on things. You saw how unhappy they were, and it affects your dating life and ability to trust the container of a relationship. Or perhaps your parents were happy. They demonstrated healthy relationship dynamics that led to relationship standards that feel hard to find in today's dating world.

You see, no matter your lineage, you likely feel the pressure and output of those who came before you. Whether positive or negative, your family's history affects you and each of your characters, and your job is to get curious about *how*. Every family has their own unique story, and unpacking these realities is critical for your characters to thrive.

Get to know your Level 3 inputs:
- → *What generational trauma may have affected how you view yourself today?*
- → *What is your family's relationship with love and relationships?*
- → *What is your family's relationship with career and money?*
- → *What characters have you given less space to because of this?*
- → *What characters have you given more space to because of this?*

Level 2: Their Inner World

How someone else's experiences affect their characters and, in turn, affect yours

There is a story from *The 7 Habits of Highly Effective People* that has stuck with me. Stephen R. Covey recounts a story of a family on a subway where a man is seemingly ignoring his children, who are being loud and disruptive. A bystander, growing increasingly irritated, finally addresses the man, asking if he could control his kids. The man then apologizes, explaining that they had just come from the hospital where their mother had died, and he wasn't sure how to handle the situation. This explanation completely shifts the perspective, replacing irritation with compassion. What if we navigated this world constantly remembering the unseen reality others are living in? The other people our characters interact with throughout their lives have different realities. Someone's inner world is derived from their three preceding realities, Societal +

Cultural + Generational, as well as their personal life experiences, relationships, and traumas. What has happened to them has shaped the person they are today. To successfully navigate interpersonal relationships for each character, one must understand the concept of the inner world. *Learning someone is the key to loving them.* Whenever you interact with someone else, you are interacting with each of their four dimensions of reality.

Let's say you go on several dates with someone, and they come off as not interested. They don't meet your energy or excitement right away. You could quickly write them off. Or you could stay in it a bit longer to understand their levels of reality. What was their experience with love and relationships growing up? How has their experience in the modern dating world shaped their ability to open up quickly? Their inner world shaped how they are as a Partner and may actually have very little or nothing to do with you.

Or let's say your boss is from another country and culture. They struggle to give praise and positive feedback. You feel as though you are never good enough, and you start to question whether this is the right job or career for you. But a closer look at their inner world might find a child who was told they needed to make their family proud. To work harder. That they were never enough. You might learn they were not given enough emotional support and affirmation, thus not equipping them with the ability to show it to others. Their inner world shaped how they are as a boss and actually has very little or nothing to do with your performance. You might even be killing it at work, and they adore you!

We need to learn someone else's inner world before we jump to conclusions. We all could stand to embrace more curiosity and empathy for the people around us before we categorize them with therapy buzzwords and toxic fill-in-the-blanks. One thing is for sure: No one has ever felt a deep connection from a surface-level judgment.

Understanding Level 2 will be a superpower for your characters. Your CEO character needs to understand someone's four dimensions of reality to manage people well. Your Partner character needs to understand the four realities of their significant other to support them and love them well. Your Caregiver character needs to understand others' inner worlds to care for someone well.

Get to know their Level 2 inputs. Think of a person in your life:

→ What experiences have affected how they view themselves?
→ What do you know about their societal inputs? Cultural inputs? Familial inputs?
→ What characters do you think they've given more space to because of this?
→ What characters do you think they've given less space to because of this?

Level 1: Your Inner World
The experiences, feelings, and relationships that have affected how you view the world

Your inner world is a culmination of the previous four dimensions as well as your own experiences, upbringing, education, relationships, and trauma. Specific things have happened to you on your trips around the sun that will ultimately shape the script for your characters. For years after my divorce, I tucked my Partner character safely in a drawer and focused on my Soloist. After a sexual assault, my Goddess felt shame and fear, so I threw myself into work and alone time. What we experience will inevitably shape how much or little screen time our characters will receive. Awareness is the key. Get curious about why, and you will unlock a path forward.

Go through your ten characters and ask yourself, *What has happened to them, and how has that affected my ability to let them develop their plotline?* This powerful question will set you up for the rest of the book, where we will define their goals and create space for them to succeed. These five realities are the writers' room of our script. Knowing them gives you a clear lens to see the world through and begin to edit the script and change the plotlines for your characters. It also sets the stage for us to understand and examine what it looks like when each of the characters goes too far and becomes toxic.

Chapter 3

Toxic Characters

We just met and examined the ten characters with a neutral lens—not assigning positive or negative emotions to the role each character plays in our lives. Just seeing them as they are with their own goals, values, needs, and the scripts they've been handed. But the flip side of these needs can reveal the root of some of our toxic traits and not-so-favorable qualities and triggers. These are also some of the qualities that keep us repeating behaviors and stuck in patterns or situations that, in our conscious-adult state, we'd never stay in.

Before we meet the toxic side of each of your characters, I think it's important to highlight the way society cheers on extremes under the guise of dedication and care. Losing your life to your job is not success, and yet we celebrate billionaires despite their six or seven divorces and estranged children. Losing your entire identity as you take care of your family is not success, yet we celebrate (dare I say, expect) women to be responsible for the entire family's emotional, physical, and mental needs without taking care of themselves. Losing your social circles to your Partner is not success, but we celebrate some pretty toxic relationships that do just that in film and media. The list goes on and on. This book is about intentional imbalance but not **extreme** imbalance. We can be aware that we can't keep all characters in equilibrium at all times while also avoiding the scale from tipping too far in one direction and creating a toxic grit scenario. Burnout happens when one character grows toxic and takes over the entire plot of your movie. We need a fully robust cast to prevent burnout in our lives and create that feeling of macro balance we are all searching for. But sometimes it's not actually society forcing us to do the tipping of the scales into burnout; it's us. Well... a younger version of us that has unmet needs and untamed fears.

Your Emotional Bus

This is the single therapy tool that changed my thinking and how I viewed my emotional triggers. Shout-out to my amazing therapist, Macy Oosthuizen (clinical social worker/therapist), who gave me this tool when I had a dire need for it. Emotions are most often activated when the brain interprets what's going on around us through our own *memories*. So when you are at work and feel extremely triggered by a colleague or boss and can't figure out why you aren't enforcing boundaries with them, use this tool. Or when you are with a partner and they do something that triggers a big reaction from you even though the thing itself probably warranted a size 4 or 5 reaction, not a size 9. When the reaction outweighs the cause, it's time to use this tool.

Macy tells us to picture a bus. Every version of you from growing up has filled up the seats on the bus. At any given time, (current) you should be driving the bus. **Current You** is an adult with logic and reasoning and goals and boundaries.

However...

Sometimes a situation will stir up six-year-old Amanda. Little Amanda is scared of being abandoned and alone. She spent a lot of her time alone as a child living in the middle of nowhere with nobody to play with. So when Adult Amanda experiences something that feels even remotely like someone may get mad at me and leave me, six-year-old Amanda hijacks the driver's seat and starts to drive us all to spiral city to avoid being abandoned and alone. Little Amanda is not equipped to be driving. She will people-please, tear down any boundary, and allow bad behavior to avoid the possibility of someone not wanting to be around her and play with her. Adult Amanda has to tell her she will be OK and that Adult Amanda knows where we are going. Adult Amanda puts her back in her seat and takes the steering wheel back. Adult Amanda knows what she deserves, will set a boundary, and will walk away from a situation if the other person can't provide it.

Adult You should be driving at all times. Our toxic characters come out when we allow younger versions of ourselves—with all their fears, anxieties, and trauma—to take over the bus and drive us to a place that isn't healthy. To cement this reminder in my mind, I have a picture of myself as a six-year-old favorited in my phone. When I feel myself start to spiral, I look at the picture and talk to her. I remind her that she is OK and that I've got her. This is called reparenting yourself: helping to give the younger versions of ourselves the things we didn't get as children.

[Illustration of a school bus with four figures in the windows, labeled from front to back: "You now", "You as a child", "You as a teen", "You in college"]

This is an important tool as we look more closely at our characters when they take things too far and go from character to villain. So let's dive deeper into what makes each character take on too big of a role in our lives or drive us somewhere we don't want to go.

The Toxic CEO

Let's begin with the CEO character. They desire accomplishment and success. The CEO is the character that keeps you motivated to keep pushing to climb higher, take risks, and advocate for yourself in your career. But what does it look like when the CEO character goes too far? For four years of my early twenties, I planned celebrity weddings. Bet you didn't see that one coming. I traveled the world, was on a reality TV show about weddings, and managed the brand for one of those big-name celebrity wedding planners. I started to get to know everyone in the wedding industry and saw a clear path for my future. Then, after a whirlwind four-day site visit to Hayman Island off the coast of Australia with the wife of an MLB player while thirteen weeks pregnant, I hit a wall. When my rainbow baby arrived, I convinced myself I was ready to stop working and would be a stay-at-home mom. I was twenty-seven and had been working late nights and long weekends for so many years; I was tired and ready to swap out my main characters.

Or was I?

Ambition is a funny thing. At some points in my life, I've been haunted by my fear of losing my ambition—like I would lose the drive that keeps me going as easily as I lose my AirPods. At other times, I feel my ambition is like a toxic ex that wants to push me until my breaking point—breadcrumbing me just enough to keep me going to the next mile marker in hopes of getting a little more validation or love.

A mere three months after having my rainbow baby, theoretically as a stay-at-home mom, I decided to launch a tech start-up for the wedding industry. One meeting with a serial entrepreneur who wanted me as his cofounder was all that it took. My spark was ignited, and the New York City tech scene was really heating up. I saw a new goal: to be a founder. To build and sell a company. I pushed again, now with more on my plate and still lacking the tools to find intentional imbalance among my characters. And guess what? I did it. And then I burned out. Again.

Now, I can look back and see a common cycle. One that I've now seen countless times among high performers. I've coached hundreds of founders and marketers on their career growth. I've spent countless hours on social media looking at the patterns of ambitious women. I saw it play out over and over again: a five-phase cycle that our Toxic CEO is playing over and over again. One where a younger version of us takes over the driver's seat to push us to prove ourselves, earn love, and sacrifice ourselves in the hope of being seen and recognized while we drink the toxic grit Kool-Aid. When our CEO is the one taking up all screen time, this cycle can easily click into place. Let's explore this cycle more closely.

The Cycle of Ambition

Phase 1: The Spark

You envision the life you want. Perhaps you see someone with a career, status, or lifestyle, and your CEO decides they want it. You see a possible path to get there or at least know where to find the flashlight to see it. This is your high-energy, quasi-delusional state. You feel as though you can conquer the world and have an endless amount of energy to do so.

Phase 2: The Setback
Something happens along your path, and your confidence is shaken. You aren't sure if you're cut out for or even want the thing you previously set out to get. This setback has you questioning everything, and you hit a proverbial wall. You decide you can't do it. You are balancing a two-part paralysis: fear of failing and fear of what would happen if you try and move forward.

Phase 3: The Phoenix
A validating email. Leading a great meeting. Hitting a milestone. Seeing a motivational TikTok. Something pulls you out of the valley. You feel like a phoenix rising out of the ashes and push even harder than before toward your goal or dream. Phase 3 can last for months or even years, but eventually it catches up to you.

Phase 4: The Burnout
It starts slowly, almost undetected. At first it's a bit of anxiety, then it's a loss of motivation or ability to focus and prioritize. You take a day off to do your normal self-care routine, and yet it's not working. You may even take a vacation. But you come back still crippled with overwhelm and anxiety. You finally realize you can't keep pushing like you were in Phase 3. Your health is suffering.

Phase 5: The Rebalance

Acknowledging the burnout, you intentionally shift gears. Rebalancing isn't just about rest; it's a recalibration of priorities. You do all the right things. Focus on your health and wellness, take the foot off the pedal, and start to feel centered and calm. Your CEO moved over to the passenger seat, and you let someone else drive.

And then someone or something lights the spark inside you. A new mountain to climb. And here is where the cycle repeats. This is the toxic side of our CEO character: a recurring subscription to hustle culture. It's an all-or-nothing approach to success where the pendulum swings from pushing to a goal and proving to everyone we can do it to the other extreme of quiet quitting or actually quitting—that is, until something relights the spark and the cycle repeats itself. Without the tools in the rest of this book, the Toxic CEO will continue this cycle over and over again.

Ambition is not unhealthy in and of itself. But there also isn't a checklist of things you can do to find it. If you took all the ambitious humans in the world and lined them up, you'd find some wake up at 5:00 a.m. and some work until 2:00 a.m. Some eat McDonald's (paging Warren Buffett) and some measure every macro and nutrient in their body (Bryan Johnson). Most tweets of how to be successful miss the three connected qualities of an ambitious person, and I'd venture to guess these will resonate with you—the person who is reading a book about how to achieve success without burning out.

Ambitious people all share the following three traits:
1. A belief they are meant for more
2. A need to prove it to others
3. A fear they will be found out as an impostor, so they work harder to make up for it

The belief that our CEO character is here to accomplish something great and that we are meant for more than we have now is the checkered flag we race toward in life. The fear of being exposed as an impostor—the need to constantly prove we belong—is like a competing race car on our tail, pushing us to kick into the next gear. But if we don't recognize and manage it, that pressure will eventually leave us exhausted, defeated, and waving the white flag again and again. Your programming is what it is. The people on your bus, the younger versions of yourself, will be on the ride with you forever. Your job, as the adult version of your characters, is to be in control. To make decisions from a place of conscious logic and intention and not toxic, subconscious grit.

When one character takes over, it can make it difficult to access other characters. When our CEO takes over the entire plot of our movie, we may find it difficult to access our Creative, Explorer, and Goddess characters. When we embody a more dominant, powerful energy all day, it's hard to switch into a softer, more flowing, and creative character at night. I've spent a lot of time with women who have made hundreds of millions of dollars in their thirties and forties only to find themselves unable to access their softer, more receptive characters. It's kind of like the phrase "use it or lose it": if you leave a character off the script for too long, it may become harder and harder to find them. In the third part of this book, I will give you a how-to guide for switching between oppositional characters as part of your daily routines.

When one character takes over for too long or repeats unhealthy cycles or patterns, other characters can get lost along the way or even become toxic themselves. Let's examine the other characters more closely.

The Toxic Partner

We've all been there. New love. Rose-colored glasses. Lost time. Unanswered texts to friends and family. But those are not the toxic characteristics we are talking about for this character. Those are just pheromones. What we are talking about here are things like codependence, anxious or avoidant attachment styles, and a complete loss of your social life, alone time, or ability to enjoy the hobbies you once enjoyed because of your relationship status. This is for anyone who tends to lose themselves in a relationship.

Take a moment to pause and journal here. Do you tend to lose yourself or chameleon in relationships? Or, think about the last time you spiraled in a relationship. What version of you do you think was actually driving the bus? What do they need to be told?

Nothing is more of a mirror to our trauma than close, intimate relationships. I've said it before: Awareness is the greatest agent for change, but agency is a close second. Once we are aware of where *our* stuff comes from, we can operate more from our conscious, adult selves. We can make decisions from the driver's seat. It's really difficult to change when you run from difficult or toxic situations without pausing to look at what your part may be in it.

Awareness is the greatest agent for change, but agency is a close second.

Another visual helped me deal with my intense reactions when a person I was dating wouldn't match my text energy. Imagine a pot of stew inside of you. Inside the stew are all the noodles and chicken chunks of past trauma. One day, someone will come along and grab the spoon, stirring up that pot of stew, or maybe even turn up the heat on it. If they turn it up too much, the entire pot will start to spill over. This means you're now reacting from the stew of *years* ago, not the current situation. In my situation, the fact that the person I was dating was not texting me triggered six-year-old Amanda's fear of abandonment or unhealthy things from my marriage, so I was reacting with the weight of thirty-plus years of stew, not the three months we had been dating. If I let my Toxic Partner character react, I'd blame the other person and say they were emotionally unavailable and a fuckboy. But Adult Amanda (the director of the entire movie) was able to consider if there were other possible explanations, determine what I needed to feel secure, and communicate it clearly. We need to make sure each of our characters is operating from a place of the present, not the past, and these tools will be incredibly helpful for your Partner character.

A cautionary note for some: The Toxic Partner loves to pair up with the Toxic Caregiver. If you have unmet needs of care from your childhood, the Partner may embody a Caregiver role that extends beyond the container of a healthy partnership. You may be searching for someone to take care of so you can recreate the thing you didn't have as a child. But picture a wall that is leaning and starting to fall. Now imagine you use your strength to hold up the wall. For a while it is manageable, but over time, the weight of the wall is too much. You can't hold it up forever. Eventually, the wall is going to crush you. This is similar to what happens when your Partner and Caregiver team up and go to the unhealthy extreme. You are not strong enough to hold up the full weight of someone else. Your Partner character should care for your person but not be their Caregiver (a.k.a. parent). When your Toxic Partner starts to take over the movie of your life, ask yourself: *Who did they invite on the bus, and who is driving? And what do they need?*

The Toxic Soloist

The Soloist wants to experience independence, growth, and freedom, so naturally the extreme scenario for this character is hyperindependence. This toxic character tends to take over the script after a Toxic Partner storyline. After my divorce I went through a long stretch of time when I thought *I don't need anyone. I can take care of myself.* And while those empowering mantras got me through some extremely dark times, they quickly became the core theme of the entire movie of my life. The Soloist was growing more toxic and taking over the script. She was quick to assess any new relationship as unreliable and a foregone conclusion, so she parroted her mantra, "I don't need anyone. I can take care of myself." When the Soloist grows toxic, it's easy to lose the ability to connect with others. We are skeptical of anyone being who they say they are and are quick to distrust, so we actually start to lose the Partner and Socialite characters when the Soloist has established these unhealthy thought loops. She likes to push everyone away.

The emotional bus is a powerful tool when you feel your Soloist trying to take over your Partner or Socialite's storylines. You have to trust that the adult, current version of you will be wise enough to wait until someone actually wrongs you rather than preempt the wrong. Trust yourself to know the adult version of you is strong enough to walk away when it happens. The Toxic Soloist wants to tell you everyone is fucked up, so why bother? The antidote is having the adult version of you calmly tell her, "Well, let's see what happens."

We are starting to see some toxic characters are best friends, and the Toxic Soloist loves the CEO. When hyperindependence is the goal, throwing yourself into work is the logical next step. You can rationalize your busyness with deadlines and the promise of more money, which leads to more freedom and less reliance on others. Those two characters are quick to reinforce each other's toxic behavior.

Have you recently gone through a period of hyperindependence? Picture the bus. Which version of you was driving it when you shut out people and the world? In the next chapter, we'll talk about how to slowly ease our way out of these unhealthy cycles using our other characters.

The Toxic Caregiver

Oh, the martyr. She is doing everything for everyone else and just can't get a break. Everyone needs her. No one is doing anything for her. She's exhausted but keeps pushing beyond her limits because "who else is going to do it?" This is the Toxic Caregiver, and a character I became all too familiar with when I became a mom, but let's remember that you don't have to be a parent to experience this character and her unhealthy extremes. Are you the person always coordinating the trips and making sure everyone is OK when you go out? Are you always making sure everyone else has the information and updates they need? Do you know when their birthday, anniversary, or kids' birthdays are? I'm not saying any of these, in a vacuum, is wrong. But when you are consistently pouring from an empty cup (and becoming resentful for it), it's time to check your Caregiver. She's gone too far.

Visualize a pitcher of water. Every day you start with a full container of water, and as you go throughout your day, you find people who need some of your water. The more you pour into others, the less you have. Eventually, your pitcher becomes empty. You have nothing left to give, but you still try. You turn the container upside down and shake the last drops to the next person. And then try again with the next person. This is what it looks like to let your Caregiver character take over. She isn't slowing down to let anyone or anything pour into her to fill her back up.

Some signs your pitcher may be running empty and your Caregiver character is becoming toxic:

- **Constant Exhaustion:** You feel perpetually tired and drained, both physically and emotionally, from constantly tending to others' needs.
- **Overextension:** You frequently push beyond your limits, taking on more responsibilities than you can handle because you believe no one else will do it.
- **Lack of Reciprocation:** You notice that while you are always doing things for others, no one is doing anything for you in return.
- **Neglecting Self-Care:** You seldom take time for yourself, neglecting your own needs and well-being to focus on others.
- **Feeling Indispensable:** You believe that everything will fall apart if you are not the one coordinating, managing, or taking care of things.
- **Unrecognized Efforts:** You feel unappreciated and taken for

granted despite your continuous efforts to help and support others.
- **Emotional Depletion:** You find yourself emotionally drained, with little to no energy left to invest in your own interests, hobbies, or self-improvement.
- **Resentment and Frustration:** You experience feelings of resentment and frustration toward others for not recognizing or reciprocating your efforts, yet you continue to sacrifice your well-being.

If any of these resonate, you are not alone. Many women find themselves in situations where the Toxic Caregiver is actually forced into the plotline. Weaponized incompetence is a common theme in relationships and work environments and can be a catalyst for the Caregiver to start to take over the script. Weaponized incompetence is a manipulative behavior where an individual deliberately performs tasks poorly or pretends to be incapable of doing them in order to avoid responsibilities and shift the burden onto someone else. This tactic is often used in relationships or work environments to exploit our willingness to take over tasks to avoid frustration or failure. When we know we can get it done the right way...we just do it.

If you haven't read the book *Fair Play* by Eve Rodsky, please do. It's an incredible tool and resource to create equity in the home. And just remember, there are two paths to having a co-parent to raise your kids with: work together to divide up the visible and invisible labor OR have a court do it for you. My Toxic Caregiver took over to the point of a breakdown with three kids under the age of four. My pitcher was empty, and I had nothing left. But, through a divorce and rebalancing of parental time, I now have a great co-parenting relationship with my ex, and my kids get a present and hands-on dad and not a full-time, running-on-fumes-and-resentment mom.

The Toxic Goddess

The nuance of anyone's relationship with intimacy and sex can and has filled shelves of books. I'm going to touch on just two symptoms of the Toxic Goddess from my own personal experience: detachment and loss of worth.

My last start-up was a wellness company that empowered women to take control of their sleep, sex, stress, and strength through originally formulated CBD gummies. It was a product wrapped in a promise: permission. Through research, we found women were subconsciously looking for permission to take care of themselves (see Toxic Caregiver for more info), and this start-up was my attempt at helping someone give themselves that permission. I worked with sex therapists and spoke on a lot of sexual health and wellness podcasts and panels. We were one of the first libido-enhancing products on the market for women. The timing of my start-up coincided with my post-divorce, rediscovery chapter.

Being raised Catholic and getting married at twenty-one didn't allow for a lot of sexual discovery. My Goddess had always been confined to the container of my Partner character. But this new season of life opened that container and allowed my Goddess to be free and explore what desire looked like for her. I joined a bi-curious social club called Skirt Club. Had my first one-night stand. I was drinking up my newfound autonomy and sexual independence. And then, my Goddess started to grow toxic. I was struggling to connect emotions to sex. I had swung the pendulum so far in the other direction that I no longer associated sex with love but rather, solely, pleasure.

This led to the second symptom: loss of self-worth. In dating, I started to lead with my sexuality before my heart, soul, and mind. I had forgotten all the other things I had to offer to someone. I started to equate my body and ability to attract as a core component of my worth. Detachment and loss of worth are two of the symptoms that revealed themselves and shined light on my Goddess growing toxic and affecting the other characters in my life. When I helped my Goddess strike the right balance of worth, desire, excitement, and love is when I started to attract people who wanted to see and love me for all of me.

We will talk more in later chapters about how this character can be easy to access in some seasons of life and harder to access in others. We will establish tools and transition techniques for navigating between the various roles you are embodying throughout the day, but right now it's important to pause and see what came up for you when reading about my experiences. Does any of this resonate? Again, awareness is the first step toward rebalancing a character.

The Toxic Lazy Girl

Even the most ambitious people love a lazy day. We stay in sweats all day and binge a show. We order Uber Eats for most meals and exhibit less human, more raccoon-like qualities. We will discuss how important rest is for our movie to progress. Imagine watching an action movie where the characters jump from high-speed chase to massive explosion to fight scene and over and over again. No quieter scenes for the storyline to progress and develop the characters. We would be exhausted by the end of that movie. That's kind of what life looks like without allowing your Lazy Girl to get some screen time. However, there are times when this character starts to affect our ambition and slows the development of our other characters. A common symptom of the Toxic Lazy Girl is a loss of the Doctor, Creative, Socialite, CEO… Well, almost all the other characters are affected when the Lazy Girl grows toxic. Loss of momentum and a goal of shutting out the rest of the world to fall deeply into the digital worlds and forget about all responsibility can go from necessary (you need a break) to dangerous (you're broken). When the Lazy Girl is taking over and you can't find a way back, routines are her kryptonite. Whenever I feel myself wanting to go from bed to couch to bed for more than just a weekend, I create a high-five list: five things that will make me feel a little higher when I'm feeling low.

My High-Five List:
1. A walk to a coffee shop
2. Getting two things done for work
3. An afternoon walk
4. Taking at least one supplement
5. A 9:00 p.m. bedtime

These things all feel very manageable and start to force the Toxic Lazy Girl back to her designated part of the movie of my life. Take a moment to grab a journal and create your list of five easy, accessible things you can do in a day when you feel your Lazy Girl trying to overstep.

The Toxic Doctor

As a former fitness professional and someone who has struggled with my own relationship with my body in various seasons, I can confidently say there is such a thing as letting your health-focused character go too far. For example, when your health and wellness routines consume your thoughts and restrict your ability to find joy in life, your Doctor has started to tip the scales to the extreme (pun intended). This toxic character can lead to a loss of your Socialite because being around people becomes harder to endure out of fear of slipping on your routine. Social media is the gateway drug to this toxic character, as we are fed a visual diet of endless picture-perfect lifestyles and bodies that, upon further interrogation, would be found to be staged or altered for content and not real life and, definitely not, scientifically proven. Toxic wellness culture can have negative effects on mental health and lead to body dysmorphia and shame, so we must understand and identify when this character is going from a leading character to a villain in our lives. Prioritizing health and wellness is important for ambitious people, but when left unchecked, it can become a form of punishment rather than self-love.

Proactive defenses against this toxic character include self-talk and flexibility. Self-talk is your internal dialogue. It's influenced by your subconscious mind and reveals your thoughts, beliefs, questions, and ideas. We all have an inner voice that tells us we aren't as good or why we shouldn't be doing something. Give it a name (Cindy or Karen or Bob or Fred), and every time it pops into your head, acknowledge Cindy, thank her for stopping by, and show her off your bus.

When I became a fitness professional, one of the first things my instructors taught me was how to shift someone's thinking to be aligned with their identity. Studies show people are more likely to quit smoking if they start identifying as a nonsmoker: "Oh, I don't smoke" rather than "I'm trying to quit." The shift in identity keeps alignment with their goal. When we want someone to embody a new lifestyle, we help them change their self-talk to be coded as a healthy individual. When things veer off course, I usually pull back the layers to hear how that person is actually talking to themselves. There are four types of negative self-talk, and understanding them will help you identify which are starting to bubble up from your Toxic Doctor.

1. **Personalizing:** When "It's not you, it's me" becomes your mantra. If something bad occurs, you automatically blame

yourself. A workout gets skipped. A routine gets missed. You immediately make it personal. You blame yourself, not the external situations that factored in.

2. **Magnifying:** You focus on the negative aspects of a situation, ignoring any and all of the positives. Instead of celebrating the ten-minute walk you got today despite a busy day of work, you tell yourself you fell off your routine and are back to the beginning.

3. **Catastrophizing:** You expect the worst, and you rarely let logic or reason persuade you otherwise. Your toxic character prevents you from achieving your goals. Why bother? I'm never going to stick to this.

4. **Polarizing:** It's either good or bad. No middle ground. One "poor" decision and you call the whole day a wash and continue on a self-shaming spiral of poor decisions.

When you notice one of these types of negative self-talk happening, congratulate yourself. Noticing is the first step in rewiring your brain. The next step is to assess the actual situation versus the perceived one in your head. Is there any evidence to support these thoughts? What are three things that actually went right? What would it look like to show grace in this moment?

The Toxic Doctor tends to be strict and inflexible, so the natural antidote is compassion and flexibility. Most people overestimate what they can and should do in a day but underestimate what they can do in a year. A wellness journey is a marathon, not a sprint.

James Clear, author of *Atomic Habits*, refers to this underestimate as the power of tiny gains. He explains that in the beginning, there is basically no difference between making a choice that is 1 percent better or 1 percent worse. (In other words, it won't impact you very much today.) But as time goes on, these small improvements or declines compound and you suddenly find a very big gap between people who make slightly better decisions on a daily basis and those who don't. If you get 1 percent better each day for one year, you'll end up thirty-seven times better by the time you're done. So when your Toxic Doctor berates you for not sticking to your twenty-seven-step skincare routine or missing your ten thousand steps, remind them: "One percent better a day equals thirty-seven times better in a year." Wellness is meant to be about self-love, not self-hate.

Wellness is meant to be about self-love, not self-hate.

The Toxic Socialite

This character is the hardest to spot when she grows toxic. On the surface she is loved and wanted by everyone. Her calendar is packed with events, dinners, and places to be. This toxic character can sometimes team up with the Toxic Caregiver: "Everyone needs me." But when everyone needs you, you end up pouring from that empty pitcher.

Complete this sentence: "I'm too busy for ___." The Toxic Socialite can take over and cause a loss of alone time, wellness routine, creative outlets, and possibly finding a partner. The other problem? When we are constantly moving and growing our network without an intentional prioritization of depth and quality of connection, it can lead to a lot of surface-level interactions and relationships. All of a sudden you have to keep your light shining bright to ensure the moths keep close when, in reality, you might actually be looking for just a few lightning bugs—people who bring their own light and don't feed off yours. Later in this book we will dive deeper into the supporting cast and how to assess which roles people are playing in your movie.

The Toxic Creative and Toxic Explorer

The Creative and Explorer characters tend to get the least amount of attention and screen time in an ambitious woman's life. I'm usually pushing someone to access them more. The extreme scenarios for these characters usually are a result of someone running from herself rather than seeking to find herself. She's catching flights, not feelings, and always on the move looking for creative outlets or places to explore. When these toxic characters team up with the toxic Soloist, we find a movie without much of a supporting cast. When these characters grow toxic, it can also cause immense financial impacts, so we will talk more about how to rotate these characters in as a means of supporting your other characters, not depleting them.

Building Healthy Characters

If any of the toxic character descriptions resonate with you and you feel you've allowed a character to tiptoe near the extremes, you are now one step closer to achieving intentional and controlled imbalance. If you ever feel the scales tipping too far for a character, come back to this chapter and reference the following chart to see which of your characters may be taking things to the extreme.

An unhealthy dose of one character can starve other characters from getting their time and space in the movie of your life. It's important to understand the interplay between characters. Some characters starve others, and some are extremely compatible—where the focus on one creates a gateway to another. There will be times in life when we need help unlocking or finding a character. They got lost on their way to the movie set, or a toxic character has stolen their screen time. Proceed to the next chapter to understand how to find some of the characters that have been pushed out of the script.

Character	Healthy: What drives the character	Unhealthy: When the character goes too far
Character #1: The CEO	Accomplishment Achievement	Hustle culture Burnout / Imbalance Loss of Creative character Loss of Explorer character Loss of Goddess character
Character #2: The Partner	Companionship Support Connection	Codependence Anxious attachment Loss of Socialite character Loss of Soloist character

Character	Healthy: What drives the character	Unhealthy: When the character goes too far
Character #3: The Soloist	Freedom Independence Growth	Hyperindependence Loss of Socialite character Loss of Partner character Loss of Goddess character
Character #4: The Caregiver	Being helpful Providing care Feeling needed	Martyr mentality Lack of reciprocity Pouring from an empty cup
Character #5: The Goddess	Desire Passion Intimacy	Detachment Feeling shame or guilt
Character #6: The Lazy Girl	Rest No responsibility Cozy self-care	Loss of momentum Shutting out the world Loss of connections Increased screen time and loneliness
Character #7: The Socialite	Friends and fun Social calendar	Overscheduled Surface-level relationships Loss of Soloist character
Character #8: The Creative	Creation Passion Creative spark	Loss of social connections Financial concerns Loss of CEO character
Character #9: The Doctor	Inner caregiver Feeling good Emotional, physical, and mental wellness	Restrictive routines Addiction to exercise Punishment Loss of joy and pleasure Loss of Socialite character
Character #10: The Explorer	New experiences Curiosity Fun and freedom	Loss of stability and roots Financial impacts Running away from problems (e.g., catching flights, not feelings)

Chapter 4

Character Compatibility

I started my corporate career at a Big Four accounting firm in the heart of Chicago. I spent my days in a male-dominated work environment (mortified one day for being sent home for not wearing pantyhose with my pencil skirt). From morning until evening I was hardening enough to follow the prescription society had given to me—hard enough to break glass ceilings, climb the ladder, and hang in the boys' club.

But when I got home from work, I found myself unable to soften, which is a necessity for me to feel sexual (I need to get out of my head to get into my body) or creative (I need to turn off logic to turn on the right side of my brain) or even lazy (lying on the couch turns into a shame spiral because I'm still in execution mode looking at every email notification that hits my phone). My Goddess, Creative, and Lazy Girl characters started to shrink in direct correlation to the expansion of the Zara pantsuit collection for my CEO character. I remember wondering, *Do I need to lose the other parts of myself in order to succeed in my career? Is this the sacrifice working women have to make to have it all?* I'm thankful for the years that have followed since my days at that accounting firm, with so many women showing the multitude of ways to achieve and define success. That you do not need to lose all parts of yourself for one to succeed. The new definition of success is allowing all of your characters to develop on their own timelines. To let go of toxic grit. To develop the movie of your life *together*.

I remember a particularly stressful season of work in my twenties. I was heads down at work, and everything was revolving around this super-important project that, almost two decades later, I couldn't tell you what it was about or for. My friends had planned a night out. We were going to get dolled up and go dancing. Those who know me know I love a good night of dancing. But work was so intense. A huge part of me wanted to say no because I needed to stay focused on the project. Then I realized two things: my then-husband and I weren't really connecting lately, and I hadn't seen my friends in a while. So I said yes. Determined to be home and in bed by 1:00 a.m. We drank and danced, and I felt young and sexy and alive. Allowing my Socialite to come out unlocked other characters that were harder to access thanks to my CEO. That night allowed me to process things that I had been shutting down and blocking with work. This is the power of character compatibility. Some characters are the gateway to finding the not-so-compatible ones for your leading characters.

When life gets stressful and quickly becomes a string of "if I can just get through this next week, things will slow down and I can refocus," it's time to intentionally write a different character into the scene. We all go through weeks that turn into a series of groundhog days, the same day repeating over and over again, and feel unable to switch into any other characters. But when we find a character has been left off the script for too long and starts to feel inaccessible, we can use the power of character compatibility to help them get back in the spotlight. When you find yourself unable to find or access a character, use the following descriptions of compatible characters to lead you back to them.

When You Lose Your CEO...
Focus on Your Creative
Studies show that when we lose our spark at work, building new neural connections through play and non–work-related problem-solving can help us break through work-related stress and problems. Spend time doing creative work and hobbies to unlock ideas for your business and career.

Focus on Your Socialite
You can't open new doors if you aren't in the room. It can be easy to isolate ourselves when we feel shame around stunted career growth or a loss of spark with work-related burnout and fatigue. We don't know what we can't see. The Socialite will help remind you of other career paths, options, and opportunities and relight

the spark by feeding off others' energy. The Socialite will also help remind you that not everyone is "killing it" like you see on social media. Everyone has their own form of career self-doubt and struggle, and your Socialite will help lead the way back to your CEO.

When You Lose Your Partner...
Focus on Your Socialite and Caregiver

When we start to veer into the lane of hyperindependence, it's important to focus on characters that value connection. We need to surround ourselves with people to remind us of the energy and expansive feeling of connection and pouring into others. We may not need someone, but it feels good to have someone. These connection-seeking characters are helpful in that reminder.

One note: It's important to balance the types of people you surround yourself with when you have lost your Partner character. You, like all humans, have a tendency to surround yourself with like-minded, similarly staged people (being the single girl looking for single girls to go out with), but your Socialite needs to support your Partner character by getting away from the cynical and getting closer to the type of connections you hope to find (go ahead and be that third wheel).

When You Lose Your Soloist...
Focus on Your Lazy Girl

The Lazy Girl and the Soloist are best friends. When you feel like you can't get alone time, your Lazy Girl will happily find a day to curl up on the couch, binge a show, and eat nothing that resembles a full meal. The goal for the Lazy Girl is to help the Soloist understand the world will not fall apart if you aren't helping everyone around you. The Lazy Girl is the most selfish of all your characters. Her MO in life is 100 percent unbothered. In this character you will be reminded how good it feels to be alone and possibly start planning other fun solo adventures to help your Soloist expand on that freedom and growth.

Focus on Your Explorer

When you feel like you can't find yourself, go find yourself. Solo travel can be a great reminder that being alone doesn't equate to being lonely and can be an incredibly energizing opportunity for your Soloist. You can experience the world around you and immerse yourself in new cultures and energies without the need to perform or be "on" for anyone else. The Explorer can help you reconnect to yourself and your inner Soloist.

When You Lose Your Caregiver…
Focus on Your Doctor

When we struggle to find compassion and the energy to take care of others, we must start by taking care of ourselves. Every airplane ride starts with the announcement that in the event of an emergency and a change in cabin pressure, oxygen masks will drop from the overhead compartments. You should put on your own oxygen mask before helping others. Why? Because if you don't, you will run out of oxygen and be unable to help anyone else. When our cup is empty, how the hell are we supposed to pour into anyone else? If you are struggling to show up for those you love, you need to start by asking, "How am I showing up for myself?"

When You Lose Your Goddess...
Focus on Your Explorer
There is nothing sexier than a new place. You can be whoever you want. No one needs to know about the piles of laundry on your floor. The unanswered texts and emails. You are living in the moment, relishing the novelty and exploration of the world around you. When you explore the world, you are actually exploring yourself. New experiences shine a bright light on the parts of yourself that may not get illuminated often. Travel and exploration can be the fastest gateway to your inner Goddess. And a friendly reminder: Travel can be to a new country or just to a new part of town. Novelty isn't based on radius.

Focus on Your Doctor
The other access point to your inner Goddess is your wellness character. When we pause to connect with our bodies, we become more aware of them. Aware of their energy, needs, and tension. Releasing tension with a wellness routine can make it easier to release tension in other ways (you get where I'm going). For women, desire and sensuality are mental first, physical second. We have to slow down

our brains and anxiety to unlock access to pleasure. Using your wellness-centered character to slow down your brain is a great way to unlock your Goddess.

When You Lose Your Lazy Girl...
Focus on Your Doctor
Your Lazy Girl character is one of the easier to access, unless you are overly stressed and anxious and can't calm your brain down. When I got my first puppy, I remember someone saying, "A good puppy is a tired puppy." Long walks and workouts and leaving your phone in another room are healthy access points to your inner Lazy Girl. When we lower our cortisol levels through time outdoors and movement, we give ourselves the space and permission to get restorative downtime (not the sit-and-scroll while watching TV and never-fully-relax downtime).

When You Lose Your Socialite
Focus on Your Creative
Passion and curiosity are the keys to unlocking energy, especially when we feel withdrawn from ourselves and those around us. If you are struggling to access your inner Socialite, start with the Creative. Find a class or group or online community talking about the thing you are interested in creating and focus on the creation, not the people. You are there to learn and create, not to socialize. But when you remove the focus from something, it tends to happen more naturally.

Focus on Your Doctor

Being active releases endorphins and serotonin. These chemicals are the perfect social cocktail. Go to a class or outdoor meetup with a focus on mental and physical health, and watch your social health increase as a by-product. Come for the workout, stay for the people. I love having a standing yoga date with my friend. Some days I don't have the energy to socialize, but just by having the time and workout locked in, sometimes we grab coffee or lunch after. It takes way less energy to be social when the person is already in front of you. This is why working from home has also led to a lot of lost Socialites. Proximity and ease are the grease to our social wheels, so it's important to use your Doctor to create more intentional social opportunities.

Focus on Your Explorer

There are many compatible characters to the Socialite. When you are struggling with connection to people, seeking connection to new experiences and places can open up the gateway. Some of my favorite conversations in life happened when I was exploring a new city, looking for recommendations and historical insights. Sometimes it's easier to open up to strangers we may never see again, so go out in the world to explore and connect or use a trip as a reason to bring your friends together.

When You Lose Your Creative...
Focus on Your Explorer

Nothing lights a creative spark quite like novelty and exploration. Seeing new art, decor, landscapes, or trying new food and nightlife will help you create a list of things you want to incorporate into your life. Sometimes you need to go out into the world to come back to yourself.

When You Lose Your Doctor...
Focus on Your Socialite

Accountability is the greatest lever in establishing a wellness routine. Grab a friend and make a plan to meet up at a yoga class, go for a long walk, or even just sit outside together. If you're in a wellness rut, your Socialite character will happily round up the troops and pull you out.

When You Lose Your Explorer...
Focus on Your Socialite or Soloist

The Explorer is highly compatible with the Socialite and the Soloist. These two oppositional characters are both motivated by connection and growth: The Socialite wants to connect and grow with others, and the Soloist wants to connect and grow with herself. Both of these characters are looking for opportunities to go deeper with these connections and will pull you out of your routine to go find something new.

Accountability Checkpoint

It's time for a quick accountability checkpoint. Which of your characters feels inaccessible at the moment? Based on the compatibility descriptions, what is one actionable step you can take with a compatible character to start unlocking the door to your lost character?

Making intentional trade-offs is a core theme of this book, and now that you understand the ten characters in the movie of your life, it's time to honor the beauty of imbalance in your life. Not everyone gets the spotlight in every scene. Toxic grit is when we feel like we should be able to keep all characters' plotlines developing at the same pace. Imagine trying to tackle ten projects at work at once. You will likely move each of them forward 10 percent every month. But if you prioritize two of them this month and keep the others in maintenance mode, you've now made 50 percent progress in one month, which would have taken you five months with the original strategy. The ability to honor the imbalance of life and prioritize characters is key in having it **all**. Just not all at once.

Part 2

Honor the Imbalance

Chapter 5

Imbalanced.
I'm Balanced.

Life is full of different character transitions and trade-outs sparked by canon events. A canon event is an important event in your life that shapes who you are and what you become, and one that can add, remove, or drastically alter the main characters of your life. Canons... I've had a few. Infertility. Miscarriage. Having three babies. Divorce. Building companies. Quitting jobs. Selling companies. Discovering my sexuality. Character theory is *not* about balance. Imbalance is inevitable, especially following a canon event. When you meet the love of your life, it's common to see your friends less. Imbalance. When you get a new job, you have a period of time to prove yourself to your boss and teams.

Imbalance. When you have a baby, you are operating on little sleep and wacky hormones. Imbalance.

But without awareness and adjustment, the scale will tip too far...and break. One woman may focus on her career for twenty years and wake up realizing she has put her friends and dating life on the back burner. Another may focus on her family for so long and realize one day she's not sure who she is outside of taking care of other people. One may have traveled the world collecting passport stamps and experiences but realize she hasn't built roots or developed deeper relationships and community.

In my years of working with female founders and high-achieving women, I've learned there is usually a canon event that causes them to reevaluate the weight they've placed across their characters: things like burnout, the end of a relationship, depression or anxiety, the loss of a loved one, or a desire to start a family. This book is about proactive, not reactive, rebalancing. It shouldn't take a massive and/or traumatic circumstance in someone's life to make them reevaluate their energy expenditure and which character they've been prioritizing, but, unfortunately, that's the pattern many follow.

But what if we didn't wait for a canon event? What if we spent time understanding where we want to go in our lives before the universe decides to change the plotline for us? What if we designed our lives and intentionally embraced the imbalance at the micro level so it doesn't happen at the macro?

Intentional imbalance is knowing there are trade-offs in each season, and it's OK to develop a few characters more than others. Intentional imbalance is about proactively assessing which path you are on and if that path is still getting you closer to the thing or things you want for your life. But how do you know which characters to develop and when to switch? Welcome to part 2 of the book: mastering and honoring the imbalance of life.

I forgot they existed.

After my divorce and the pandemic, I was starved for community. My Socialite and Partner characters had been left off the script for so long, but I didn't have the tools of character theory to understand that. I just felt alone and didn't know what to do about it. At the start of COVID in 2020, I left all my friends in NYC and rented a small temporary home in Charlotte, North Carolina, to save money, isolate and homeschool my children, and get some more space. A year later we decided to move to Miami to be together as a modern family (their dad was moving there) and start a new chapter. All of the moving and working from home while single parenting had me feeling really disconnected from others, beyond superficial likes and DMs on social media. One day, as I was building my venture capital–backed health and wellness start-up from my kitchen counter in Midtown Miami, I received an email from one of my investors asking for some of my product to give away at a female founder retreat in Tulum. I checked my co-parenting calendar and realized it was in three weeks and I was kid-free. I replied, quickly asking if I could send the products…and myself.

Three weeks later I found myself on the beaches of Tulum for a three-day, two-night retreat. I was surrounded by female founders of brand names you most definitely have heard of, as well as investors and authors. On day two we sat in groups of four, gearing up to do a meditation/exercise. Let me preface this by saying I'm from the Midwest, and meditation/manifestation was still tucked perfectly in the "woo-woo" folder of my personal values filing cabinet. I was more of an "if I want it, I will make it happen by sheer force" kind of gal. But I was in such a weird place in my life. I felt stuck. Being a founder and CEO and trying to raise a third round of capital with talks of an impending recession was depleting everything within me. I was living in CEO Amanda's plotline most of the time. My time with the kids was frequently interrupted by Slack messages, calls, and the ongoing list of to-dos in my head. The scale had tipped too far.

As I wiggled my toes in the sand, nervous of what we were about to do, our guide came over to explain the exercise. "For the next ten minutes you are going to close your eyes and imagine your most perfect day. Money is not an object. You can live anywhere. You will close your eyes and then imagine waking up on the most perfect day of your life. What does your room look like? What do the sheets of your bed look and feel like? What's the weather outside? What do you smell? What do you do first? Who is there? Think of every single detail of the day as if you are actually living it. Proceed to walk through every moment of the day, until your head hits the pillow again at night."

Imbalanced. I'm Balanced.

I woke up in a home that felt like a treehouse. Palm trees swaying outside. It was a modern but open house with warm accents. Perhaps because I was in Tulum when I did the exercise, I saw terra-cotta planters holding fiddle-leaf plants and woven rattan light fixtures throughout my bedroom. I woke up and had a partner. I couldn't see the partner, but I had the idea of one on this perfect day. I could hear my kids already rummaging about, and my chef was waiting for us with breakfast. (Hey, she said money was no object!) We all sat down in this nook surrounded by windows and talked as the kids got ready for school. They walked out the door and headed to school, and I got ready to meet a friend for coffee. After coffee I hit the gym and did an awesome workout and came back to do a sauna and ice-bath circuit in my backyard. Around 11:00 a.m. I sat down to write and made a few calls from my Pinterest-perfect desk before signing off at 3:00 p.m. I took a walk with a group of friends who came back, and we had smoothies from my chef. Then hair and makeup came, and my daughters got glammed up with me in this huge bathroom vanity area while the house was being set up for a party. All of our friends were coming over for a backyard hang. Cafe lights lit up our large backyard, and the smell of brisket and steak was taking over the home. We laughed and ate and danced the night away. Magically, my home was clean and quiet by the time I tucked my kids into bed, and I crawled into the arms of my partner, made love, and fell asleep. Wow. What a perfect day.

Ten minutes later I am shaken back to reality by an iPhone alarm. Back in Tulum, it was now time for the second part of the exercise: to share our perfect day with the other women of our foursome. I went first and recounted the flow and softness of the day. Quality time with my friends, partner, and children. The ability to work out, do some work, and be in control of my time—something I didn't currently have as the CEO of a fast-growing start-up. The end of my perfect day included a gathering at my home, dinner under garden lights in my backyard, and kids running around. The irony was I hadn't had any time to make close friends in Miami yet. I could count on one hand the number of people who would come hang with me *and* my kids. I shared about having a partner, something I wasn't sure I wanted because my CEO and Soloist were toxically tag-teaming and reinforced my "I don't need anyone" thought patterns. It was interesting that my calmed brain pictured sharing my perfect day with another person.

Then the woman next to me shared her perfect day. She was a founder and CEO of a beauty start-up, and it was a rocket ship. She had already secured Sephora and Ulta purchase orders, and her 200k followers on Instagram adored her and loved cheering her on every step of the way. She was a mom of two, had full-time nannies, and had a place in the city as well as the suburbs for weekends and summer. It was a level I had not achieved yet idolized from afar.

I listened as she recounted her perfect day. She woke up in

Imbalanced. I'm Balanced.

her NYC penthouse, and hair and makeup was there. She had an appearance on the *Today Show* followed by a magazine shoot. She was being featured on the cover of *Forbes* as the CEO of the fastest-growing beauty brand. Her day was about power and the empire that she was building. The end of the day was spent with her husband and children.

Well, *fuck*.

Had I done the exercise wrong? Can I try again? I felt so much guilt. I wanted those things as well, but my brain forgot them! I felt small at that moment. I totally had forgotten the CEO/founder character on my perfect day.

And then it hit me.

That was the point of the exercise. The perfect day helped shed light on the lack of alignment between the life I had and the life I wanted. I had spent so much time in my CEO's storyline that my Partner, Caregiver, Goddess, and Socialite were screaming for attention. I almost forgot that they existed. I left that trip and made the decision to sell my company and completely step away from it. I took on consulting work and rearranged my characters to start to align more closely with the perfect day I had envisioned that day on the beach. Throughout the next year, I found love again. Moved in with my partner in a townhome with palm trees swaying outside the window. Planned trips to reconnect with my closest friends. I found alignment for that season in life.

Finding and honoring this intentional imbalance is ongoing

work. Two years later I repeated the perfect day exercise on a solo weekend trip. I sat in a park, put in my AirPods, opened Spotify's "Peaceful Meditation" playlist, and set my timer for ten minutes. This time my brain played a story of my family walking with me into Barnes & Noble to sign copies of a book I had written. I pictured my children and partner coming with me to give a keynote speech in front of a large audience before heading back to our huge hotel suite, where we ordered room service and laughed and played together. I was ready to spend a little more time on CEO Amanda's storyline again.

You see, the perfect day exercise illuminates agency, alignment, and intentional imbalance—three of the key takeaways of this book. If you understand where you want to go, you can take the steps to get there. You get to decide how much attention you give to the various characters of your life and switch them before the scale tips too far in one direction.

Whether you feel stuck, out of balance, or just want to check where you are at, this ten-minute exercise can be the catalyst for making changes to a character's screen time. Let's imagine your perfect day and figure out which characters are ready for more or less screen time.

This exercise is best performed when you are rested and away from your everyday life. Head to a park, plan a staycation, or perform it on your next vacation in the quiet hours of the morning. Removing yourself from your existing characters' plotlines creates freedom to explore the potential for your life.

The Perfect Day Exercise

You will need a timer, pen, paper, ambient music, and a clear head and heart.

- **Step 1:** Set aside one hour.
- **Step 2:** Remove all distractions; silence notifications.
- **Step 3:** Put in headphones and turn on meditation music.
- **Step 4:** Set a timer for ten to twenty minutes.
- **Step 5:** Close your eyes. Begin visualization.
  - *Imagine your most perfect day.*
    - *Money is not an object.*
    - *You can live anywhere.*
  - *Picture waking up on the most perfect day of your life.*
    - *What does your room look like?*
    - *What do the sheets of your bed feel like?*
    - *What's the weather outside?*
    - *What is outside your window?*
    - *What do you do first?*
    - *Who is there?*
  - *Proceed to walk through every detail of the day until your head hits the pillow again at night.*
- **Step 6:** Open your eyes. Write down everything you just saw.
- **Step 7:** Evaluate.
  - *How far is your current life from this life?*
  - *What characters showed up?*
  - *What characters didn't show up?*
  - *What changes need to be made to take steps toward that life?*

The Character Stovetop

Let's now double-click into character theory Law #3: Characters vary by season, based on the changing needs of your life and the fact that not all characters will get the same amount of screen time in any given episode. You can have it all—just not all at once.

Can you imagine if a movie had a plotline with ten main characters in it? Pure chaos and confusion to the audience. The same is true in character theory. We may be playing ten characters in the story of our lives, but we cannot give *equal* weight to each storyline. Some characters only make a cameo appearance for a few minutes a day, a week, or a month. Getting comfortable with imbalance and prioritization will set you up for less stress and guilt in your day-to-day. A reminder: Balance is unachievable.

A reminder: Balance is unachievable.

I like to picture my life as a stovetop, one of those fancy five-burner stovetops that you see on HGTV kitchen makeover shows. Every month I proactively assess which five characters are on the stove and specifically determine which characters are on the front/biggest burners (a.k.a. the main characters) and which are on the back/smaller burners based on which of my needs are feeling unmet in that season. It's unrealistic to develop ten characters all the time, so this exercise also highlights the intentionality and permission to say "not right now" to a few characters. Every month I take a moment to move things around so nothing gets too cold or too burned (out). When I pair this monthly exercise with an annual perfect day exercise, I get better at proactively switching burners around. Awareness is a superpower and the antidote to toxic grit.

[Illustration: A stovetop with burners labeled LAZY GIRL, DOCTOR, CEO (center, largest), PARTNER, and CAREGIVER.]

Even now as I write this book, I know that my CEO, Caregiver, and Partner are on the front/bigger burners. I have a deadline to hit, and because I care so deeply about this book helping women feel less guilt and burnout in their lives, I want to make sure I take the time and energy it deserves. So that means The Doctor and Lazy Girl are on the back burner. I still need to keep my relationship and health in focus, but I also know my main focus for the next month is writing and momming. Characters like the Explorer and the Socialite are left off the stovetop entirely. I am intentionally saying I can't focus on them as much right now. My Socialite may make a cameo appearance for a quick coffee date, but I won't feel guilty if I don't connect with my friends this month. Next month, however, I will likely find through this analysis that I'm under-indexing on fun and connection, so I will need to bring the characters back onto the burners and plan a night with friends or a weekend getaway.

This exercise is about alignment, intentionality, and, most importantly, anti-goals. So many of us go through life without giving ourselves permission for imbalance. Knowing what you are *not* focusing on for the next month is just as important as knowing what you *are* focusing on. This is a core component of relieving guilt and avoiding toxic grit. I have intentionally said I am not doing a lot of social activities this month, so I won't feel guilty or berate myself when I scroll Instagram and see everyone going out and hanging out or even force myself to go out despite not feeling emotionally and physically available for it. Because of this exercise, I am saying my Socialite is just not on the stovetop right now. And that's OK. She will be back on the stovetop shortly.

What's Cooking?

Based on your perfect day, think about the characters that need more camera time in the movie of your life and place them on your stovetop for the next month.

→ *Which ones are getting the front/larger burners?*
→ *Which characters are getting back/smaller burners?*

→ *Which characters are intentionally off the stovetop and waiting on the counter? Perhaps they will make cameo appearances in the movie of your life but will not get a lot of screen time this month.*

We will use the rest of the chapter to help you create goals for each of your main characters in your day-to-day to ensure we make the most of their time in the spotlight. If you are giving them a burner, then let's make sure they are cooking up something great! Later in the book we will gather the tools necessary to transition among the leading characters in your day-to-day as well as those with supporting and cameo roles.

Big Dock Energy

Sometimes the movie of our life feels so imbalanced and blurry that we struggle to picture our perfect day. We no longer feel agency over our plotline. My amazing therapist, Macy Oosthuizen, clinical social worker/therapist, gave me this analogy and it has stuck with me.

Picture a boat floating in the water with no anchor. It drifts around and around, until an anchored boat invites it over. So, the anchorless boat ties up and joins the party and people. Then the party ends, so they untie the boat, and it drifts away. Then the anchorless boat sees another group of boats. It drifts over and ties up to one of them, joining those people and their party until they decide they are done and untie it. And the anchorless boat drifts away again, waiting to see who it can anchor itself to.

This is what it feels like to navigate life without a defined set of core values.

Core values act as a filter for the decision-making of each character, how they spend their time, the opportunities they take, the content they consume or create, and the relationships they allow in their life. Without core values, every passing thing can pull you in, creating a false sense of safety and stability for a short time. This is exactly what my post-divorce era felt like. My leading characters were my CEO, Caregiver, Goddess, and Socialite. But I didn't have clear values defined for any of them. This led to toxic relationships that fucked me up even more than my divorce—friendships that turned out to drain me more than they filled me. And every moment with my children, I was trying so hard to be the perfect mom that I overplanned and overextended my time with the kids, leading to extreme exhaustion and guilt.

Growth and contentment require you to be a dock, not a boat.

After you picture your perfect day and arrange your character stovetop, you've got to build your dock. Unlike the anchorless boat, a dock is a person with a defined set of values that pulls in the right people and the right opportunities. It's stable. Others come to it. Let's make sure each of your characters is a stable dock, not an anchorless boat.

This is where I find most of my coaching clients need help. They don't have clarity about or know how to prioritize what they value in a job or career, so they float from job to job repeating similar patterns and feeling stuck or unhappy. They don't know what they value in a relationship (romantic or platonic), so they don't take the initiative to end toxic ones but rather hang with whoever is close in proximity or initiates contact. They float through life without being at the helm. Imbalance is happening *to* them, not *by* them. Values and actions are tightly linked—what we value and believe influences how we act. And character theory Law #1 (you write the script) reminds us you have agency over the movie of your life. You have complete control over the actions of your characters. But many people are anchorless boats. Their actions aren't filtered through a set of core values, which ultimately won't get them their desired outcome.

Imbalance is happening *to* them, not *by* them.

It's time to set your characters' values and give them big dock energy. It doesn't take years of self-reflection or therapy to define a character's core values. This simple exercise will help you create the values so you can start aligning your character's actions with the right people, decisions, and opportunities.

Go through each character. Reflect on your life *as that character* and answer the following four questions for each of them:

→ *When was that character happiest in my life, and what was I doing at that time?*

→ *When was that character least happy in my life, and what was I doing at that time?*

→ *How do I want to spend my time as this character?*

→ *What people would I want this character to emulate?*

Based on those reflections, choose ten to fifteen words that best represent that character's values. Don't overthink. Once you have a list of words, you can start to bucket them into a few categories.

Consistency	Friendship	Trust	Fun
Stability	Empathy	Thoughtfulness	Playfulness
Communication	Balance		Passion
	Ambition		

Once you have your categories, you can write out short, impactful statements to create a set of values for your character.

My Partner character:

- Desires **consistency** in the relationship.
- Seeks a deep **friendship** to grow with.
- **Trusts** herself and her partner.
- Generates and seeks out fun and **playfulness.**

Imbalanced. I'm Balanced.

Congrats! You just created your characters' core values and can start aligning your actions with the right people, decisions, and opportunities. With these defined values, you can properly set your stovetop and clear your doorway. Yes, your doorway. Let me explain. When I first moved to Miami, I was dating a person who was mysterious and fun but never consistent. The dopamine hits I would get when I saw them kept me addicted but never feeling safe or stable. One night I was out with a group of friends, and this woman was asking me about my dating life. I said, "I'm seeing this person, but it's not serious," to which she replied, "Are you looking for serious?" At that point, four years after my divorce, I was. To which she replied, "Get them out of your doorway." I stared back with as puzzled of a face as my Botox would allow. She looked at me and said, "This person is blocking the doorway for anyone else to enter or exit. You will be stuck exactly where you are until you remove them from the doorway." I was an anchorless boat. I didn't have any defined values for my character, so I was just drifting.

I ended that relationship shortly after and realized that if I had established a set of values for my character, I would have quickly assessed this person through that lens.

- Desires **consistency** in the relationship.
  - → *There was no consistency whatsoever.*
- Seeks a deep **friendship** to grow with.
  - → *We were not building toward a friendship.*
- **Trusts** herself and her partner.
  - → *I definitely didn't trust them.*

- Generates fun and **playfulness.**
  → *Sure, it was playful, but really with one goal in mind.*

You are now embracing imbalance by moving characters around on the stovetop based on your perfect day. And those characters are anchored in their values—no longer drifting from place to place, person to person, or job to job. This chapter is all about intentional imbalance in our lives. But if we are imbalanced, doesn't that mean we can't have it all?

Having It "All"

We haven't started to unpack the thing that likely brought you to this book: having it "all." As a starting point for your quest to have it all, we've got to keep underlining that your characters have competing objectives. Different puzzle pieces that don't always fit perfectly together. The goal for one character may compete head-on with the goal of another. After divorce, my life was like a bad Netflix series: every episode had a different plot twist, cast of characters, and disconnected storyline. You knew the main character would be OK (it's not HBO), but you weren't sure what was happening in the show or where it was headed. I needed to create a stronger plot for my cast of characters so they worked together rather than stepping all over one another.

The best analogy I can think of to describe our internal conflict of character storylines comes from my professional career as a CMO. Leading a marketing department, something I've done for over twenty years, is a lot like juggling my internal characters. The entire team is working toward the same goal for the company (grow the company) in the same way all your characters are trying to work together to achieve your perfect day and, ultimately, life. But when you zoom in on each owner of a marketing channel, you see competing objectives. The head of PR wants buzzy headlines, but the head of Content wants traffic. The head of Social has their goals and doesn't genuinely care if they drive traffic to the website as long as the social content goes viral or gets engagement. The SEO and Paid teams are at odds with my creative director because that perfect keyword title lacks any sense of brand voice and tone.

Let's try another example. Juggling your internal characters is kind of like planning a trip for a large group of girlfriends. You know everyone has the same goal: to have fun. But fun to some looks like getting up early for a sunrise yoga session and green juice, while others want to sleep in and lie around until it's time to get ready to go out again. Some want to spend every moment together, while others prefer downtime.

So how do you get alignment across a leadership team or large group on a girls' trip? The same way you will get alignment across your characters: by setting the plot and creating goals that ladder up to the larger vision for the company or group or, in this case, your life.

The Character Plot Equation

In order to set the plot for a character, you need to understand the plot equation. Welcome to character theory math class. I don't know how I still remember PEMDAS from my tiny grade school in central Illinois (shout-out to Mrs. Francis), but it's an acronym that determines the order of operations for a math equation. It stands for: parentheses, exponents, multiplication, division, addition, and subtraction. Calculate them in the wrong order and you get the wrong answer. The same goes for the character plot equation: the culmination of a strong vision, clear values, and clear goals over a defined period of time. Remove one part of the equation and you will get the wrong answer: living a life you didn't necessarily want.

$$\text{Character Plot} = \text{Vision} + \text{Values} + \text{Season} + \text{Goals}$$
$$P = V+V+S+G$$

- **Vision:** Where you see your life going as determined by your *perfect day exercise*
- **Values:** The *values* you've outlined for each of those main characters
- **Season:** The lead characters you've selected for a set duration of time as determined by your *character stovetop* exercise (front burner + back burner)
- **Goals:** The goals for each of those main characters to achieve *(we will do this next)*

What About the Other Characters?

Just because you've selected four or five characters to be on your stovetop for this current season of your life does not mean the others don't exist or have goals or need attention. But the reason we, as women, are facing extreme burnout and toxic grit is no one has given us permission to say "not right now" or "not as much right now." We just keep pushing through, feeling like we are "supposed" to be able to figure it out. Let's look at a few scenarios to further illustrate how all your characters exist even if you have not placed them on the stovetop for this set period of time.

Scenario 1

You've determined your perfect day is waking up, working out, and leading your team through a big project, followed by dinner with friends and a relaxing night by yourself (vision). You've placed CEO + Doctor + Socialite + Soloist on the stovetop, and you've set the duration for two months until you reassess (season). Does that mean you're not allowed to travel or go on dates or be in a relationship? No. It just means that you won't be dedicating the majority of your energy to those characters. So, if your Partner starts scrolling Hinge one night or your Socialite bumps into a cute human, follow that energy! Do you see the difference between active and passive characters? If not, let's try it from a different angle.

Scenario 2

You've determined your perfect day is waking up with a partner and having a slow day in a foreign country (vision). But you are currently single and don't have the funds to quit your job and backpack through Europe. So, your CEO character still very much exists, but for the next month (season) you've placed Partner + Doctor + Explorer + Goddess on the stovetop. Does that mean you've stopped working? No. It just means that you won't be withdrawing as much energy for work, and it will be on "maintenance." Instead, your energy will be around intentional dating and the work necessary to prepare yourself for a healthy relationship. You are setting aside time to research and plan your next trip while also working on your mental and physical health.

Scenario 3

You've determined your perfect day is hanging all day with your girlfriends laughing and playing, then exploring your sexuality with some hot guy or girl (vision). Again, unless you have savings and can step away from work, your CEO character still very much exists, but for the next month (season), you've placed Goddess + Socialite + Explorer on the stovetop. Does that mean you won't find a partner or work out or do the work to prepare for a healthy relationship? No. I went through a period after my divorce where I just needed to feel desired without the emotional intensity or investment required of a relationship. Putting a duration on it alleviated any guilt or emotional overhead of needing to date with the intention of a relationship. That season also helped me better understand what I needed for a long-term relationship. I also had a full calendar of social events, which brought so many great memories and bonding with friends, but it paved the way for another season of appreciating my Soloist character. I learned that being alone didn't equal being lonely. Fueling one character's needs actually helped me learn about and grow another character.

Scenario 4

Your perfect day involves intentional time with your children and partner as well as lunch with your friends and a great workout sprinkled with some beautiful solo time (vision). Great. We see Caregiver, Partner, Socialite, Doctor, and Soloist on the burners. For the next year (season), you've decided you aren't going to focus all your time and energy on your work. Does that mean your CEO character is gone? No. Your perfect day may change in one, two, five, or even eighteen years. I was a stay-at-home mom working on a side hustle for one year with my first child. I had used fertility treatments to get pregnant, and something inside of me desperately wanted the freedom to soak in every moment since I was unsure I would be able to have another. My CEO character wasn't gone. I went on to build and sell another company. Acknowledging your vision + duration helps remove guilt from your script. Intentional pauses can be powerful. The characters not getting as much screen time are still there, but you've made an intentional decision to focus your energy to achieve the current vision for your life.

Last Stop: Goals

We've reached the fourth and final stop in our PEMDAS character plot equation. It's the last ingredient you need for a character to ensure their storyline progresses in the right direction. Intentional imbalance means you aren't developing ten characters at once, but when you have intentionally placed a character on the stovetop, you're using that time to develop that character and story arc.

Character Plot = Vision + Values + Season + Goals

As a reminder, you've already set the vision (V) by completing the perfect day exercise. You've set the season (S) by placing main characters on the stovetop and set a duration of time until you reassess. You now have the values (V) defined for those characters to give them a lens to see the world and make the best decisions. Now it's time to give them goals (G) to achieve during this season.

Ninety percent of people fail at achieving their goals. After hundreds of hours coaching people, I've distilled the top reasons people fail into the following five categories.

Reason #1: Fear of Failure

We are primal creations wired for survival and safety. Our brains are literally designed to avoid fear and discomfort and, heaven forbid, failure. Yet my greatest strengths today came from failures of the past, so I no longer fear failure, as I know it will always bring learning and change.

Great days bring memories.

Good days bring joy.

Bad days bring learning.

Horrible days bring change.

Reason #2: Self-sabotage

You have to believe you deserve something better. So many of us get in our own way without realizing it. Peeling back the layers to reveal what your subconscious (those on your emotional bus) is thinking might help you discover years of programming leading you to believe you don't deserve something better. Get curious about who from your past may have led you to believe you didn't deserve something better. A helpful way to begin identifying forms of self-sabotage is to frame your situation using the following sentence: "I want to achieve (goal), but I keep doing (behavior)." Get closer to and more familiar with your limiting beliefs and actions holding you back from achieving your goals. Later in this book we will give you more tools to allow your characters to take up more space in the world.

Reason #3: We Try to Change Too Much

We've referenced it before, but it's worth repeating: In his book *Atomic Habits*, James Clear says if you get 1 percent better each day for one year, you'll end up thirty-seven times better by the time you're done. Small changes make for big gains, but inaction is sure to result in no change. None of our characters can do a one-eighty overnight like a '90s rom-com makeover scene. It will take time. One percent better most days is better than zero percent better every day. Realistic goals are key in actually moving your characters forward.

Reason #4: The Wrong Motivation

The thing that motivates you will determine your ability to take action and maintain it. Losing steam usually comes from having the wrong motivation. Ask yourself: *Am I running from something or toward something?* Did you place the character on the stovetop out of shame and guilt or because you are excited to see what things could look like if you level up in that characters' plotline?

You also must distinguish between loving the outcome and loving the process. If you want to become a creator, you have to fall in love with creating, not just the idea of quitting your job. If you want to build muscle, you have to fall in love with the process of working out, not just the idea of looking good next summer. Fun fact: I set a goal to run a marathon before every baby turned one year old. And I did it. I ran the Chicago marathon for Hadley, San Francisco for Lincoln, and New Jersey for Greyson. How? My goals were aligned with the process, not the outcome. The training process was the thing that I actually desired and needed. The breaks and alone time helped me process my thoughts and helped with postpartum depression and anxiety and work through the feelings

I was having with my partner, which helped give me the space and clarity to file for divorce (thanks to a great therapist as well). My point is this: Motivation to achieve goals has to come from loving the process and person you are becoming during it.

Reason #5: Comparisonitis

Are you comparing yourself to someone who has been doing the thing for years? You can't compare your day 1 to their day 10,000. It will be important for your character to find others on a similar journey. Look to those ahead of you for inspiration but to those around you for support and motivation.

Character OKRs

Now that we know the pitfalls of goal setting, it's time to take the characters you've placed on the stovetop and determine what they are trying to achieve during the defined season of your life.

This next section will be especially useful if you are:

- Feeling lost or have lost your spark
- Embarking on a new chapter
- Spending a lot of effort but not seeing the impact
- Struggling to identify or stay focused on priorities
- Stalling in personal or professional development

I first learned about OKRs (**O**bjectives measured by **K**ey **R**esults) when I was leading a team of fifty at The Knot. Our CEO, Mike Steib, brought over the methodology from when he worked at

Google, and it changed everything for me. Rather than executing random marketing campaigns that didn't connect to the larger goal for the company, we now had a system to keep all teams moving in the same direction toward the same larger goals. It gave us a lens to see if the work we were doing was impactful to the business, not just the brand. I've worked with many start-ups who use OKRs as a check-the-box activity. A "hey, look, we can do this thing too" moment in the calendar year. The problem? They never revisited those docs until the next year's goal-setting process, so they didn't actually provide a guardrail throughout the year. The same happens for individuals. I absolutely hate New Year's resolutions for this reason. The process is a performative act to oneself signaling the hope for change but without the tactical planning necessary to enact it.

Goals are not a one-and-done moment in time. They are a GPS destination for your day-to-day activities to allow for each character to move forward in their plotline. Imagine if you got in the car, set the GPS, and then never looked at it again. You may know where you want to go, but you stopped looking at the thing that is going to ensure you get there. This is what OKRs need to be: Your GPS. Every quarter (or when I make major shifts to my character stovetop), I sit down and assess what I want my characters to achieve over the next three months. Then every month I review what's working and where I'm falling short in moving their development and storyline forward. Let's walk through how this works.

Imbalanced. I'm Balanced.

OKR

OBJECTIVE — **KEY RESULTS**

I will accomplish (**OBJECTIVE**) as measured by (**KEY RESULTS**).

Step 1: Select a Character

Choose from the set of characters you've put on your stovetop for the next month, quarter, or other defined season. I typically designate my main characters and their goals for a quarter but review and assess at the end of every month.

I will continue my example with my Partner character.

Step 2: Create Objectives

Based on your perfect day exercise, create two to three goals for the character to work toward over the next one to three months. Objectives should be aspirational and inspiring and *not* quantitative. (That comes next with the key results.)

Given my values of desiring **trust** and **consistency** in the relationship, seeking a deep **friendship** to grow with, and generating fun and **playfulness**, I've come up with the following two objectives to grow my Partner character over the next quarter.

O1: Discover more opportunities for fun and play.

O2: Grow our friendship through deeper conversations.

Step 3: Set the Key Results

Key results are now the quantifiable measurements that will give you a binary "yes or no" when you ask the question "Are we meeting our objective?" They should be reasonable so as to not discourage you or demotivate you. Try to have one or two key results for each objective.

O1: Discover more opportunities for fun and play.

KR1: Try one new class or non-restaurant date night a month.

O2: Grow our friendship through deeper conversations.

KR1: Do one lesson a week in a relationship health app.

KR2: Keep a no-work-or-kid-talk date night every Wednesday.

Step 4: Schedule and Delegate

Now that you have the results you want to hit, it's time to look at your calendar, schedule the time, and make sure it happens. The date nights won't magically happen. We have to assign a person to make a plan. We have to determine who is arranging the sitter. So we scheduled a planning night to choose the dates and activities and determined who was planning what. We also started a shared note to drop ideas into when we see something on Instagram or TikTok or hear of a recommendation from a friend. Without these tactics, these intentional date nights likely wouldn't happen amid our busy schedules. If you've decided to grow your character by setting these objectives, make sure you give them the tools and resources they need to achieve them.

Step 5: Repeat and Review

Go back through this exercise with each of your other characters on the stovetop. Does the collective set of goals look reasonable and manageable? Have you set aside the time and clarified the tactics in which you will achieve them?

If you do this properly, you will start to see how you can create space for each of your main characters to grow and develop. You are becoming a master in character theory and honoring the imbalance of life. You've now got a clear equation to follow for creating the plotlines for each of your main characters and understanding the trade-offs necessary to move things forward to work toward achieving your perfect day.

Up until this point, we've kept things neat and tidy, but let's go ahead and address the elephant in the room. Ninety percent of you reading this book likely put the same time-dominant characters on the stovetop. I like to call these the Big 3. These three characters tend to take over the entire script for most women, so let's meet them, examine why this happens, and give you guilt-free permission to optimize them and give them a little less screen time.

Chapter 6

The Big 3

Imbalance is key to alleviating guilt. We can't be everything to everyone all at once.

We are unlearning the goal of balance and honoring the intentional imbalance that has to happen for our characters to grow and succeed and unsubscribing to the hustle culture and toxic grit narratives. But we will ultimately lose a connection to ourselves and feel completely out of alignment when we tip the scale too far in the direction of one of our characters. We've already examined the toxic extremes of each character, but there are three characters that, no matter what ambitious women do to optimize their lives, tend to make up the majority of their movies when they've been written into the script. I call these the Big 3: the CEO, the Partner, and the Caregiver.

A caveat for this chapter: You may decide to not have one or any of these three characters play a dominant role in the movie of your life, and that's perfectly OK. Please don't take this chapter's focus as shade or a prescription. Perhaps you've decided to step away from your career to help take care of your children, partner, aging parents, or even yourself. Perhaps you've decided you don't want to have children. Perhaps you've decided to not have a partner. This book is about paving a realistic path to having it all, but *all* is subjective and based on the person writing the script (character theory Law #1: You write the script). This chapter is designed for the person who says, "I feel like I'm failing at everything" and is attempting to juggle work, family, and a relationship. It will also be helpful to someone who eventually wants to juggle the Big 3 but is fearful of how feasible it will actually be in their life. When you've been dedicating a large part of your life to one cast of characters, it can be difficult to visualize space for anything or anyone else. I get so many DMs from women in their twenties saying, "I have no clue how I will do all of this AND have kids!" This chapter will help us establish some boundaries and guardrails for the Big 3: CEO, Partner, and Caregiver.

 I had a call recently with a dear friend and former direct report. She worked for me when I was navigating three small children and a divorce. A time in my life when I would leave work every day at 4:00 p.m. so I could see my kids since they went to bed so early. Fast-forward five years, and she went on to work for a larger company, reporting to some incredibly successful and powerful women. She took the job because both of the women were moms, and she thought she would be able to navigate the push to the next level of her career while also being present for her toddler. She explained how the women she worked for sent emails and Slack messages at all hours of the night and scheduled meetings during dinnertime. They both had full-time support at home with their children and had (from her perspective) prioritized work most of the time. After explaining her frustrations, she flat-out asked me, "Is this what it takes to get to the next level? Do I need to sacrifice the type of mother I want to be?" My response was simple: "No. No, you do not. But you do need to acknowledge two things: intentional imbalance is important, and every woman will choose their own version of that imbalance. **Someone else's choice does not have to be yours. And yours doesn't have to be theirs.**" The women taking a pause in their career should be celebrated and supported right alongside the women pushing in theirs.

Intentional imbalance is important, and every woman will choose their own version of that imbalance.

There are two reasons women feel resentment in an intense season of life:

1. **Unintentional imbalance:** They don't feel in control of the tipping of the scale.
2. **Character autopilot and absence:** The feeling when you are showing up as a robot, going through the motions, not feeling present in your other roles.

In some seasons of life, you may move work to the front burner and prioritize it above everything else. Big projects. Deadlines. Big campaigns. But you do it with intention and with checkpoints. In other seasons, you may move your CEO to the back burner or even take it off the stovetop entirely. Either way, *you* have to choose those seasons. Honoring the imbalance is knowing that every season and day is a choice, choosing which character is going to get the attention and energy in that moment. There are days when I'm kicking ass and taking names at work, and I show up as a mediocre mom while Bluey and Uber Eats shepherd my children from school to bedtime. There are days when I'm determined to be a present and fun mom, and work is relegated to set blocks of time and minimal project movement. There are days where I'm present for my partner and relationship and focused on connecting with him. We get a babysitter, and I turn off my other two characters so we can give my Goddess a chance to come out and help reconnect with my Partner. (Let's face it…my Goddess really doesn't love being around children.)

The Big 3

Juggling these three consuming characters is a result of mastering the following essentials: non-negotiables, boundaries, and managed expectations.

Three essentials for juggling the Big 3:
1. Non-negotiables
2. Boundaries
3. Managed expectations

Setting non-negotiables allows you to create boundaries. Your non-negotiables should be connected to your perfect day (vision for your life) and character stovetop (priorities for the season). Where most people fail is allowing the scales to tip too far in one direction without communicating your priorities to a boss, team, or family and partner and, yes, even to their children. There are two certainties in life: Without boundaries, people want more. Without context, people assume the worst. In the absence of information, people make up their own, and human brains are wired to assume the worst and take it personally. They only see or know what you tell them. But with boundaries and context, people can support you in your goals and make sure one or all of your Big 3 don't suck all the energy and joy out of your life. I reminded my former direct report that she needed to communicate her needs and boundaries instead of accepting someone else's and then growing resentful because of it. "Hey, I'm stepping away from five to eight to focus on the kids but will check back in and respond to urgent priorities after that" is a way to communicate your boundaries. Now you can see if the other person can and will honor them.

Ten percent happier—Enjoyment creates greater effectiveness. When you enjoy the character you are embodying (rather than resenting them), you will lead them more swiftly to their goals. Take a moment to think about how you could make yourself 10 percent better and happier in any of the (applicable) Big 3 roles in your life?

→ *What is something you could do to be 10 percent happier at work?*
→ *What is something you could do to be 10 percent happier as a parent?*
→ *What is something you could do to be 10 percent happier as a partner?*

Ten percent happier at work for me means doing deep work in the morning when my brain is clear. That's how I can ensure I'm moving my work goals forward. I need to guard that time and have no meetings before 10:00 a.m. For my Caregiver to be 10 percent happier, I want to be fully present with my kids from 5:00 to 8:00 p.m. That's how I can ensure I'm moving my parenting goals forward. I find it's the time my kids are most open to talking—during long car rides to after-school activities, during dinner, and at bedtime. I turn off notifications on my phone during this time to ensure there are no interruptions from work. For my Partner, we take morning walks to Panther Coffee and keep our weekly date nights. We honor 8:00 to 9:00 p.m. as time to reconnect emotionally and physically. I guard those times from any other characters and communicate them to my teams and clients. My Slack is set to "away" when I'm with my kids and partner. If someone has an urgent need, they know to ask me before 5:00 p.m. Otherwise, it will wait until the following morning. When I take on new marketing consulting clients, I explain my values and non-negotiables. Feel free to steal my script:

I'm so excited to work together and bring my twenty-plus years of marketing and start-up founder experience to this project. Transparency and presence are two key values for me in my work and life. Every day I will be unavailable until 10:00 a.m. every morning, and every night I will be unavailable from 6:00 to 9:00 p.m. EST to focus on my health and family. I will check Slack at 8:00 a.m. and 9:00 p.m. EST and respond to any urgent items at those times. These blocks allow me to show up fully to work when I'm at work and fully to my family when I'm at home.

The second component to mastering imbalance is actually **holding these boundaries.** How many times have you blocked lunch on your calendar or blocked time to get a workout in and then Nick in Sales or your boss books a meeting over it? A weak boundary is a high-speed interstate to resentment. If you deemed something important and declared it non-negotiable, it's important to never weaken it. Once someone sees the non-negotiable is actually, well, negotiable, they will never respect it. Being realistic with your non-negotiables and starting with 10 percent improvement will help you start to alleviate the guilt of juggling the Big 3.

Hey Nick, I'm unavailable at that time for the meeting. I can review the notes after or am available at the following times: 3:00 p.m. and

4:00 p.m. EST. Thanks for your understanding. (Side note: Please notice there was no apology.)

Realistic boundaries are key to all of this. I've managed people at various stages of their careers, and, as their boss, I've seen both realistic and unrealistic situations. Asking for no meetings during core meeting hours or doing a two-hour workout in the middle of the day every day might be pushing it for most bosses. This is where 10 percent happier meets communication and managing expectations.

If you still struggle to uphold your realistic boundaries, the next chapter will be a magnifying glass on the deeper reasons we struggle with this, thanks to limiting beliefs, but right now we will stay focused on tactics. The last step in juggling the Big 3 is reinforcing and **managing expectations** with those around you, including yourself. When my kids are beating down my door wanting to play Apples to Apples but I need to finish a work project, I set the Alexa timer for a set amount of time and explain to the kids when I can play with them, why I'm excited to work on this project, and what we are going to play when I'm done. Managed expectations lower stress and resentment. For everyone.

Everyone wants all they can get from you. Kids want more no matter how much you give. Your boss wants more no matter how much you give. Your Partner wants more. The less you manage their expectations, the more they will bang on your door or inbox. I was once told at a performance review that I was exceeding expectations and hitting my goals, and my boss said, "Just think what you would accomplish if you worked more!" More is more. That is correct. But more will never be *enough*.

I saw your email and will be able to get to this by EOD tomorrow is a perfect response to your colleague.

I'm setting a timer for twenty minutes to send three emails, and then we are going to build that Lego set is a perfect response to your kid.

I'm heads down on a work project and will text you later this week is a perfect response to friends and family.

Now they aren't pinging you every two minutes wondering what the status is. If you set non-negotiables, hold your boundaries, and manage expectations for everyone involved, you will be able to juggle the day with a bit less guilt and stress.

And this is where realism really comes into play. There are roughly 83.8 million families in the nation. In married-couple families with children, 97 percent had at least one employed parent, and 67 percent had both parents employed. If you've decided to place these three consuming characters on the stovetop, you know there are trade-offs. Equity is not realistic. You won't be able to spend eight hours a day with your kids, eight hours at work, and eight hours with your partner. Imbalance is necessary and inevitable. But there will never be enough hours in the day if the CEO character takes over all of the time and energy.

The 25 Percent CEO

I believe the biggest problem we're facing right now is that people are waiting to live their nonwork lives on the weekends. Every other character is relinquished to two days a week. Think about the last few weeks of your life. How many times did you say, "If I can just get through these next few weeks of work, things will get better"? "Once I get through this project, I can start to focus on my health or get back to the gym or see my friends or start dating." But how many times did those statements turn into months or even a year of "just get throughs"? Work has taken over our Monday through Friday, which ultimately takes over our lives.

How many times did those statements turn into months or even a year of "just get throughs"?

Let's zoom out and look at our time here on earth, since I've always found mortality and the finite value of life to be the biggest wake-up call to live the present day I've been given. Let's say we live to be eighty years old. That means we will have lived for 4,160 weeks.

The first twenty years, we're learning to become an adult. The last twenty years, we will be slowing and reminiscing about our

The Big 3

time as an adult. Many of us are in what I call the peak "adulting" years of life: the forty years (or roughly two thousand weeks) we get to take the clay of life and mold it into the statue that will live on beyond us.

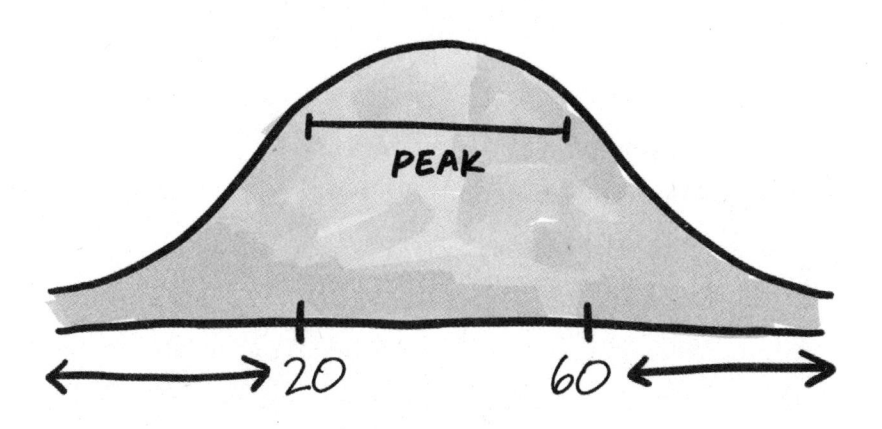

Forty years is about fourteen thousand days. But if you are only living for the weekends, you quickly reduce it to about four thousand days. The goal of this section is to teach you how to love work and honor your inner CEO *without* losing ten thousand days of your life.

Full human experience = 80 years = ~4,000 weeks
Peak "adulting" experience = 40 years = ~2,000 weeks = 14,000 days
Minus Monday-Friday = 10,000 days
= 4,000 days to live a life outside of work?

No thank you. I want more!

Let's look at what percentage of your peak "adulting" years is *actually* spent working (a.k.a. in your CEO character). Two thousand weeks (your forty peak adulting years) is 336,000 hours. If you work forty hours per week, you will have worked 80,000 hours during that time. That's only 25 percent of your peak human experience as your CEO character, yet so many of us are living lives that look more like a 75/25 CEO-to-other-characters split.

> Peak adulting years = 40 years = ~336,000 hours
> Working 40 hours a week = ~80,000 hours
> Work = ~25% of Peak Adulting Years

Let's take this math lesson a step further. We all have to sleep. If we remove sleep from those two thousand weeks at seven hours a night, we will remove another 98,000 hours of your peak human experience time.

> Peak adulting years = 40 years = ~336,000 hours
> Working 40 hours a week = ~80,000 hours
> Sleeping 7 hours a night = ~98,000 hours

That leaves us with a grand total of 158,000 hours (that you're awake) to give time for the other characters' storylines to develop. The anxious person will say, "But I only have 158,000 hours to do something with my life!" Whereas the grounded and present person will say, "I have 158,000 hours to do something with my life. LFG."

We need to guard those hours from time warp and energy creep

The Big 3

because our peak human years shouldn't be an endless string of "getting through this week" and losing ten thousand days to your CEO character. Review the previous math lesson and use it as a wake-up call to stop "getting through the week" or holding back other characters' development. Many of my DMs from women in middle management or those who are close to their thirties say, "I'm just waiting until my career is in a good place before I have kids." Let me reframe this. Are you willing to hold back 50 percent of your life for a 25 percent character? There's a saying: "If you want something done, give it to the busiest person in the room." Becoming a mom made my CEO character learn boundaries, cut through the corporate bullshit, and kill it in my job in fewer hours a day. Many of the tools I'm about to teach your CEO character came from my time as a mom building and selling companies. It's why I started a community and coach working parents to navigate the BS and get more time back in their week so they can build without burning out and take back their nonwork time.

Are you willing to hold back 50 percent of your life for a 25 percent character?

"How do you find work-life balance?" If I had a dollar for every time I was asked this question on a stage or podcast as a founder and single mom of three, I'd likely be writing this book from a bigger house with a chef calling to me that my breakfast is ready. My CEO character is the character most eager to tip the scales, so I created a system to pull back to a more acceptable imbalance: I reclaimed my 5:00 to 9:00 p.m. If you find yourself going from a medium-sized screen at a desk during the day to collapsing on the couch to watch a big screen while scrolling your small screen, putting other characters on hold, and feeling really unfulfilled in your life, it's a good sign you need to take back your 5 to 9.

The 5 to 9 Cycle

In order to rightsize the CEO back into their 25 percent position in your life and discover you have another 50 percent of your peak adulting years to devote to other things, it's important to take back your 5 to 9: the four hours every day when you can and should give energy to another character. Whenever I teach someone this protocol, I see a common pendulum swing. They feel empowered to take back their life and rebalance from a "CEO takes all" to a more diverse cast of characters in the first week. But then they overschedule themselves, leading to guilt and shame when they, inevitably, don't uphold the new jam-packed Google calendar of events and go back to the big screen, medium screen, small screen evening cycle.

The 5 to 9 Burnout Cycle:
Stage 1: Feel imbalanced
Stage 2: Overbook calendar
Stage 3: Feel exhausted
Stage 4: Shut out world, refocus on work
Stage 5: Repeat

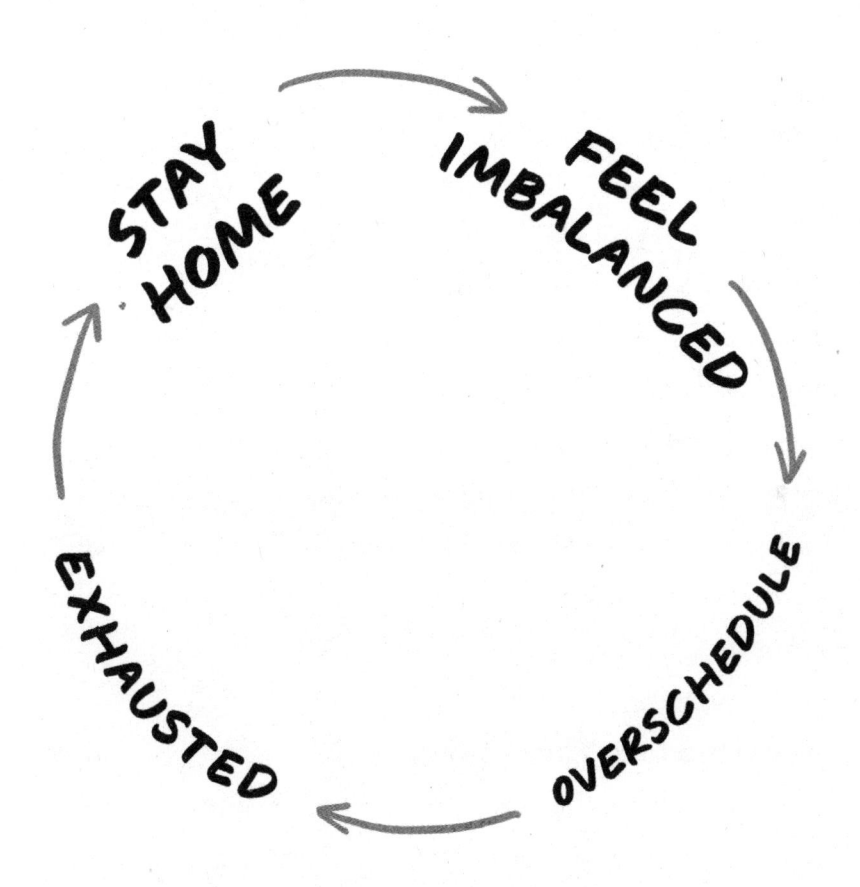

STAY HOME → FEEL IMBALANCED → OVERSCHEDULE → EXHAUSTED → (repeat)

Not every character requires leaving the home and seeing people. Character theory removes the guilt of staying at home by giving intentionality to restful and lazy evenings. The goal for your 5 to 9 planning is to separate from your CEO character so that 25 percent role doesn't seep into the rest of your day…or life. Use the following 5 to 9 schedule to brainstorm a few ideas for each of your characters. Once you've made a list, start with just one night a week and work up to your own 5 to 9 routine.

Let me give you an example of how I try to strike my personal balance.

My Weekly 5 to 9 Schedule

Monday 5 to 9: The Soloist
I start my week with a solo/self-care night. After my kids go to bed, I do a full-body shower, do my skincare routine and red light mask, and read before bed. I go to bed early to ensure I have enough energy for the week. I struggle to do a full skincare routine every night, but I can handle one night a week as a treat to myself. My partner knows he won't see me on Mondays. I need to shut out the world for one night.

Tuesday 5 to 9: The Caregiver
Tuesday nights are for Taco Tuesday and quality time with the kids. We make dinner together and talk and play games or turn on music and dance. It's my intentional night of fun with my kids amid a busy week.

Wednesday 5 to 9: The Goddess

Wednesdays are for transitioning into my Goddess character and going on a date. Whether I was single, casually dating, or in a committed relationship, I tried to go do something that would make me feel young, sexy, and alive in the middle of the week. My Goddess gives me the burst of energy I need, as well as slows down the week from becoming a blur of Slack and email and driving the kids around and picking up the house.

Thursday 5 to 9: Doctor + Lazy Girl

To gear up for the weekend, I use Thursdays to get a workout and sauna blanket session in and then be lazy and binge a show and go to bed early. My kids are included in this Thursday ritual, but I'm more intentional about making sure I'm honoring my inner Doctor and Lazy Girl.

Friday 5 to 9: The Socialite

To start the weekend, I love to schedule something for Friday, like a dinner or drink with friends. I want to be home by 9:00 or 10:00 p.m. so I can be rested for the weekend, but I've always found that getting out on Friday after work gives me the momentum I need to be out and about on the weekend. A socialite in motion stays in motion.

Go ahead and take a moment to plan out your new 5 to 9. Does it include time alone? Does it include time with friends? If you are in a relationship, do you feel guilty that every night isn't devoted to your partner? Let's unpack that.

The 100 Percent Partner

Now that we've rightsized our inner CEO to just 25 percent of our life, let's move our focus to the next Big 3 character: your inner Partner. The single most important decision you can make in this life is who you will spend your life with. It's scientifically proven. According to the American Time Use Survey, our partner is the person we will spend the most time with other than ourselves. But this fact can also lead us to make some drastic changes to our supporting cast when we meet the person we want to spend the rest of our life with. All of a sudden, we confuse the rest of our life with all of our life.

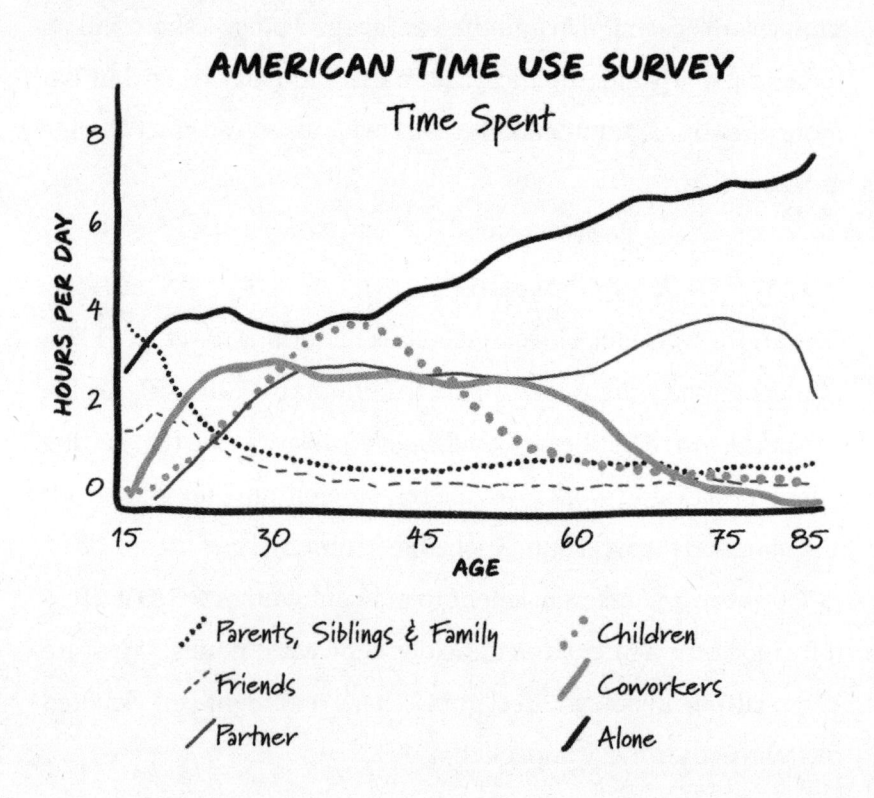

AMERICAN TIME USE SURVEY
Time Spent

Legend:
- Parents, Siblings & Family
- Friends
- Partner
- Children
- Coworkers
- Alone

All of a sudden, we confuse the rest of our life with all of our life.

Cast Replacement Fallacy

"You complete me." Not only a line reserved for the 1996 movie *Jerry Maguire*, but also a narrative throughout the dating world. Prior to finding a partner, many of us have a whole cast of people who fulfill different needs. You have your workout buddies. The people in your industry you talk about work and trends with. You have foodie friends to go try out the latest restaurants. You go on vacations with others. But then you fall in love and try to jam all of those needs into your partner. You expect your partner to become your workout buddy, vacation buddy, foodie friend, and person you talk to about all your work drama. It's important to understand this common cast replacement fallacy because the feasibility of one person replacing ten-plus people in the cast of your life is not realistic at best and, at worst, unfair. The fastest way to resentment in a relationship is expecting one person to meet every single need of your characters.

CAST REPLACEMENT FALLACY

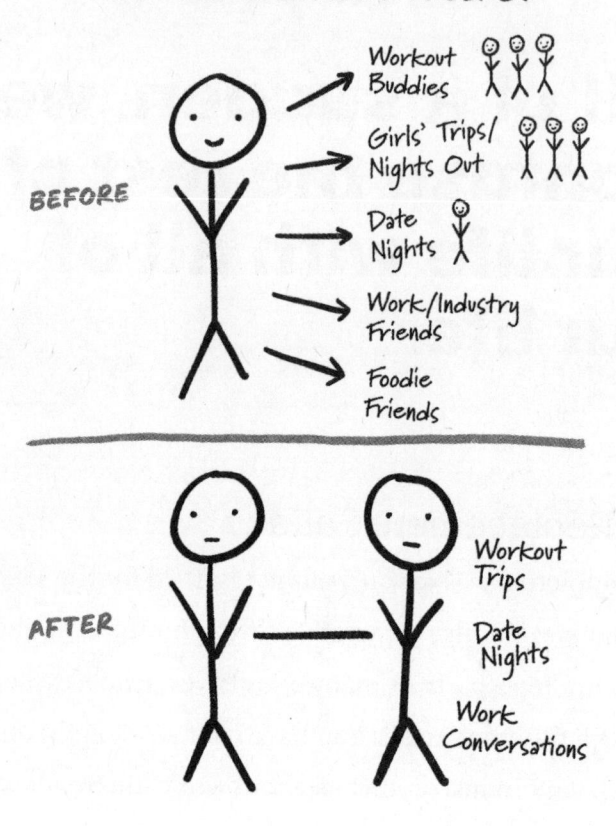

BEFORE
- Workout Buddies
- Girls' Trips / Nights Out
- Date Nights
- Work/Industry Friends
- Foodie Friends

AFTER
- Workout Trips
- Date Nights
- Work Conversations

If I could go back and tell nineteen-year-old Amanda anything, it would be these three things: First, find the person you can see yourself drinking coffee with when you are eighty years old. The person who makes you smile and laugh, and you can talk with for hours. Because according to that chart earlier in this chapter, it's going to be a lot of hours together. The second thing I wish I could tell my younger self? A relationship takes two complete individuals. It's a 1 + 1 = 2 situation and not 1 + 1/2 = 2. No one is completing (or fixing) anyone. It is our job to address our trauma and put in the work. Remember that wall we discussed when the Toxic Caregiver and Toxic Partner team up—the wall that we attempt to hold up for someone else? For a while it is manageable, but over time, the weight of the wall is too much. You can't hold it up forever. Eventually, the wall will crush you. That's what it's like when we don't show up as two whole individuals doing their own work, patching up their own walls before they crush anyone. Lastly, I would tell nineteen-year-old Amanda to keep an active supporting cast. Your partner doesn't need to be the only person in your life, but over and over again I would let love overshadow important friendships. Keep those workout buddies. Go on girls' trips. Make industry friends. Choosing a partner for the rest of your life does not mean every hour of your life.

Review your 5 to 9 schedule. If you are in a relationship, did your Partner character take over most nights of the week? What changes do you want to make to ensure you aren't confusing showing up as a full person for your partner as showing up 100 percent of the time with them?

The Worst Plot Twists

From the moment you say "I do," a timer begins. When the timer goes off in seven years, half of the couples will be divorced. Getting a divorce is one of the biggest derailments in a person's life. Was it the best thing that happened *for* me? Yes. But it was also the worst thing that happened *to* me. Something can be amazing for your future while also being miserable for your present. For most people who get divorced, it takes years to recover from the financial and emotional setbacks. It took me five years to feel back on track financially and emotionally. Divorce derailed many of my characters from their plotlines. Knowing what to look for in a partner and what you need from them could prevent this.

Getting engaged at nineteen meant I never had a season of being alone as an adult. As soon as my divorce was finalized at age thirty-four, I started to spiral. Who is going to take care of me? Who is going to care *about* me? The crazy thing is that when you are in a toxic relationship, no one is actually taking care of you or caring about you. It's an illusion. **Security doesn't come from relationship status. It comes from emotional safety and stability.** I had to learn to feel safe while independent of another person. I had to learn that being alone wasn't synonymous with being lonely. I had to learn to provide that stability and care to myself.

But then something happened. I swung the pendulum too far in the opposite direction. I learned to meet my own needs of safety and stability, so dating became a thing that was only for fun and pleasure, not partnership or peace. I was on the dating scene for six years after my divorce. I know it's rough out there, but let's talk about toxic independence for a moment. When you've been hurt by someone, it can harden you to the idea of depending on someone again. But needing someone and wanting someone are two very different things. When you accept this, you take back your power. You hold boundaries and stop allowing toxic behavior in a relationship because you know you will be OK on your own if it ends. Be strong enough to not need someone, but soft enough to want someone. Yes, you will be OK on your own, but you can only find something if you remain open to the idea that you may not have to be. You may find a person who wants to see the world with you.

Oranges, Birds, and Butterflies

The Gottman Institute predicts divorce with 90 percent accuracy. As part of his research, Dr. John Gottman conducted a study with newlyweds and then followed up with them six years later. Some of the couples remained together. Some had divorced. The couples that stayed married were much better at one thing: turning toward one another versus away. Emotional bids are little moments throughout the day where we are looking for connection with our partner. A bid is another way of saying one person is looking for some attention, affirmation, affection, or any other positive connection. An example list of bids from Dr. John Gottman follows. At the six-year follow-up, couples that stayed married turned toward one another 86 percent of the time. Couples that divorced averaged only 33 percent of the time.

Dr. John Gottman's List of Minor Bids for Emotional Connection

1. Pay attention to what I say.
   "How do I look?" "Did you see that squirrel?!?"

2. Respond to simple requests.

    "Could you take Pooh for a walk?"

    "While you're up, can you grab the salsa?"

3. Help or work with me.

    "Let's help Grandma outside."

4. Show interest or active excitement in my accomplishments.

    "Do you like my drawing?"

    "How were the cookies?"

5. Answer my questions or requests for information.

    "Phoebe's on the way. Can you give her our address?"

6. Chat with me.

    "Let me tell you what happened when he came back..."

7. Share the events of your day with me.

    "What've you been up to?"

8. Respond to my joke.

    "Did you hear the one about...?"

9. Help me de-stress.

    "I've been cooking all day. I'm so tired."

10. Help me problem-solve.

    "Greta wants to go on a walk, but my foot hurts."

11. Be affectionate.

    "Come cuddle with me while I read."

12. Play with me.

    "Let's get the chessboard!"

13. Join me in an adventure.

    "Do you want to explore the woods tomorrow?"

14. Join me in learning something.

"Let's go to that ice-skating class!"

One of my favorite Gottman tools is called bird theory. When one partner points out something that "could be deemed insignificant" to the other person, such as seeing a bird nearby, does the other person respond with genuine interest? I'm as excitable about most things as a puppy on cocaine. One day I was sitting on the couch in my Miami townhome and saw a butterfly outside our window. It was yellow and black and floating gently in and out of the palm trees. I said, "Oh my god, there's the most beautiful butterfly in the backyard!" and my partner looked up from his phone and gazed out the window with me and shared the moment. We looked up the type of butterfly together. We watched it for a while until it flew away. That's when I knew we could grow old together. Watch the kids grow old together. He wanted to experience life with me, through my eyes, leaning in. Months later I laugh about this moment because he is very color-blind and was truly just matching my excitement about the beauty and colors. He couldn't even see them. Love is (color) blind.

Choosing a partner is choosing the person you are going to spend the most hours of your life with. But don't confuse *most* with *all*. And don't confuse *want* with *need*. Your movie needs to maintain a strong supporting cast to ensure your characters develop. Find a 100 percent partner for some of the time.

The 18 Percent Caregiver

If you're a parent, you've likely heard the phrase "the days are long, but the years are short." And when this Big 3 character is on the front burner, it can be all-consuming. Every minute is accounted for. The first few months of having a new baby might take over your stovetop. That's a very common experience and a canon event that causes predictable imbalance. I was diagnosed with postpartum anxiety with my first baby. What this meant for me was my brain was on a constant loop of all the ways my baby could get hurt. This led to me not leaving the house (by house I mean studio apartment in the Upper West Side) for ten weeks. The days were excruciatingly long, and yet those weeks now feel like a blip on my timeline.

If you look at the chart from the American Time Use Survey shown earlier, you can follow the intense spike and fall of time with children. For math to easily math, let's say we live for one hundred years. Eighteen of them will be focused intensely on raising children. And, as someone with preteens, eighteen is generous. My kids are starting to want to be with their friends more than me, at their after-school activities and heading to summer camp.

But this is the job of our Caregiver. To honor the rapid acceleration and rapid deceleration of this role. It's the only job we want to get fired from. When our kids desire to leave the nest, it shows we did our job and our children are strong and confident enough to go out in the world without us. **We go from home to home base.** They go out and return. Out and return. Every time, we wait with open arms, eager to hear what they learned about the world.

When your Caregiver character is on the front burner, acknowledge the imbalance. It's an intense role for 18 percent of your life. Eighteen summers. Eighteen holidays. The years are short. Set those non-negotiables and hold those boundaries.

But the days are long.

For those of you in the throes of raising young children, it's hard to fully embrace the beauty of this short stint in our lives. It's the fastest eighteen years you will ever experience. But we are too busy in the minutes: making food, doctor's appointments, cleaning, ordering supplies, and researching activities, all while juggling the other roles in our lives.

When I find my Caregiver struggling to see the beauty and brevity of this season of life, I use a visualization exercise. I picture my ninety-year-old self sitting in the corner of the room. Thanks to the TikTok age filter for making this visualization exercise way more realistic.

All of ninety-year-old Amanda's characters have retired, one by one. She now spends her time reminiscing about the characters that came before her and sits in the corner watching the present moment, soaking in every detail. The way Greyson twists his hair with his tiny hands while I read *Goodnight, Goodnight Construction Site*. The townhome we decorated together and the astronaut statue that fell, and I never superglued it back together. Every detail. Ninety-year-old Amanda sits and remembers it all with the type of nostalgia that warms your entire body. If I find myself on autopilot and unable to soak in the moment, I change the lens. Everything seems a lot sweeter when you live the present moment like a fond memory.

Take a moment to think about yourself as a ninety-year-old.

Ninety-year-old you is nostalgic for the life you have now. She misses this chaos and fun and wishes she still had all the time ahead of her to live this life again and soak everything up.

It's not lost on me that our peak CEO years and peak Caregiver years usually line up right on top of each other. Be kind to yourself and know there is only so much you can do in a day, so it's crucial to focus on the most important things.

The Two-Do Matrix

This tool has had the greatest impact on my Big 3. We can't do it all every day. So I created this tool after years of studying productivity and realizing many productivity blogs and gurus are wrong. Long to-do lists are hurting you. To-do lists are dopamine creators. When we scroll a long to-do list, we look for the easiest thing to do so we can get that dopamine hit. But usually, the easiest thing isn't the most important thing. The easiest thing doesn't move our characters toward their larger goals. So, let's reframe it: Keep your ongoing list of things as a "parking lot," not a to-do. Every day, you are going to choose *two* things to do every day for each character and consider the day "successful" when you've accomplished those. This is now your two-do list. See what I did there?

Go back to your non-negotiables and ask yourself:

→ *What are two things I want to do tomorrow to push my career goals forward?*

→ *What are two things I want to do tomorrow to push my relationship goals forward?*

The Big 3

→ *What are two things I want to do tomorrow to push my parenting goals forward?*

At the end of every day, I create this Two-Do Matrix. If I get two big things done a day, that's ten things done per character per week! Most people are so paralyzed by the thought of all their long lists of to-dos and tasks and notifications that they won't even finish two things in a week, let alone ten.

The Two-Do Matrix: Example

	CEO	Partner	Caregiver
Two-do #1	Finish deck for client	Coffee walk	Make dinner together
Two-do #2	Write newsletter	No phone cuddle session before bed	Pre-bedtime talks

Your Turn: Create Your Two-Do Matrix

	CEO	Partner	Caregiver
Two-do #1			
Two-do #2			

Pay It Forward

When we talk about the brevity and intensity of eighteen years of parenthood, it can conjure up feelings of guilt for wanting to use any moment of it on something other than being with our kids. But I want to share a final thought about the beautiful imbalance of the Big 3: We are paving the way for our children to understand what it takes to honor all the characters inside of them. If we don't honor our other characters and the imbalance of work, relationships, and fun, our children won't know how to establish their own boundaries and create space for their various characters. I don't want my daughters to feel the guilt I feel as a working mom thanks to my mom being a stay-at-home mom. I was never taught how to balance ambition with motherhood, so with every boundary I set, guilt follows.

Juggling the Big 3 is a constant pursuit of 10 percent more enjoyment and rightsizing each of the characters appropriately. We take back our 5 to 9 and make sure our CEO doesn't take over the whole script. We show up as two whole individuals in a relationship and don't confuse the rest of our life with every moment of our life. We honor the brevity and intensity of the eighteen years of raising children while demonstrating what it looks like to honor the imbalance so future generations can feel less guilt and burnout.

Cure Comparisonitis

The last tip for allowing the Big 3 to thrive is to cure comparisonitis. If we don't, we will struggle with procrastination and fear of failing in every task in front of us as we obsess about not being as good as the person next to us. Over the last twenty years, the digital age has broken down the barriers to information, and we can see what options are available to us in this lifetime. The year 2004 was my freshman year of college and the launch of Facebook, our gateway drug to putting our lives on display and paving the way toward the concept of a "personal brand." Before social media, celebrities were people on movie screens and in the newspaper or in advertisements. They were untouchable and, thus, incomparable. Their life was Hollywood. Mine was Main Street. Apples to oranges. But the rise of social media has shown us that even the girl on Main Street can gain attention, influence, and power. She can throw the best birthday parties while juggling a career and having the perfect relationship and body. Our careers, parenting styles, and relationships now feel immense pressure to be more. They are now a means of self-expression and a personal brand rather than a paycheck, relationship, or role as a parent.

Prior to the 1990s and 2000s, your neighbors' American dreams weren't on display in front of you every day. Your work stayed at work. Their work stayed at work. Their parenting style stayed on their lawn. Yours stayed on yours. But once we got access to information and an endless scroll of each other's accomplishments, the pragmatic approach to life moved up the Maslow hierarchy of needs into connecting our work, parenting, and relationships to fulfill our full potential as humans. What does my career success say about me as a human? What does my success say about my worthiness of love and attention? What does my parenting style say about me? What does my relationship say about me? This explains, in part, why so much of our energy goes to the Big 3. We've been led to believe every single choice is a connection to our identity and self-expression.

The cure for comparisonitis is tucked neatly into the pages of this book. *Your* perfect day. *Your* stovetop. *Your* boundaries. *Your* two-dos. When you have a clear vision for your life, you aren't as influenced by others. This is easier said than done, thanks to the programming of our characters and how we view ourselves in each of the roles we play. We will cure comparisonitis by giving our characters permission to take up the space they need to fulfill *their* goals and plotlines.

Chapter 7

A Bigger Role

You've set the plotline for your characters and understand the tropes of the Big 3. But when things aren't going as planned and your characters aren't developing, it usually comes back to one thing: You don't *believe* your characters deserve what's waiting on the other side. Believing your characters deserve better is actually the biggest step in getting it. You are not your beliefs...but you do become what you believe.

You are not your beliefs...but you do become what you believe.

Now that your characters are defined and you've created room in your day for them, the next part of the process (the one most forget) is to give them permission to take up more space as they move through the world. Permission leads to action.

There's an old allegory about a baby elephant tied to a fence post. As the baby elephant tugs and pulls, it fails to break the fence or the rope. It tries for hours a day until eventually it gives up and makes peace with its fate. It stops trying to break free. Over time the elephant grows up and becomes a big, adult elephant with huge legs and sharp tusks and a strong trunk. It could easily break the rope and walk away from the fence if it wanted to, but it believes the fence to be some immovable thing due to its past experiences as a child with it. The adult elephant remains tied to it, believing it can never get away.

Limiting beliefs are the stories each of our characters tells themselves that prevent them from getting what they want out of life. Setting goals for a character won't matter if they have internal headwinds and narratives causing constant turbulence, making them unable to reach their destination (and worse, find themselves landing at the wrong airport). Just like the elephant, we all have things we were led to believe when we were younger that prevent our adult characters from breaking free. A key part of character development is identifying and changing these narratives before they hold us back from breaking free and living the life we want.

What we believe, we think.

What we think, we value.

A Bigger Role

What we value, we say.

What we say, we do.

What we do, we become.

What we believe will eventually become our reality. Our destiny.

The funny thing about limiting beliefs is that we usually don't even know we have them or believe them until someone points them out to us. Hi. I'm Amanda, and I'll be your mirror today. I will reflect some of your limiting beliefs to you to help you break free from them and allow your characters to go after the life they want.

The first step in evaluating if you are stuck in place thanks to a limiting belief is looking at the effects these beliefs can have on your life—kind of like how my stomach problems couldn't be solved by eating Tums with every meal. After further examination, I was diagnosed with celiac disease. No amount of Tums could solve the inflammation I was experiencing from gluten. Limiting beliefs are the gluten in this scenario, yet we go around jumping from relationship to relationship and job to job, struggling with financial security and taking Tums in hopes of offsetting the stomach pains. Continuing to live with your own version of gluten-filled limiting beliefs can have a lot of negative consequences for your character. You need to get to the root of the problem and stop just treating the symptoms. Where you go is where you are. You can't run from the root issue when it's coming from within.

Think of a specific character in your life that feels stuck right now. Your career? Your love life? Your sex life? Your social life? Your health? Look at the following list and see if you are experiencing any of these symptoms. If yes, you need to stop focusing on treating the symptoms and start treating the cause: the stories you believe about yourself.

Symptoms of limiting beliefs:
- Poor decision-making
- Staying in unhealthy patterns
- Feeling unable to find or take on new opportunities
- Low motivation
- Low creativity
- Feeling unable to reach full potential
- Negative thought cycles

The Self-Worth Iceberg

Whoever does the PR for impostor syndrome deserves a raise, because although impostor syndrome is just one of several types of limiting beliefs playing on loop in our heads, it's the one we talk about most. Impostor syndrome is when we feel anxious and can't experience success internally, despite being high-performing in external, objective ways. This condition often results in people feeling like "a fraud" or "a phony" and doubting their abilities. With impostor syndrome, inadequacy and competence are symbiotic. You attribute external success to things like circumstance or luck. You say things like "I got that promotion because the company had a good year and I've been in this role for a few years" rather than attributing it to your hard work and growing expertise in your field.

But not all limiting beliefs come with a side of high performance.

A Bigger Role

Another common type of limiting belief is the worthiness-to-sabotage cycle: This cycle happens when someone has a subconscious belief they're not actually worthy of something, so they eventually self-sabotage before they achieve it.

All limiting beliefs are rooted in self-worth. Hear this: You aren't doing any of this consciously. Limiting beliefs come from below the surface. Our programming is a culmination of things that have happened to us. When you haven't done the work to understand the stories your characters are telling themselves, they will operate daily from their subconscious—the 95 percent below the surface that we don't see.

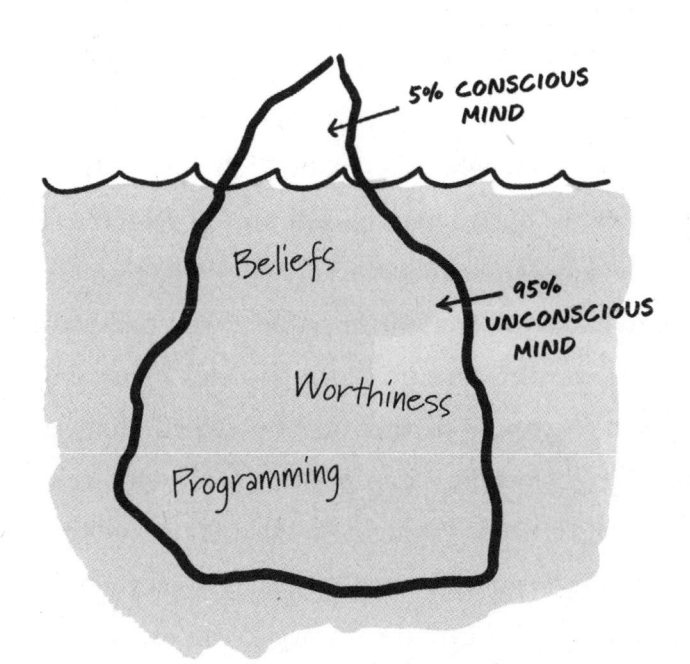

THE SELF-WORTH ICEBERG

Two examples I see often with this flavor of limiting belief (the worthiness to sabotage cycle) are money and dating. If you were raised in a home where rich people are considered evil or taught from religion that your time on earth is meant to be spent in suffering while happiness is reserved for the afterlife, then each time you come close to a monetary breakthrough, you will sabotage it. Subconsciously, you don't believe you deserve it. In dating, you may have been raised in a home where your feelings or needs were not valid. You may have had emotionally volatile parents or a sibling who required a ton of attention, so your survival skill was to be perfect. You didn't need anything. You made yourself smaller. You didn't have too many emotions. So, as an adult, you choose partners who affirm these stories in your head—people who make you feel small or needy. Or you may find someone who is a great match and makes space for your emotions, but you start a full-on FBI search to find one piece of evidence to corroborate your story that they too will not be able to make you feel safe or stable. If you find yourself in a healthy relationship and are starting to pick fights and looking for ways to prove your partner can't be trusted, chances are you are operating below the waterline of the self-worth iceberg. Your (relation)ship is headed straight for the iceberg, and yes, you will take everyone down with you. Our goal is to get you more aware of what's lurking beneath the surface so you can operate from a conscious and current state of mind.

Common stories from the subconscious:
- I'm not enough.
- I'm not worthy.
- I don't have enough experience.
- I'm powerless in this situation.
- I don't have what it takes.
- I don't have enough time.
- I'm not talented enough.
- I'm not strong enough.
- I'm not smart enough.
- Everyone else knows what they are doing.
- I can't handle conflict.
- I'm too old or young.
- I don't deserve love.
- I'm not good at X.
- I always fail. What's the point?
- I'm too shy.
- Bad things always happen to me.
- I don't have enough time.
- I'll be alone forever.
- Relationships only cause pain.
- I'll never be as good as them.
- It takes money to make money.
- Money is the root of all evil.
- I can't afford to be happy.

LEVEL 5 Society
LEVEL 4 Culture
LEVEL 3 Generational
LEVEL 2 Their Inner World
LEVEL 1 Your Inner World

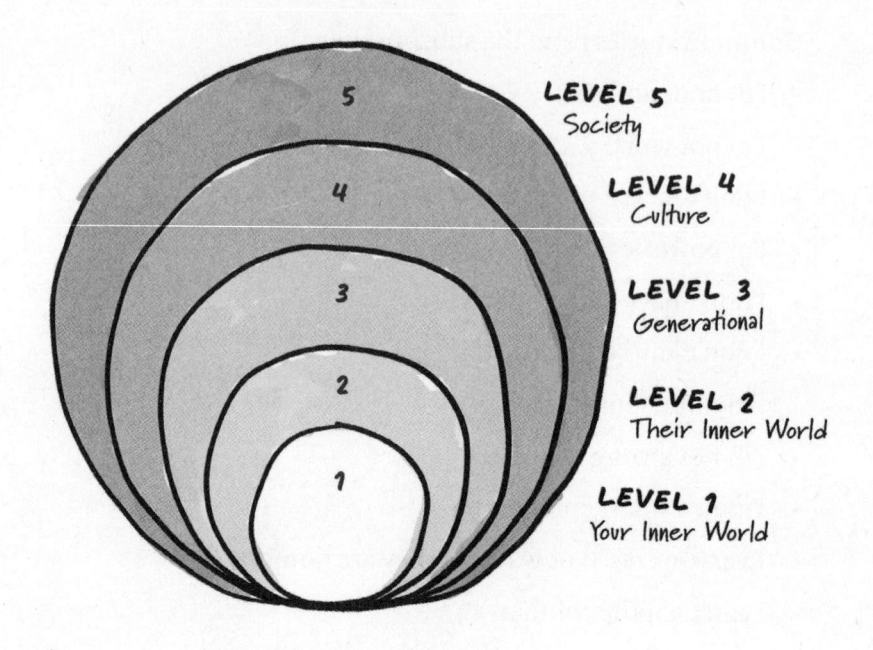

Origin of Limiting Beliefs

To understand where our limiting beliefs come from, we just need to recall the five dimensions of reality from part 1 of this book. These realities our characters exist within are also the same realities our limiting beliefs come from. These narratives create the programs from which our adult software runs. Without any software updates, you will be running from this below-the-surface, subconscious, and outdated software. Pause here and think about the following.

→ **Level 5: Societal.** *What did society tell you about your worthiness?*

→ **Level 4: Cultural.** *What did your race, gender, or community tell you about your worthiness?*

- → **Level 3: Generational.** *What did your family dynamics tell you about your worthiness?*
- → **Level 2: Their Inner World.** *What did your relationships tell you about your worthiness?*
- → **Level 1: Your Inner World.** *What experiences or stories about your life do you tell yourself that keep you trapped in a state of feeling unworthy?*

Making the subconscious conscious is what inner work is all about. This is the key to allowing our characters to achieve their goals and allowing their movie to play out in the way we want. Since many of us weren't raised in perfect societal or familial realities or without experiencing traumatic relationships or toxic jobs, it's important we reprogram our characters with more confidence.

Character Confidence

According to studies circulated by *Harvard Business Review* and *Forbes*, a woman will look at a job description and apply only if she meets 100 percent of the criteria, whereas a man will look at a job description and apply even if he meets only 60 percent of the criteria. If we develop our characters and give them the right tools, we will be able to step out of these limiting beliefs and take up more space, owning the outcomes of our lives.

I was at a venture capital event in Miami while I was building my second start-up. The event was held in a club, and due to the pedigree of the VC, most of the attendees were male. The firm hosting the event hired Instagram models to walk around as eye candy to make the event feel "cooler" to the male founders it was trying to impress. I found out because I tried to talk to one of the models, thinking she was a female founder, and she said she was just hired to attend. This was in 2022. *It's still happening.* Every time I walked up to a group of men, they thought I was hired to be there for their viewing pleasure, and their goal was to hit on me versus network with me. So here's what I did: I acted like someone they would be stupid not to know. I channeled a forty-year-old white dude who had exited four companies. I had done my homework on some of the founders and knew their investors. I dropped names. I talked numbers. I acted like I was supposed to be there, even though I definitely didn't feel like I was. My inner CEO was trying to crawl into the corner and wait for the perfect time to exit, but she has goals to achieve, and she isn't going to achieve them by sitting in the corner and leaving early. Granted, once I realized this about this VC, I never took any further meetings or went to any events they were a part of. Don't confuse finding confidence in a situation with condoning these kinds of behaviors. In a famous clip, Rihanna is asked, "What do you do on those days you don't feel confident?" Rihanna: "Pretend. I mean, it's either that or cry myself to sleep. Who wants to do that? You wake up with puffy eyes the next day; it's a waste of tears."[1] Now, we could argue that these rooms shouldn't exist or you shouldn't attempt to find a seat at a table like this, but the road to character success may lead you through some of these moments, and I've created tools to help you tackle them head-on.

Change Your Mindset

The funny thing about pretending is that one day you will wake up and not feel like you are pretending anymore. You actually embody the characteristics of the person you were pretending to be. Method acting encompasses a range of techniques actors use to inhabit their roles fully and bring their characters to life. Actors who follow "The Method" want to give a performance defined by authenticity, believable realism, and the expression of sincere emotions. In this book we will create our own definition of method acting: allowing your characters to take on additional characteristics they haven't quite mastered. It's a controversial method in the acting world because of its intensity and the all-consuming toll it takes on the actor. In this chapter we will refer to method acting as an exercise in building character confidence: *finding* a confident self rather than losing ourselves.

Before we dive into the steps of method acting, you must first understand and master four mindset shifts. In order for your characters to stop shrinking, take up more space, and own their success, we must change some narratives that have been given to women.

1. Impact > Comfort

The rise of women's clubs and women-only dinners and events has created safe spaces for women to share their struggles and experiences and give one another the cheat codes from others who have beat the levels in the game of life before you. This is important. But if you want to play the game, you have to know the players and the rules they *all* play by. And most games today aren't female-only. You are learning the rules from only half of the players. Part of my success has been making sure I get the invites to the dinners that have the best founders, VCs, and minds—not just the ones that I feel the most comfortable with. You have to shift your mindset and use the following method acting steps to get your seat at the table with the most impact, not the most comfort. This may read as controversial, but that's not my intention. I support and am involved with many women-only groups. I just make sure they're not the only source of my learning and support. Many doors of my career were opened by men, from rooms or situations that were not the most comfortable. But changing the narrative of comfort to impact helped me get into those rooms, stay in them, and reap the benefits from the people inside.

2. Expansion > Exclusion

Why do we shrink? Where does that come from? What is it doing to you and your energy? Most of the time we are scared of taking away something from someone else. Expansion mentality is remembering there is enough to go around. Enough love. Enough success. Enough attention. Enough money. Your success does not take away from someone else's. Your needs do not take away from the needs of your partner or your family or your company or your friends. We tend to operate with a zero-sum mentality with our characters: Whatever is gained on one side is lost on the other. If I ask for more from my relationship, my partner will be exhausted, or I'll be "too much," or I'll be seen as "not able to handle it all." If I ask for more money when the company is cutting budgets, I'll be seen as greedy and not appreciative.

If I ask for time to myself, my kids or friends will think I'm selfish or a bad friend or bad mom. Shift your mindset to expansive thinking. Instead say: *I will be able to give more to them if my needs are met. I will feel more valued and connected to my work if I am given the raise I deserve and am able to build more for the company. If I take time for myself, I will be calmer and present for those who need me. If I grow on social media, I can use my platform to highlight others.* Your expansion = their expansion.

3. Assumption > Permission

Method acting operates from a mindset of assumption and not permission. We assume we deserve the thing we are going after and aren't slowing down to ask if it's OK with everyone else. Many of our characters get stuck waiting for permission to proceed when the only person who can give you the permission is you. Success unlocks when you stop asking for others to open the door for you and find your own key or break the door down.

4. Vulnerability > Oversharing

With method acting, you will step out of your comfort zone a lot. Stepping out often triggers a need for immediate connection. Oversharing seems like vulnerability, but it's not. Vulnerability is the organic result of a relationship growing closer. You've built trust and familiarity over time and share things within that context. But when we feel uncomfortable in a situation, we can use oversharing in an attempt to get closer to someone without matching the current level of connection. In those awkward or silent moments, we might unleash a torrent of TMI, hoping it'll bring us closer. Every person is different in what they consider "private." I'm known for talking openly about my fertility treatments and divorce and even started a sexual wellness company for women, but the number one thing to remember: Check in with yourself before you share something. *What is my motivation for sharing? Am I trying to manufacture intimacy? Am I doing this to get the other person to open up to me?* This is a great reminder for online conversations as well. Method acting requires familiarity before vulnerability.

Grab Your Spotlight and Head to Cringe Valley

No one cares what I have to say.

Those people are way more qualified.

Everything I say is so cringe.

Everyone feels this in the beginning of method acting. I call it "Cringe Valley" because it feels as though you are wandering around questioning everything you say. It feels icky and self-absorbed to take up space. It feels selfish to sit back and ask for your needs to be met. But eventually you climb out of Cringe Valley and get to a more stable and confident place. A place where you are proud to take up space and set boundaries.

The spotlight effect is a great antidote to Cringe Valley. The spotlight effect describes how we tend to believe that others are paying more attention to us or are thinking about us more than they actually are (in their "spotlight"). This bias shows up frequently in our day-to-day lives, in both positive situations (like when we launch a new project and think our boss must be singing our praises to the leadership team) and negative ones (like when we do something clumsy in front of people and are scared to show our face again or are wearing a wrinkly shirt and can't stop thinking about it during a conversation). The truth is: Everyone is blinded by their own spotlight. No one is looking that closely at your every move (unless you are Taylor Swift… and if you are Taylor and you are reading this book, I'm not OK). So grab your own flashlight, start walking through Cringe Valley, and get ready to learn how to fake it till you make it.

As If

If the term "faking it" feels like a misleading deception, then you can reframe the sentiment as acting "as if." You visualize what the person you want to become would do, and do that thing. Act "as if" you've already obtained that experience and confidence. Once you put in enough reps of acting "as if," you eventually become the person you want to be.

There is science to prove this. A study was performed to prove the "As If Principle." This principle states that if you act as if you feel a certain way, you'll start to actually feel that way. The research was performed on two groups of speed daters. One group was told to treat their partner as if they were already in a relationship and romantically involved, even though they'd just met. The other group was told to act like they would on a typical first date: awkward and guarded. At the end of the study, the "faking it" group felt more attached to their partners and expressed more interest in seeing them again.

A few years ago I learned about a placebo effect study done in 2002. In the study, 180 patients with knee pain were randomized into groups. One group received a procedure to fix the pain. Another group underwent simulated surgery; small incisions were made, but no instruments were inserted and no cartilage was removed. Before undergoing surgery, participants wrote in their chart, "On entering this study, I realize that I may receive only placebo surgery. I further realize that this means that I will not have surgery on my knee joint. This placebo surgery will not benefit my knee arthritis." They knew they might not get an actual procedure. During two years of follow-up, patients in both groups reported moderate improvements in pain and ability to function. However, no one reported less pain or better function than the placebo group. The placebo patients even reported better outcomes than the actual patients at certain points during follow-up. They believed they were better, so they were. Feels superhero-esque, right? Allowing (tricking) your characters to believe they can do something, feel something, or achieve something is all in the power of the mind.

They believed they were better, so they were.

So how do we do it? How do you move from faking it to acting "as if" you deserve it?

Past Facts + Future Vision = Present Confidence

- **Facts** = What do I know, and what got me to this place? What data points and experiences have given me knowledge about what I do and don't want?
- **Vision** = Think about the person you want to become or find a person who thrives in that situation. This is the vision for who you are meant to be in that character.

When you combine the facts of who you are with the vision for who you want to become, you can harness confidence in who you are today. The speed daters knew they are good people who desire an amazing partner, so they felt more confident and attached to the people they were talking to. The patients knew they had knee pain and a fifty-fifty chance of getting treatment, and all had a vision for living a more pain-free life, so they felt more confident in their recovery, regardless of the facts.

The Four Quadrants of Character Confidence

Each of your characters will journey through varying degrees of confidence based on their ability to outline the facts of their situation and the clarity of their vision.

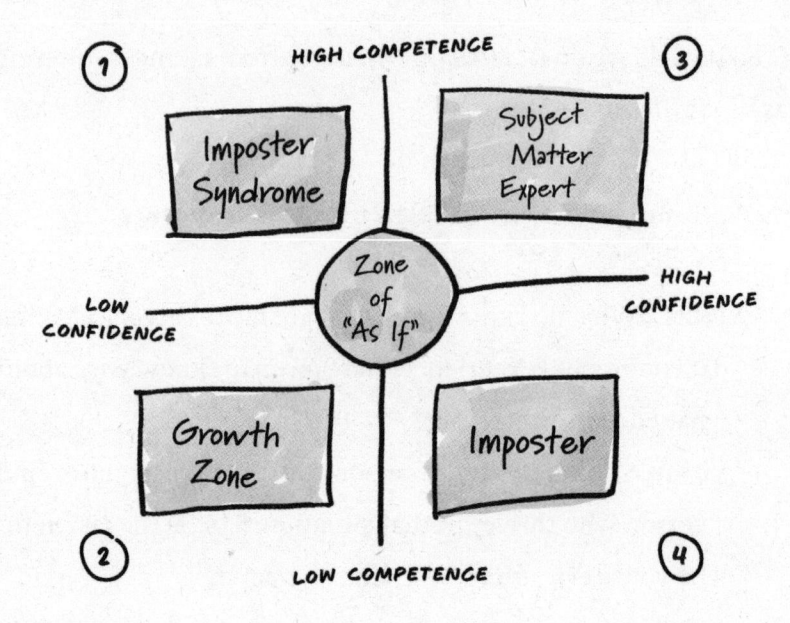

[Diagram: A 2x2 quadrant chart with axes labeled HIGH COMPETENCE (top), LOW COMPETENCE (bottom), LOW CONFIDENCE (left), HIGH CONFIDENCE (right). Quadrant 1 (top-left): Imposter Syndrome. Quadrant 3 (top-right): Subject Matter Expert. Quadrant 2 (bottom-left): Growth Zone. Quadrant 4 (bottom-right): Imposter. Center: Zone of "As If".]

Quadrant 1

Strong Facts + Weak Vision = Impostor Syndrome. When you logically know you can do something but struggle with feeling like you should be the one doing it, your character will stumble. You have all the experience and knowledge, but you can't see yourself taking up more space. Act as if you are the person you admire or want to become. We will study the steps of method acting in the following section and start allowing your character to embrace their expertise.

Quadrant 2

Strong Facts + Strong Vision = The Expert. Step into your power. Once you have the facts, competence, and vision for where you want your life to go, you will squarely find yourself in Quadrant 2:

The Expert. Your CEO will lead meetings with ease. Your Partner and Goddess will set boundaries and ask for what they want. Your Socialite and Soloist will have check-ins to ensure one doesn't overpower the other. You are in your flow.

Quadrant 3

Weak Facts + Weak Vision = Growth Zone. If you are early in your career or dating or wellness journey, it's hard to see where you are going or how you are going to get there. Seek more experiences to learn from rather than acting as if you are someone else. It's hard to act "as if" if you don't have enough data points to pull from. Study more humans. Collect more experiences. Keep learning and growing. Consistency and exposure are the keys to moving out of this quadrant.

Quadrant 4

Weak Facts + Strong Vision = Actual Impostor. Since you are reading this book about growth, you are not in this quadrant. You're putting in the work to gather the facts and data points about your characters. This quadrant is reserved for a few of my ex-boyfriends. You may know them. The guys who pursue you hard with the goal of validating their own delusional self-image. ("If I could get *her*, then what does that say about *me*?") These are the people who will love-bomb you until they have you and then slowly try to break you down in hopes of controlling you as the ultimate sign of power. These are the companies that posture incredible growth when in fact they are weeks away from missing payroll. The Twitter gurus who talk about life lessons when their own life is not something anyone wants to imitate.

Most people have a set of values and a moral compass that provide the guardrails to prevent them from falling into Quadrant 4. It also explains why many at the top of the proverbial business food chain and most billionaires are narcissists and on the spectrum of sociopathy. Narcissism and sociopathy are part of a class of personality disorders. I've found it essential to have a basic understanding of these disorders while navigating the business world and incorporate that knowledge into my mental models. Knowing people is crucial, even the ones you don't want to emulate but will, in fact, encounter. Quadrant 4 is one that some of your characters will encounter. Be on the lookout.

Fake feelings can lead to actual feelings. Fake surgery can lead to actual relief. Fake confidence can lead to real confidence. Just don't fake knowledge, experience, and connections. Those are for you to collect along the way. You can, in fact, rewrite your script and assign your characters bigger roles than they may have been led to believe they deserve with the right assessment of facts and a clear vision for who they want to be.

Five Steps to Increase Character Confidence

Daniel Day-Lewis, one of the most celebrated method actors of our time, famously used an immersive approach to portray President Abraham Lincoln in the 2012 historical drama film *Lincoln*, directed by Steven Spielberg. To prepare for the role, Day-Lewis delved deep into historical research, studying Lincoln's speeches, mannerisms, and personal accounts. He even reportedly remained in character throughout the filming process, addressing his co-stars and crew members as if he were the sixteenth president of the United States. You may not feel like you are preparing for a Steven Spielberg movie, but for your characters to level up and take up more space in the world, you will need to take on some characteristics that may not be 100 percent formed in the current version of you.

Welcome to character theory acting school, where we teach each of your characters how to display a mastery of their skills before they have had a chance to truly master them. I will use two examples throughout the steps to make the process feel more tangible. The first example will be for your career. The second will be in your love life.

Example (CEO): I've been feeling really unmotivated at work lately and don't know why.

Example (Partner): I'm really frustrated with dating and keep finding myself in situationships.

Step 1: Pattern Recognition

The first step in method acting is recognizing patterns, loops, or mud that our characters keep walking through and we'd like them to stop. This is when the stories we tell ourselves in our head become louder and louder, and in order to do anything about them, we must first notice them.

Create a note in your phone titled "Stories vs. Facts." Create one for each of your main characters for this season of your life. Whenever you catch yourself in a moment where a character feels triggered or stuck, I want you to pause and ask yourself, *What story am I telling myself right now?*

Character/Example	Step 1: Pattern Recognition
CEO: I've been feeling really unmotivated at work lately and don't know why.	The story I'm telling myself is that my work doesn't matter. Other people are seen as having more important roles at the company.
Partner: I'm really frustrated with dating and keep finding myself in situationships.	The story I'm telling myself is I'm not good at dating, no one wants to commit to me, I'm too needy, and there are no emotionally available people these days. Everyone wants to have their cake and eat it too. They want me without committing to me.

Step 2: Future Casting

With method acting, you have to picture the fully formed version of the character in your head. How do they go through life? What does success look like? The good news is you've already done this with the perfect day exercise in chapter 5, so before we sift through these stories and go hunting for the facts, let's zoom out. Close your eyes and picture that perfect day again, and say it out loud as if it's actually happening right now to your current character. If you've already pictured the perfect day for that character, let's cast that future into the present:

Character/Example	Step 2: Future Casting
CEO: I've been feeling really unmotivated at work lately and don't know why.	I'm being promoted to a manager role and in charge of the next big project.
Partner: I'm really frustrated with dating and keep finding myself in situationships.	I feel secure with an amazing person, and I know my worth and boundaries.

If you are struggling with seeing this, sometimes it helps to picture the person you want to emulate in your life. Study them. Use them as your source of inspiration, just like Daniel Day-Lewis studied every mannerism of Lincoln. This is like a real-life version of an alter ego. When I was at The Knot, I loved to study our CFO, Gillian Munson. I didn't work directly under her, so I watched her from afar and thought she was a badass. A former Morgan Stanley executive, she later sat on the board for companies like Duolingo and Vimeo. She walked into the room and took no bullshit. Men immediately respected her. She took up space with grace, confidence, and intelligence. She was a great leader. Whenever I am struggling to picture what "future CEO me" would do in a situation, I channel Gillian. Side note (and forgive me for this alt take): I think this is why it's important to work in an office at some point in your career or attend more in-person gatherings and networking events. I studied how leaders walked into a room. Where they sat. How they interrupted someone. How they disagreed with someone. Their body language when they were upset or happy or tired. You can't future cast what you haven't seen, so get in a room with people you want your characters to emulate.

Step 3: Fact-finding

Grab your boots. It's time to go fact-finding. Pull up the same notes app and look at the stories you've been telling yourself while in this character. It's time to combat the stories with the facts. Think of the concrete examples that balance out your story. Acknowledge black-and-white thinking and add some gray to the mix. Recognize the external factors affecting your situation.

Character/Example	Step 3: Fact-Finding
CEO: The story I'm telling myself is that my work doesn't matter. Other people are seen as having more important roles at the company.	I've repeatedly done great work for the company. My feedback and reviews have all been positive. My boss and I have a good relationship. The company is going through a tough climate right now.
Partner: The story I'm telling myself is that there are no emotionally available people these days or everyone wants to have their cake and eat it too. They want me without committing to me.	I've been in healthy relationships before. I've met healthy couples. There is someone out there who will choose me. I just haven't met my person yet.

Step 4: Reframe + Action Plan

Reframing is a powerful tool that looks at a situation, thought, or feeling from another angle. In changing the framing of a thought, we change the meaning of it. Reframing is *not* about invalidating or minimizing your feelings. Your feelings are valid. They are what you feel. No one (yourself included) should tell you that you shouldn't feel the way you feel. Once you have the facts, you can reframe your situation and add an action plan.

A Bigger Role

I've studied children of divorce ad nauseam due to ending my marriage with three kids under the age of four. A common reframe that parents miss is when children start acting out. We think: *My child keeps pushing my buttons; they need more discipline.* Reframing this narrative to *My child must be craving more of my attention. How can I give them the connection they seek?* fundamentally shifts the parent's mindset and approach and allows them to take back internal agency of control and move toward a constructive action plan.

Now that you have the facts from step 3, you can reframe and move forward.

Character/Example	Step 3: Fact-Finding	Step 4: Reframe
CEO: The story I'm telling myself is that my work doesn't matter. Other people are seen as having more important roles at the company.	I've repeatedly done great work for the company. My feedback and reviews have all been positive. My boss and I have a good relationship. The company is going through a tough climate right now.	My career is in my own hands (agency). I'm not feeling connected to the success of the company and will use the next quarter to use my 1:1s to ask for additional context and connection.
Partner: The story I'm telling myself is that there are no emotionally available people these days or everyone wants to have their cake and eat it too. They want me without committing to me.	I've been in healthy relationships before. I've met healthy couples. There is someone out there who will choose me. I just haven't met my person yet.	I'm choosing to wait for the person who chooses me and is emotionally safe (agency). I will move slowly with dating until I see a person worthy of my full love and attention.

Step 5: Repetition

Increasing character confidence takes time and practice. Daniel Day-Lewis didn't wake up on day one and embody Lincoln. You can't expect to start playing the game of life at an expert level immediately, but these five steps will develop your characters and give them the practice they need to master the skills that will get them to where they want to go.

Character/Example	Step 5: Plan + Repeat
CEO: The story I'm telling myself is that my work doesn't matter. Other people are seen as having more important roles at the company	- Every week you send a Managing Up Monday email to your boss telling them what you are working on and how it connects to the larger goals of the company. - Every 1:1 you ask for context as to how your work is impacting the company. - Every day you focus on the most impactful work first rather than starting your day in meetings, emails, and Slack.
Partner: The story I'm telling myself is that there are no emotionally available people these days or everyone wants to have their cake and eat it too. They want me without committing to me.	- You create a list of questions to vet potential partners. - You go slower in your next relationship and sit back, letting them show you how they are as a partner. - Every week you set aside one night for a date to help increase your dating surface area so you don't ascribe false hope to a person due to scarcity thinking.

When you use these five steps, your characters will start building the confidence they need to break through the cycles of limiting

A Bigger Role

beliefs and narratives that have been holding them back. They will operate from the tip of the self-worth iceberg rather than hidden, below-the-surface beliefs they were programmed with. They will break free from the fence post that once held them back as a child. They will start moving through the world with more confidence and ready to take up space

Chapter 8

The Spin Cycle

Taking a pause isn't a reward for work; it's part of the work. December 2021, 2:00 a.m. I stared up at the fluorescent lights of a Miami-Dade hospital emergency room after an ambulance ride where I found myself explaining NFTs and bitcoin to a first responder shortly after he stuck me with an EpiPen because my throat was closing up.

It had been ten-plus years of my inner CEO pushing for the spotlight of the movie of my life. Becoming the youngest VP of a public company while navigating a divorce and three babies. Launching a start-up, raising millions of VC dollars, and growing it to millions in revenue while navigating a global pandemic and homeschooling three babies. My CEO character had stayed on the front burner and was refusing to budge.

The first responders didn't know what was wrong with me, so

they treated me for a possible allergic reaction, and I slept it off in the emergency room, heading home as the sun was coming up. Three days later I found myself back in a different Miami ER after my entire face and arms went paralyzed at my daughter's holiday concert and I was rushed to the hospital by my ex-husband. This time they gave me a diagnosis: panic attacks.

My first reaction? *I thought I was stronger than that.* (Glimpse into my former self-talk. Something bad happens. Time to shame myself.) Growing up, I knew I had to work harder than others to get ahead. I was already behind from the start as a first-gen college grad from rural America. So I trained myself to push and push and then push some more. Stressed out and busy were badges of honor I wore with pride. My CEO character demanded the spotlight because she feared stepping away would send her sliding back down the imaginary corporate ladder as if it's a game and one misstep takes you back to the start. My Caregiver character was on the stovetop making sure my three kids had everything they needed and were supported emotionally, physically, socially, and mentally, but my inner CEO made sure everything stayed out of her way while she was laser-focused on her goals.

Many of us can handle a lot of pressure. In fact, some of us believe it's our superpower. We save quotes like "pressure creates diamonds" and "grind now, rest later" to reinforce an unhealthy narrative and lack of empathy and grace for ourselves. We confuse rest for weakness while pushing ourselves to a point of burnout. This is toxic grit. The inability to see when resilience becomes

The Spin Cycle

restriction. The inability to see when the drive to persevere turns into self-destruction.

Being ambitious and pushing hard toward a career goal is not inherently bad, but when you constantly move the goalpost of "enoughness," you will never visit a destination long enough to enjoy the view. The finish line becomes a mirage that always moves when you appear to be getting closer to it. And your body, like mine, will force you to slow down. The irony in hitting a point of burnout and being forced to slow down is you actually lose way more time in the long run. If the goal is progress, burnout is the antihero. Proactive rest is more efficient than reactive rest. When you train for a marathon, there are built-in rest days to repair the damage and toll the running is taking on your body. Skip the rest days, and you will find yourself in physical therapy with mandatory weeks off from training. One vital rest day skipped leads to weeks off. It feels like burnout is a buzzword of the twenty-first century, but it's important to understand the nuance of our environment and why we struggle with taking the proactive rest we need and why our bodies are reacting accordingly.

Proactive rest is more efficient than reactive rest.

Burnout: A "Workplace Phenomenon"

The World Health Organization describes burnout as a "workplace phenomenon" characterized by feelings of exhaustion, cynicism, and reduced efficacy.[2] "Workplace phenomenon" makes me laugh. Like it's a magical creature that jumps out of Zoom and makes you not able to text your friends back or fall asleep. But today's generations have a lot of things past generations can't claim:

Performance-Based Rewards

Today's generations were raised to believe our level of worth is directly tied to our level of productivity and performance. Good grades? Reward. Perfect attendance? Reward. Five extracurriculars? College acceptance. We've carried this into adulthood where we now tie our identity to job titles, follower counts, and hustle culture. The 6:00 a.m. club is now the 5:00 a.m. club. You have one side hustle? I will attempt to have two. When identity is tied to performance, rest is reserved as a reward. "When I hit this milestone, I will take a day off." "I will decompress on my next vacation." So we keep pushing and moving the "enoughness" goal line, reserving rest for a future moment of celebration.

Unprecedented Times

The second thing facing today's current generations is increased access to disturbing news coupled with an endless newsfeed of the rise in housing costs, inflation, and high interest rates, which make the American dream rat race feel like an ultramarathon that no one trained us for. Every day feels like an "unprecedented time." We thought we were playing one game of life—go to college; get a job; work hard and get a house, retirement, and healthcare—but it feels like boomers keep adding new spaces to the board so we will never get to pass Go, collect $200, or buy one property, let alone own a whole row of real estate. But we keep playing the game. Keep chasing that illusive American dream of owning a home and one day retiring while being fed narratives that avocado toast and expensive coffee are the reasons the younger generations can't buy homes. Well, I made my coffee from home for a year, and I wasn't any closer to buying a home, Bob. Alas, we keep pushing and chasing the elusive American dream in hopes of finding affordable homes, childcare, and healthcare right next to some unicorns and rainbows.

Addiction to Stress

Our subconscious programming tells us if we aren't stressed out, then we aren't pushing enough, and thus we aren't enough. If we aren't moving forward, we must be moving backward, so we don't allow ourselves to rest. We confuse movement for progress. So instead of allowing ourselves to rest, we pick up our phone and scroll. We say yes to everything. We jam-pack our calendars. Our neural connections are now hardwired for constant inputs. And thanks to social media's addictive DNA, our brain's wiring is being reinforced to crave dopamine hits and constant activity. It actually feels unnatural or difficult to slow down. We have formed an addiction to stimulation and stress. This is not conscious. We can realize we are stressed, know we need to slow down, and still pick up our phone to scroll while watching TV and shaming ourselves for not doing the dishes or putting that pile of clothes away.

Information Overload

Another thing our generation can claim louder than prior generations is the amount of information we consume in a day. Imagine saying out loud all the things you read and consume online. Before 9:00 a.m., you'd likely be talking about a new beauty trend, another shooting in America, a celeb couple's latest outing, what that influencer eats in a day, the fall of another crypto firm, how to get the perfect glow, your friend's new baby, the end of the world, and when WW3 is happening...and that was just your first ten seconds. Our brains have not caught up to the technological advancements of the last forty years and are still closer to caveman brains than computer software. We are not built to consume this much info. The next time you sit and scroll, take a moment when you are done to say out loud everything you consumed and imagine how it would be received if you were to say all of that in a conversation. You'd overwhelm the person on the receiving end. Yet we do this to ourselves every day, multiple times a day.

Misalignment

Fifty years ago, jobs were for financial security and stability. People stayed in the same job for their whole career. With the invention of technology, social media, and an outward-facing, aesthetically pleasing "personal brand," misalignment often leads to burnout. You push yourself to meet external expectations without pausing to consider your own needs and desires. That's the thesis of this book: Alignment and intention are the treatment for a prescriptive society. When the activities you dedicate your time to don't match your values anymore, stress and burnout will ultimately follow. It's a good thing we've already established your vision and plotline for your characters. When you start to experience burnout, you know where to go back to and check on your alignment.

All of these factors are making it difficult to rest while accelerating the need for us to. This chapter will be especially impactful if you answer yes to any of the following questions:

- → *Have you accepted that it's normal to be permanently stressed?*
- → *Are you constantly tired but finding it hard to give yourself a break?*
- → *Do you sacrifice a lot to be successful at work?*
- → *Are you easily annoyed?*
- → *Are you struggling to find motivation to do anything?*
- → *Are you noticing that job satisfaction is practically nonexistent?*
- → *Do you have a lack of motivation to carry out usual activities?*
- → *Are you keeping people at a distance?*

We can all agree that the game of life is coded for stress and burnout. We are swimming against the stream of all the aforementioned programming. Before we dive into the tool I developed to build proactive rest into my life, let's understand the different types of rest.

The Five Kinds of Rest

Most of us think of rest as sleep. Are you rested? Let me count the number of hours of sleep last night. But **physical rest** is only one type of rest. When I was going through my divorce, I was sleeping ten hours a night and waking up exhausted and depleted. I have friends who tell me they can drink coffee before bed and it doesn't do anything. But based on every study and sleep scientist I worked with to create House of Wise sleep gummies, caffeine *will* stay in your body for up to ten hours and will affect your depth of sleep and how you move through the various cycles of REM and non-REM. Many people confuse quantity of sleep with quality. Physical rest needs to be looked at alongside the four other forms of rest that are equally as important when our characters are teetering on the edge of burnout: sensory, mental, emotional, and social rest.

Sensory rest is a break from the constant sensory input we face every day. My oldest daughter was diagnosed with sensory processing disorder in preschool, and, upon learning much more about this relatively new disorder, I came to realize I have a lot of the same extreme sensory responses as she did—sometimes overstimulated, sometimes understimulated. When a person's senses take in more information than they can process, it can result in a sensory overload, which causes the brain to respond as though it were experiencing a life-threatening situation. Sensory rest is about giving your senses a break from the constant stimulation they encounter throughout the day. This type of rest is essential for maintaining mental and physical well-being, as sensory overload can lead to stress, fatigue, and burnout. It's important to reduce visual stimulation, minimize auditory and olfactory inputs, and give your body a chance to engage in natural and calming sensory activities.

The second type of nonphysical rest is **mental rest.** Do you ever walk into a room and forget what you came in for? Or lie down at night and your brain feels like Times Square at rush hour? You might be in a mental rest deficit. When we rest mentally, we give our brain time to recharge and process information, which helps us stay focused, productive, and alert. Mental rest is allowing your brain time without additional inputs so it can process the information it has been presented. It's time to reframe our thinking of boredom and seek out moments of reduced inputs.

Next, we need **emotional rest.** This is the act of taking a break from emotional demands that we face every day. An analogy I love (and you've seen before): We are all holding pitchers of water and sometimes we are full and pour into others...and sometimes we are empty, needing others to pour into our pitchers. Emotional rest is about creating space to refill your pitcher, either yourself or by letting your support system pour into you instead of you always just giving to them. If a particular character is making this difficult to do, go back to learn how to rebalance toxic characters. Of course, if you have a friend going through something difficult or your partner's job is really stressful, you should still sit down and fill their pitchers. They are running empty. So, you pour into them. But eventually you will find yourself just as empty, and you should make time and build a support system that also pours into *you*.

Emotional rest is figuring out who or what has the capacity to pour into you. Your Soloist is great for these times as well. Sometimes you don't need anyone else; you just need to switch characters.

Lastly, **social rest** is about understanding that not all social situations are created equal. Social rest isn't about pausing your social life. It's about the intentionality of your social life and auditing your connections. Superficial connections where you have to be "on" deplete your pitcher, whereas deep connections where you feel able to let your guard down and be completely yourself without fear of judgment refill your pitcher. Social rest usually means less time with the superficial connections and more intentional time with those who fill you up.

Building a life with appropriate and differentiated rest is critical for avoiding or recovering from burnout. Learning to optimize the push and pull of life is the secret to achieving your characters' goals. Understanding where our stressors are coming from is the first step in building a system for managing them. The next step is making space for rest in our daily lifestyle.

The Spin Cycle

During a washing machine's spin cycle, all the heaviness from the water is removed so the load of clothes is lighter when it heads to the dryer. Without a spin cycle, the clothes will be soaked and heavy and take forever to dry. Burnout is similar to a washing machine without a spin cycle. When we complete a particularly intense period of time, we feel heavy. And without an intentional moment to remove

The Spin Cycle

the heaviness, we take all that with us to the next project, job, relationship, or meeting. A spin cycle for your characters is where you allow yourself to extract all the heaviness after a push period. Spin cycles may come after a big milestone (like a work project or birthday) or transition (quitting a job, ending a relationship, etc.), but they are also needed throughout your day-to-day. Without intentional spin cycles, it's way too easy to neglect the characters that fuel our energy, spark, and passion and give us the mental, social, sensory, and emotional rest we need. Without pausing to check in, a character may stay on the front burner too long and burn (out).

The Three Stages of Character Burnout

I like to think of burnout as "death by a thousand paper cuts." It's not one thing that causes it. It happens over time. But anytime a character is starting to burn out and needs a spin cycle, you will experience the following three stages.

Stage 1: Annoyed

Do you find yourself annoyed at every meeting or task or interaction with your friends or partner? Are you assuming people are out to get you? You are in the early stages of burnout. Everything is getting on your nerves.

Stage 2: Overwhelmed and Numbing

When I was a CMO at a ketamine therapy company, the number one sign we monitored for when someone might need to talk to a therapist was screen time. Screen time goes up when we are burning out and avoiding our life. Scrolling more, playing video games, and finding other ways to numb yourself are signs you are moving to stage 2 and starting to distance yourself from the world around you.

Stage 3: Physical Response

When people are under stress, their bodies undergo changes that include making higher than normal levels of stress hormones such as cortisol, adrenaline, epinephrine, and norepinephrine. These changes are helpful in the short term—they give us the energy to power through difficult situations—but over time, they start harming the body. Signs your body is displaying a stage 3 response to stress include:

- Difficulty falling asleep yet feeling exhausted
- Sleeping a lot yet still feeling exhausted
- Headaches
- Tummy troubles (nausea, gas, or indigestion)
- Headaches
- Early signs of depression: general discontent, guilt, sadness, hopelessness, apathy
- Early signs of anxiety: shortness of breath, dizzy spells, headaches

How to Run a Spin Cycle

If any of this resonates, it's a sign you are in desperate need of a spin cycle. When you are in the stages of burnout, a spin cycle allows you

The Spin Cycle

to make more intentional time for the more easily forgotten characters, the ones who help you reignite your flame when you're burning out: the Creative, the Explorer, and the Goddess. These three characters are screaming to get out when they see the movie of your life headed toward an Academy Award–winning drama. They want to bring back the laughter, the levity, the curiosity, and the passion.

Benefits of a spin cycle:

- Time to bring down your cortisol levels
- Time to slow down the number of stimuli to your brain
- Time to pause from the heaviness of life
- Time to evaluate how you are spending your energy
- Space to analyze and switch your burners
- Time for your Explorer
- Time for your Creative
- Time for your Soloist
- Time for your Goddess

Spin cycles are not just for big life moments. Reminder, we want to build a system for *proactive rest*. Every day can build up with the heaviness of life, so we need to pause and extract it before moving on or we will take all that heaviness with us.

I use a 2:1 cadence for proactive rest. It's the cadence I've used to be a present mom to three amazing kids, build and sell companies, maintain my workout regimen, have an active sex life, and stay close to my friends. Here are the four spin cycles I run using this 2:1 cadence:

Spin Cycle #1:
Two hours of hard work, one-hour break

From 5:00 to 7:00 a.m., I do my focused work (from my two-do list). From 7:00 to 8:00 a.m., I am either on kid duty or I go to the gym. I will push for two hours and come up for air for an hour. I switch to Caregiver or Doctor for mental rest. In the afternoon, after two hours of deep work, I will switch to my Soloist and just walk alone for emotional and social rest. Or my Goddess may want a little attention, partner optional.

This 2:1 cadence has proven over and over again to allow me to hit my flow state fast because I know a break is coming. Two hours. I can do anything for two hours. For the Google Hangout and Zoom days: If I have hours of meetings, I make sure every third hour is taken during a walk outside or on the couch, where I can change up the physical and cognitive inputs. On the weekends, I will have two hours of Caregiver time and then have a one-hour break for another character. What would happen if you broke up your day with a 2:1 cadence? And if you start to say, "I could never do this," then pause and ask if you are reading off someone else's script. I understand this won't apply for people with infants or children who require constant supervision or with jobs that require you to be on for a full shift or in an office or other space like a classroom, hospital, or retail space, but if you work from home or have more control over your calendar, why aren't you writing your own script?

Spin Cycle #2:
Two weeks "doing," one week "creating"

Two weeks doing, one week creating. This does *not* mean I'm taking every three weeks off (wouldn't that be nice?), but rather: I prepare my work for the week ahead of time. I punt nonurgent meetings to the following week. I restrict meetings to two days that week.

Now I've freed up three days to create and focus on deep work. This allows me the time and headspace for my CEO to create a strategy, think about where I'm going with my business, get inspired by others' work, or go heads down on a bigger project. It allows my Creative to step in and choose something fun to do to create new neural connections in my brain, which ultimately makes me better at work. It allows my Explorer to start dreaming or planning where I'm going next. It gives my Goddess the ability to slow down and get back into her body with slower days and less intensity. We have to proactively break up the intensity of the workweeks, or else we will find ourselves on a fast track to burnout.

My days on my "off" week usually consist of:
- Longer writing sessions
- Extra sessions with a coach/therapist
- Long walks
- Drawing classes on YouTube
- Trying something new (workout class, art class, etc.)
- Being away from my phone and social media as much as possible
- Planning or dreaming of my next vacation

Spin Cycle #3:

For every two months of being heads down, one month of exploring

Every three months, I need to have something that breaks up the intensity. Again, this isn't about taking a full month off work. I have bills to pay. Babies to kiss and feed. This also isn't about building a life you have to escape from. This is about proactive rest and not letting a quarter go by without fun and exploration. Don't string 365 of the same days together every year and call it a life. If you feel like you can't remember the last time you saw your friends, had a good laugh, or tried something new, it's time for a spin cycle. We have to ensure we are breaking up the intensity with levity. Every quarter I'll come up for air and make a plan that leans more heavily on the adventure side of life. I won't let a third month go by without one of the following:

- A full day with friends
- A trip somewhere or intentional day exploring my city
- A staycation with my partner
- A training or conference to get creatively stimulated and explore a new topic

---

Don't string 365 of the same days together every year and call it a life.

Spin Cycle #4:
What about taking years "off"?
The average career is now forty-plus years. It's not feasible to push for that long. Additionally, life expectancy has a lot to do with how we think about responsibilities—work included. Research shows that teens are in no hurry to embrace adulthood. Welcome to an extended adolescence era: twenty-five is the new eighteen. Thirty is the new twenty. We don't have to be pushing all the time. It's not sustainable for all the reasons we outlined at the beginning of this chapter. So far, I've taken three years "off" in my twenty-year career. This doesn't mean I quit my job, but it does mean I'm embracing the intentional imbalance and, for those periods of time, took career goals off the stovetop entirely. Some may call this quiet quitting, but I call it driving the speed limit.

Slowing Down the Ferrari

I'm a *Formula 1: Drive to Survive* nerd and have had the opportunity to ride in some pretty fast cars. I don't particularly feel the desire to own one, but I can appreciate them. When you are in a luxury car, 100 miles per hour feels like 55. You have no clue you are going as fast as you are. And when you slow down to the speed limit, it's torture. The same is true in life as an ambitious person. If you've been going over the speed limit for many years, driving the speed limit will feel like a snail's pace. But going the speed limit is perfectly acceptable and fine for getting to where you need to go. Yeah, you may take a little longer, but you won't crash into a wall. Even F1 cars need at least two pit stops in every Grand Prix.

Throughout my twenty-year career, I've taken three longer spin cycles.

1. After baby #1
2. After divorce
3. After selling my company

Each of these cycles wasn't a "work-free" period. I don't have the financial safety net to allow for something like that. But rather it was a time to wring out the heaviness and embrace the switching of priorities on the stovetop of life. After baby #1, I left my job traveling the world working for a celebrity wedding planner to learn how to build companies. I joined a leadership program and owned my schedule after years of being in charge of schedules and never getting a weekend off. I told myself that for one year I would leave corporate America and focus more on learning and leaning into the entrepreneurial side of my brain while making money as a consultant. After my divorce, I drove the speed limit at work, moved dating to the back burner, and ran a spin cycle. I allowed myself to focus on my Soloist and Socialite and worked through the heaviness that came from divorce. When I sold my company in an equity deal, I needed to make money. I hadn't paid myself much in the three years of building House of Wise, so I took the first VP of marketing role that came across my desk. I spent seven months doing work that didn't excite me, but I had stable income and stable hours. I put ambition and my desire to build something meaningful on the back burner and let my Explorer and Creative and Partner characters get way more screen time.

Spin cycles aren't about throwing responsibility and jobs out the window. That is a luxury only a few can afford. They are an intentional moment to seek out the physical, mental, social, emotional, and sensory rest we require to avoid burning out.

The Four Parts of a Spin Cycle

If you are realizing you've been driving too fast for too long or just "adulting so hard," it's time for a spin cycle. The longer you go without a spin cycle, the longer it will take to extract all the heaviness that's built up over time. A common mistake I see when someone attempts a bigger spin cycle is they say, "I need to take the foot off the pedal," and then they spend all of their spin cycle time stressing and planning about what they are going to do with their life. They force themselves to still wake up and sit at their computer, perhaps this time at a coffee shop. But regardless, they are still reading from an old script when they are trying to change the plot entirely. To run a successful spin cycle and extract the heaviness from your life, you need to progress through the following four steps.

Part 1: Identify you are in one.

The first step is acknowledging you are going to take a larger spin cycle and deciding what that means. Which character are you pushing to the back burner or removing from the stove?

Part 2: Identify how long it will run.

Next, you must identify a time frame. Will this cycle run for a week? A month? A quarter? A full year? Setting a time frame allows two things. First, it allows you to fully reset because your brain knows when you are going to return to pushing. Otherwise, you will spend the entire cycle adding water and not extracting any. Second, it creates the deadline for when you will check in with yourself and start making decisions.

Part 3: Let it run.

Now it's time to let it run. For as long as you just determined, start creating space for your other characters. The ones for whom you haven't allowed much camera time. Let your Lazy Girl sleep in. Let your Explorer roam a city. Let your Goddess lie around and pleasure herself. Whatever it is, let these other characters take over. Guilt-free. You know the cycle will end, so let them enjoy their time in the spotlight.

Part 4: Schedule a check-in.

If you start asking yourself what your perfect day looks like at the beginning of the cycle, you won't get a clear answer. You are depleted of all spark and motivation. You have to wait until the cycle is almost complete and then reassess what you want for your life and what changes you want to make. Schedule time for the check-in, and then don't think about it again until that moment. Let the cycle run.

At the end of a successful spin cycle, you will have allowed yourself enough mental, social, emotional, and sensory rest to see your path forward with clear eyes and a clear heart. You are no longer looking at your situation through a lens of burnout and scarcity but now from a place of abundance and energy. The best decisions are made when you are running toward something, not away.

The Second Mountain

We can be broken, or we can be broken open.
—DAVID BROOKS

Every time I've experienced seasons of extreme lows, I find there is a breakthrough waiting on the other side of a spin cycle. Because of those data points, I've learned to embrace the walks through each of these valleys, knowing that they will eventually lead me to a new mountain. In his book *The Second Mountain*, David Brooks talks about the two mountains we all climb. The first mountain is one of hollow and individual success. We climb for achievement and self-worth. Then, as Brooks describes, we reach a valley of disconnection. We feel lost, so we start looking around for someone to help us out. Rather than doubling down on individualism and ego, we seek help from those around us and climb the second mountain with a community. We care about shared success and impact.

Let's look at this from the lens of all your characters. Throughout your life you will experience a version of this first mountain, valley, and second mountain for each of the ten characters. Spin cycles will be a key tool in identifying and navigating each of these journeys.

For Your CEO

At some point in your career, you will question your path and, if you are like me, may decide to embark on an entirely new path. I left corporate America as a CMO to build a consulting, coaching, and writing career. Your first mountain will likely be about titles and paychecks. And that's OK. But there will come a point where choosing your company, your boss, and your career may not feel like it's enough. This is where you will run your spin cycle. Walk through the valley and consider what more you need from your career. This is when your second mountain will likely appear and involve impact, growth, and giving back in ways you hadn't been cognizant of in the first leg of your journey.

For Your Partner

Psychotherapist and *New York Times* bestselling author Esther Perel once said, "Most people are going to have at least two marriages or committed relationships in their adult life. Some of us will just have them with the same person." For me, and half of marriages in America, it won't be the same person, but we see the same pattern of first mountain, valley, and second mountain. Your Partner character needs to run their own spin cycles to allow for space to understand where on the journey they are. If you are in a relationship: Who are you with today? Is it the same person you met when you first started dating, or have they evolved? Reflect on how you both have changed and how you want to change for the better in your relationship. Our relationships are meant to continuously evolve, so be open to the journey through a valley and to the second mountain. If you find yourself in a valley and unable to decide if you want to continue onto the second mountain together, take time for a longer spin cycle by yourself. You won't make clear decisions out of clouded emotions. I remember my therapist telling me to wait until I could say I wanted a divorce without crying—then I was ready. I spent almost a year working on myself and preparing to embark on my second mountain alone before telling anyone. No matter where your Partner is on their journey, we must acknowledge the fact that relationships evolve and change. You either change together or apart.

For Your Soloist

Being alone is different from being lonely. Unfortunately for many of us, we have to go through the journey of liking ourselves enough to be content alone, not needing to be stimulated by other people or things. My twenties were like a marathon. I never slowed down enough out of fear of what I could feel or experience when it all got quiet. I played whack-a-mole with life. When something popped up, I ran to it. The next thing popped up, and I was on the move again. The valley for your Soloist will come when things no longer feel as exciting or fulfilling as they once did. Superficial relationships and activities that don't align with your character plots will start to lose their spice. But the second mountain leads to a new perspective: one of contentment, self-love, and as much excitement for the time spent alone.

For Your Caregiver

Whether you have children or not, we all will experience two mountains as a caregiver: the first as we mostly take care of ourselves and our needs, and the second when we get consumed by the needs of others. I'd argue there is also a third mountain waiting for us, where we no longer can take care of anyone else and have to accept the care of others and retire this character completely. The second mountain for our Caregiver can feel like Mount Everest if we experience both young children and aging parents at the same time. It's important to allow yourself a lot of spin cycles during this climb, or you will run out of oxygen on your way to the summit.

For Your Goddess

Pleasure and intimacy will also experience their own two mountains. The first mountain is about discovery, freedom, and agency over your body. We tend to focus on experiences and excitement. My first mountain actually happened after my divorce, in my thirties. It was the chapter of my life where I prioritized my pleasure, allowing myself to challenge my thinking and test my boundaries. The valley for your Goddess may happen when other characters push her to the background and she becomes harder and harder to access. It may happen when you realize the need for emotion, safety, and stability alongside pleasure and excitement—no longer finding satisfaction in the novelty of casual hookups and dating. It may happen when your hormones are fighting against the natural rhythms of pleasure. The journey up the second mountain will be with several other characters: learning to love yourself, feeling safe, and exploring what works for you in that next chapter.

For Your Lazy Girl

Your Lazy Girl is unbothered. She's not climbing any mountains. She's back at the hotel waiting for the other characters to come back with pizza.

For Your Socialite

Your group of friends will transition. The first mountain is about fun, frequency, and a mirror to the version of yourself you want to be. Your friends will be "cool." And then, at some point along the way, you will feel disconnected. Your life may even grow quieter, and you will question if you're bored or losing relationships. This is the signal for a spin cycle. Your Socialite character is preparing to climb the second mountain of friendships in search of impact, connection, and quality over quantity. These friends will play with your children or honor your decision to not have any or be there with you in your struggle to have them. They will know about your aging parents or struggles with guilt and grief. They will notice signs of depression or anxiety and lean in to help and support you. Fun nights out every week will be replaced with BBQs or long weekends with friends once a year. The second mountain hikers are with you through the rest of your journey.

For Your Creative

At some point along the way, you will feel as though you've lost your creative spark. The constant inundation by technology is accelerating this dampening of our creative energy. If you find yourself in this valley, may I offer a suggestion to check in with the five-year-old version of you? That version is ready to embrace a childlike view of the world. Maybe you loved animals. Maybe you were obsessed with holidays or birthdays. Maybe you would film feature-length scary films with your friends. Having children helped me climb my second mountain and rediscover my love of art and drawing. We watched *Art for Kids* YouTube videos during COVID, and it brought me back to my childhood days of sitting around with a sketchbook. Tap into your inner child. Reconnect with the things that once lit you up. They just might be the key to reigniting your creative outlet on your journey.

For Your Doctor

Even your inner Doctor has their own mountains to climb. Your relationship with health and wellness will need to go on its own journey. At first you may see exercise as a form of punishment. Or, it's the Wizard of Oz giving you the power to look good in your going-out clothes or bikini. But everyone will eventually tire out from these narratives. In my late thirties, exercise became a part of my lifestyle as a form of self-love, not self-hate. You become more neutral toward the changing parts and refocus that energy and gratitude on the ability to move and feel strong.

For Your Explorer

Your Explorer loves to find mountains to climb, but life can get in the way. The valley for your Explorer will happen when life hits those "peak human years"—when work, home, family, friends, and community add to our to-do lists, pushing vacation and tourist days down to the bottom. I've heard many cautionary tales of people waiting until they retire to go on that trip, only to have one of them get sick and not be able to do it. Your Explorer is a necessary character to run a successful spin cycle for your other characters. The Explorer will help your Goddess, Partner, Creative, and Soloist through their valleys and up the next mountain.

A Lookout Point

As you can see, every character will embark on these journeys, and their spin cycles will be a key tool in helping you understand which mountain you are climbing or when you are hitting the valley of disconnection.

Take a moment to pause here like you would at a lookout point on a hike to see how far you've come and where you are going and how beautiful the changing view has been. Now ask yourself: How are you going to incorporate spin cycles into your day, week, month, or even year? Now go through each of your ten characters and assess if you are on your first mountain, second mountain, or wandering around the valley.

When the movie changes shooting locations too often.
Sometimes in life we find our characters in a period of stagnation and unhappiness. The valley seems to be going on forever with no second mountain in sight. No matter how long or often the spin cycle, the characters keep seeing the same unhealthy patterns repeating. When we want our characters to grow and find happiness, we tend to look outward for the fix. It's a lot easier that way. I repeated this pattern over and over again in my marriage. Unhappy? Puppy. Unhappy? Move cities. Unhappy? New apartment. Unhappy? Have a baby. Happy in some parts, still unhappy in my relationship. Some people do this at their job: They keep thinking a new company or boss or project will help their CEO character thrive. I've watched people go through this with their Goddess and Partner characters. They bounce from person to person as they remain unsure of why they can't commit to someone and be content, always placing the blame on external factors. Or their inner Doctor keeps missing their goals, so they change gyms, find a new diet to follow, or bookmark twenty new recipes. The truth is, a new set can't fix a bad actor.

The Spin Cycle

The truth is, a new set can't fix a bad actor.

When you've changed the numerator in the equation several times and the outcome isn't adding up, it's time to find the common denominator. You. You've lost something along the way and need to go find it again. You are in charge of the movie of your life, and if your characters are lost, even after a spin cycle, it's time to go find them yourself.

Chapter 9
Lost and Found

Growing up, I read a lot of *Choose Your Own Adventure* books. They allowed you, as the reader, to make a decision at a fork in the road. For example, you can either go on the date with Dan (turn to page XXX) or stay home and call your friend Tori (turn to page XXX). Depending on what you choose, the storyline plays out with a different ending. Life is a lot like these books, and before we begin mastering the coexistence of our different characters, we must give them each the power of agency. Allowing each character to thrive also means knowing it takes active work and decision-making to find things when you lose them. Honoring the imbalance of our characters means we know that when one tips the scale too far in one direction, everyone else will come crashing down with them. When your inner Socialite feels isolated, your inner Partner can get resentful. When your Doctor feels unmotivated, your inner Goddess starts to feel inaccessible. When your Explorer or Creative has lost their spark, work for your CEO can feel mundane and not fulfilling. Staying in control of our storylines and emotions is key to living the life we want.

The Power of Neutrality

Many venture capitalists agree that second-time founders are going to be more successful than first-time founders. Second-time founders have a 30 percent chance of success with their next venture despite what happened with their first. Why? Because they know what to expect, and they don't ride the highs as high and the lows as low. They stay neutral. Levelheaded. Second-time founders understand extreme highs and lows are part of the journey. You can literally go from thinking, *I'm going to be a billionaire!* to *The company is going to fail!* in a matter of hours. Second-time founders don't allow themselves to be swung with the highs and lows, and they conserve their energy.

When I first got divorced, every "first" was like a Band-Aid rip to my heart. The kids' first vacation without me—rip. Their first haircut without me—rip. Their first tooth lost without me—rip. I will never say it gets easier, but it gets *neutral*. Neutrality is not allowing something or someone to knock our characters off track. We may not love the thing that is happening, but we accept that it is. When something happens that rocks me pretty hard, I remind myself that I'm strengthening a muscle, and the next time I have to carry this load, it won't feel so hard because I've been here before. Breakups. Career frustration. Lost friendships. They are a part of life and happen to everyone. But we are fed a lot of narratives that we must romanticize our lives. Love every minute. Self-love this. Self-love that. I want to help you understand what *self-neutrality* looks like. Self-neutrality is understanding the ups and downs of life and remaining neutral in the face of them—not shaming or blaming yourself when things inevitably dip or don't feel like the highlight reel we are fed every day on social media. We are not meant to live in a constant state of ups, but self-love programming leads us to believe that. Neutral content doesn't go viral. It's the extreme highs and lows that get the likes. A neutral day means knowing no matter what comes your way, you are going to find space, allow feelings to come and go, and get back in the driver's seat if some other version of you has hijacked the emotional bus.

There will be times when you find a character feeling lost and needing to turn your choose-your-own-adventure book to a new page to find your spark, passion, motivation, or courage. At these moments, remember to not blame yourself. We waste so much energy blaming ourselves instead of using that energy to find what we lost. You will lose things along the way. Just like I lose my AirPods every week, I also will inevitably struggle at times to find contentment or discipline. This chapter is designed to be a choose-your-own-adventure for when your characters feel a bit lost.

Come back to this when a character needs to find one of the following:

- Resilience
- Closure
- Joy
- Spark
- Contentment
- Momentum
- Discipline
- Peace
- Confidence

Finding Resilience

Those who appear to be navigating turbulence calmly have just strengthened the muscle of resilience (or they took a Xanax before the flight, but that's not really supporting my point here). In my home I have a quote framed in my bedroom. (I know, I know. But don't come at me with your "live laugh love" millennial BS. I'm a *cool* millennial. I swear.) It says, "Life is tough but so are you." I've navigated infertility, emotional abuse, sexual assault, raising three kids under five on my own through a pandemic, and much more. With each new headwind, I remind my characters of that phrase, and I take pride in two things: The first time is always the worst time, and I am tough enough to handle it. I will get through it, just like the last time. Just like all the firsts with my children and building my second start-up. Psychologists define resilience as the process of adapting well in the face of adversity. It does *not* mean you won't feel distress or experience emotional pain. Resilience is not a personality trait but rather a culmination of behaviors, thoughts, and actions. It's like building any kind of muscle. It requires exercise, practice, and intentionality. The line between resilience and toxic grit is a blurry one. When do you know when you need to keep going? A little turbulence doesn't cause the plane to not arrive at its destination, but a broken engine will. Is your adversity a normal part of the journey?

Most people struggle because they allow a bump in the road to stall their character's car. This is called rumination. It means that when something bad happens, we relive the event over and over in our heads, rehashing the pain. Many people get stuck when their character can't move forward from something because they are spinning their wheels in the mud of the past.

Which of your characters are currently stuck in the mud?

What events are they spinning on and not able to let go of?

Whenever your brain recalls something painful from the past, try to counter it with three things that have come about from it. Perhaps you grew from it. Perhaps it forced you into a new path full of new opportunities. Perhaps you built a new emotional muscle that will make it easier to navigate a similar type of turbulence in the future.

Finding Closure

It had been five years since my divorce, and I was still ruminating on what I went through and how I suffered, holding on to so much anger. My Partner character was stuck in the mud. And that affected my Socialite and Goddess characters as well. This mud was affecting the ability of all of them to move on, trust others, open up to deep relationships, and soften.

Then my therapist, Macy, asked me to write a letter.

The prompt was to write a letter to acknowledge and validate all the things I lost from the experience and learned from the experience. She specifically told me to not use the word "grateful" because you don't have to assign positive emotions to something that was traumatic. So, I sat down and wrote. I allowed myself to mourn the family I thought I'd have. The time with the kids I won't get now that I'm co-parenting. The ease at which I used to approach love and the ability to trust others. I wrote it all down.

The next part was most important: **conduct a ceremony.**

Macy's instructions were to either take the letter to the ocean and set it free or burn it. (I chose the ocean.) The purpose of this act was to create a ceremony to mark the change between the person I was before and the person I was going to be after. Kind of like a wedding. We don't magically change after the wedding ceremony, but it's a symbol of change and a new era. You are actively choosing a new way to be after the ceremony concludes. When I was leading marketing at The Knot and we merged with our biggest competitor, a consulting firm coached us on change management.

We now had two teams who used to compete working under one roof. Their first order of business in change management was to conduct a ceremony to honor the individual companies and then celebrate their union. The underlying psychology was to give the teams the space they needed to acknowledge and accept that things were going to be different from this point forward.

The ceremony of putting that letter in the ocean and letting it go marked a new chapter for me. I let go of all the pain and suffering of my past and decided to move forward. When my ex texted me, I stopped looking for signs that he ever cared about me. I now just responded with facts, not feelings. All of that was now part of my past, not my present.

Closure can only be given to you by you. Stop expecting anyone else to give it to you. If you feel like you are stuck in the mud of the past, it's time for a ceremony. Pick a day a few weeks from now and plan out how you want to do it. I've done ceremonies for situationships when my Partner and Goddess are stuck on a person and need to let go. The ceremony entails Chinese takeout + looking at all the pictures of us one last time + a letter (iPhone app note) of what I learned from them and what I want out of a relationship based on the values I created for my Partner (from chapter 5) and then finally blocking that person from everything and hiding the pictures so Google doesn't accidentally create a nostalgic slideshow. I take back my energy and honor my moving on from that person. I've done ceremonies to mark the end of jobs and friendships. Your characters have big goals that you've outlined in the previous chapters, but if their tires are still stuck in past mud, you need to conduct a ceremony and free them.

> **Closure can only be given to you by you. Stop expecting anyone else to give it to you.**

Finding Joy

Happiness is an elusive long-term thing that I like to think of as the cumulation of finding joy in the moments of life. Find enough joyful moments and you will find happiness. People experience 20,000 "moments" in a waking day and upward of 500 million moments in a seventy-year life.

One of my moments happened on March 1, 2019, when I took the subway from my Upper West Side apartment to the Beacon Theater to see modern-day philosopher Sam Harris interview Daniel Kahneman. Kahneman is a psychologist and economist notable for his work on the psychology of judgment and decision-making, as well as behavioral economics, for which he was awarded the 2002 Nobel Memorial Prize in Economic Sciences. He is also the author of *New York Times* bestseller *Thinking, Fast and Slow*.

Kahneman and Harris talked about our "Remembering self versus Experiencing self," more easily described as living life or thinking about it. According to Kahneman, we have two selves: the self that is experiencing something and only knows the present moment and the self that is recalling the memory of it. Our remembering self is a storyteller, weaving moments together and connecting an emotion to them. It got me thinking...*which is the source of truth?* The way we feel when we experience something in the moment, or the way we remember it? When we sit and scroll through pictures of our characters' past lives, we have to acknowledge the war of the two selves. Your memory of the experience may not be congruent with the way you felt in the moment. When you scroll through the photographic evidence of your life, there can be a disconnect. Your photos and social media are a highlight reel of all the joyful moments without a line of sight into the down times in between. Finding joy is about being present in the moment and allowing yourself to live for the moment, not the memory of it.

When I find my characters competing in a moment (CEO Amanda wants to review a to-do list while Mom Amanda is reading *Goodnight, Goodnight, Construction Site*), I use the ninety-year-old visualization exercise again. I picture my ninety-year-old self sitting and watching the current moment. If you are watching a sunset, would ninety-year-old you want to watch you pose to get the perfect picture, or would she love seeing you soak in the changing colors and awe of the beauty? I created a rule on vacations or family outings: *Get the shot, lose the phone.* I spend the first few minutes snapping pictures of the kids and surroundings for my remembering self and then put my phone away, allowing my experiencing self to be fully present and feel the joy of that moment. Live for enough joyful moments, and you will find happiness.

Finding a Spark

There will be times when your characters feel like they've lost their spark. When you can't access the younger version of you that had the tenacity and passion for work or life or relationships or social outings. This is where your Explorer and Creative characters shine. They are the characters most easily left off the stovetop of life, but when you lose your spark, it's time to give them the spotlight.

Every year I allow myself one solo trip, one friends trip, one partner trip, and one family trip. These usually happen at the same time every year (solo trip at the start of summer, friends trip for my birthday weekend in October, partner trip in February, and family trip in the summer). Not every trip has to be a board-an-airplane-level of vacation. Sometimes it's a staycation with a break from the daily routine. I research things in my area that I've always wanted to try, like a pottery class or graffiti class or a concert that's been on my bucket list. When we are children, we are full of spark. Why? Because so much of the world around us is new. We are constantly in our curious state of mind. Not every character is wired to be curious, which is why you need to shift into the characters with a childlike curiosity about the world. If you're struggling to find your spark, give the matches to your Explorer and Creative. They will help light up your world again.

Finding Contentment

You are likely here because you recognize your ambition in life is outshining your ability to enjoy your life. This is the plight of the ambitious and a clear symptom of toxic grit. We struggle to find contentment as we travel toward the next destination. We start to feel like a toddler on a road trip constantly asking, "Are we there yet?" But ambition is not a habit to break; it's a character trait to understand.

As an ambitious human, once you achieve something, you quickly begin looking for your next mountain to climb. But it's never about the thing achieved. It's about the process and reward of achieving.

> **It's never about the thing achieved. It's about the process and reward of achieving.**

LOVING THE OUTCOME   LOVING THE PROCESS

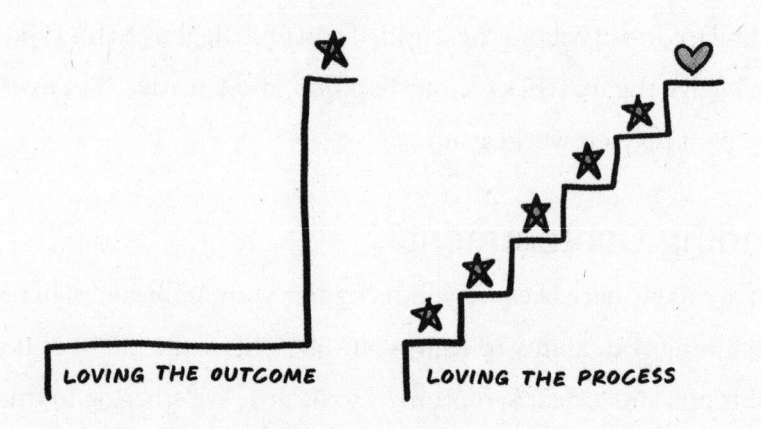

No matter what, ambitious people have a day-one attitude. A voice that tells them to keep pushing, growing, and moving toward the next milestone. That no matter what success happened yesterday, it wasn't enough. Ambition grows dark and grit becomes toxic when it becomes a constant, intense, and unrelenting sense of dissatisfaction with yourself. When the darkness follows you around and smothers your sense of self-worth and joy. The only way to conquer the shadow side of ambition is to develop gratitude. But how?

Ambitious people are not like everyone else. We want to push and squeeze as much as we can out of this life. And that's OK. But it also requires a slightly different definition of gratitude. Gratitude looks more like:

- Being aware of life's abundance
- Seeing the gift in the journey
- Realizing you will never be in this exact moment, with these people, feeling these emotions—ever again. Recognizing how cool that is.

Lost and Found

The best analogy I've been able to use in my coaching practice is around hiking. I've hiked a lot of mountains in my life, from Italy to Switzerland to even hiking Torres del Paine in Patagonia while ten weeks pregnant. The surface-level goal of hiking is to reach a destination. But hiking is full of changing landscapes and views and taking breaks to recover and look at the trail map. Here are five rules for how to climb the mountain of life *and* enjoy the view.

Rule 1: Realize the Destination Does Not = Happiness.

Many times, I get to the top of a mountain, pause and gaze at the beauty around me, and then shift my focus quickly to "how much further until the next stop?" since I still have to get back down the mountain. Life is a lot like this. The destination is not as exciting as the anticipation of the destination or the journey itself. I remember waking up one day to every single Kardashian posting my House of Wise products. Kim Kardashian giggled while holding our libido-enhancing gummy, and it was all over the press the next morning. (This was when she was first rumored to be dating Pete Davidson.) My text messages started blowing up, and I remember thinking, *I should feel more excited than this*. But then I realized the act of building toward that moment was just as fun as the moment itself. This destination was just part of a larger journey I was on. It allowed me to soak it in and keep up with the Kardashian limelight. We celebrated as a company together, and I got so much joy out of watching my team feel the pride of seeing their hard work pay off.

To help you enjoy the journey a bit more, ask yourself these questions:
- → *What am I building toward right now?*
- → *Why am I doing it?*
- → *How am I growing and learning because of it?*
- → *Who is on this journey with me?*

Rule 2: Stop to Look Up.

When you're hiking on steep or rocky terrain, you have to look at your feet. One wrong step and you can twist your ankle or fall. The only way to safely look around at the changing landscape is to pause and look up.

Here are three ways I pause on the walk of life:

1. Friday reflection walks (one to two hours with no phone) to think about the highs and lows of the week
2. Monthly reflection day where I look at my goals and growth toward them
3. Annual solo trip where I step away from my life and acknowledge the growth, milestones, and beauty of the past year

Rule 3: Look How Far You've Come.

Sometimes we only compare ourselves to those in front of us and usually the ones way ahead of us. It's important to pause and look at the things (and perhaps people) you've encountered on your journey but also the ones that are exactly where you left them. Keep a props folder in your email to look at when you struggle to feel progress. Look at emails from one year ago and realize how you no longer have to think about that thing you were once so stressed about. Look at pictures from a year ago and stay connected to those who helped you on the climb. They will be a mirror for your growth.

Rule 4: Talk It Out.
If we ever go on a hike together, you will hear me constantly in verbal awe of nature. "Look at that butterfly!" "Oh my gosh, the light hitting the trees is insane!" This keeps me grounded in the moment and signals to my brain how beautiful the present moment is. We have to do the same in this life. Stop right now and say two things out loud that are cool in this current moment. Feel free to DM them to me. I would love to hear them.

Rule 5: Climb Together.
Fierce independence is a trait many successful people have. But the biggest thing that has allowed me to enjoy the journey more is being hard enough to know I can do it alone but soft enough to accept that I don't want to. Find the people who will be there with you every step of the way. The ones who will pick you up when you stumble and remind you where the trail marker is when you lose your way.

Contentment can feel like a fool's errand when you are an ambitious high performer. But remembering to practice a slightly different form of gratitude and recognizing the intention needed for your climb to the top will bring you back to the moment and allow you to enjoy the path to the mirage of success (because I can assure you, after years of planning celebrity weddings and working with tech billionaires, no matter how high you climb, it will never be "enough" unless you practice contentment).

Finding Momentum

When your characters can't find momentum and keep having a lot of false starts, I think about this visual. The momentum equation takes all three parts: Thoughts + Goals + Actions. This is the crux of part 2 of this book. If you find one of your characters struggling, go back to the perfect day exercise. Set the plotline. Create space in your day to think about that character. Check in with them and see what they need. You can't have momentum without clear goals, aligned actions, and intention. If a character is struggling, ask yourself which you are missing.

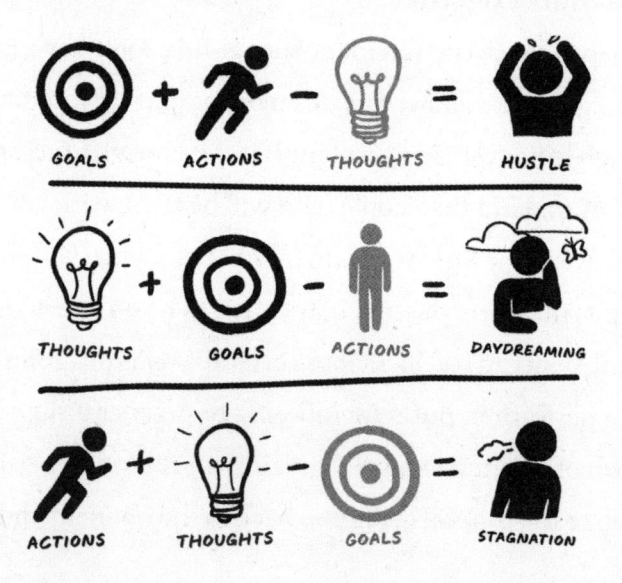

GOALS + ACTIONS − THOUGHTS = HUSTLE

THOUGHTS + GOALS − ACTIONS = DAYDREAMING

ACTIONS + THOUGHTS − GOALS = STAGNATION

Finding Discipline

Are you feeling behind but struggling to stay disciplined in the actions and goals you've set? Remember this: The most successful people don't all take ice baths, wake up at 5:00 a.m., or have Ivy League educations, but they do all share one thing: discipline.

Discipline is the bridge between wanting something and getting it. Self-discipline is your ability to manage yourself with the intent of achieving a goal. The good news? Discipline is a learned skill. The bad news? No one is going to learn it for you.

The Five Pillars of Self-Discipline

Pillar #1: Acceptance

Most fail to accurately perceive and accept their current situation. It is important to identify an area where your discipline is weakest. For example, I hate cooking, so if I don't have prepared foods in my fridge, I will order Uber Eats. Once you've accepted your weaknesses, you can begin to build up self-discipline.

Pillar #2: Willpower

Willpower is the ability to resist short-term gratification in pursuit of long-term goals or objectives. Note: Your willpower is at its lowest when you feel stressed. Do I want to get up at 5:00 a.m. every day to write? Not usually. But my desire to grow as a writer and creator outweighs my desire to get an extra one to two hours of sleep every night. And I will only be able to keep that willpower if I ensure I go to sleep at 9:00 p.m. so I'm not overtired and stressed. Many people find it hard to resist the allure of immediate comfort or pleasure, which can undermine their discipline. Growth requires you to leave your comfort zone.

Pillar #3: Hard work
Many people try to avoid this by doing what is easiest. Ever created a long to-do list and then looked for the easiest thing to check off first? Hard work is about knowing your bigger objective and choosing the path to get there—no matter how hard it appears. Many people who book calls with me are looking for the easiest ways to grow their brands or achieve their goals, so I share my playbook. I always say, "What I'm about to show you will seem simple, but that doesn't make it easy. Simple, hard work gets the results."

Pillar #4: Persistence
Persistence allows you to keep taking action even when you don't feel motivated to do so, and therefore you keep accumulating results. The number one trick for maintaining motivation is to break your big, scary goals into small, achievable goals and just keep showing up. I call it the Kit Kat strategy. When I am stalled on a project, it's a sign I just need to break it up. Every task can be broken down into smaller tasks until you achieve a size that you can handle. Break your big goal into four tasks. Still stalled? Break each of those into four more. Keep going until you find momentum. Momentum leads to motivation. Motivation leads to discipline.

Pillar #5: Patience

Success and change don't happen overnight. It can be discouraging to look around and feel like everyone else is ahead of you. Patience is putting trust in the process of how they got there and how you will too.

Discipline is the bridge between wanting something and getting it.

If your character is struggling to stay on track, remind yourself of the five pillars of discipline. Embrace the long-term goals over short-term gratification, and break those goals into smaller, bite-size pieces, and keep showing up. It's simple. Not easy. If it were easy, everyone would be doing it.

Finding Peace

Before we help your characters find more peace and stability, I want to call out one thing: When we've been living in fight-or-flight for so long or experiencing trauma or a toxic relationship, we tend to confuse peace with boredom. When we first come out of survival mode, life will feel boring. Our brain has been conditioned to experience constant stimulus and fear. My partner is the most stable person in the world, and when we first started dating, he wanted to go slow. A date or two a week. I have experienced my fair share of love-bombing: People falling head over heels on the first date. Promising me the world only to realize they couldn't uphold their end of the bargain, and those high-on-lust feelings come crashing down quickly. But with my partner it was different. He made promises he could keep—nothing more. He followed through. He kept showing up. But in comparison to what I was used to, I took it as disinterest and boredom. That he wasn't as exciting or excited by me. But guess what? Real grow-old-with-you love is about consistency and stability. He reprogrammed my brain to stop confusing love-bombing for passion and to start seeing consistency as the most exciting thing I could find.

For those of you navigating a difficult time and struggling to find peace, I've summarized seven tips I've gathered along my path to help move through it. Try these when you need to kick off the mud and get back on the road.

Tip #1: Embrace Acceptance

You may not be able to change a highly stressful event, but you can change how you interpret and respond to it. Accepting that this thing happened is the first step in moving through it.

Tip #2: Reclaim Agency

Remember, you have the power to make life happen *for* you, not *to* you. Start making small decisions about your life to take back control. Remind yourself of the previous challenges you've overcome. Reflecting on your resilience reinforces that you possess the strength and capability to navigate difficult times. Use past successes as a source of inspiration and evidence of your agency.

Tip #3: Set realistic expectations
When we are faced with a difficult situation, it's important to reassess what's possible. Former you may have wanted to get a lot done, but current you can only manage to do 30 percent of it. Break your big goals into smaller, more manageable to-dos to help you feel like you are still moving forward, even if a little slower than you originally desired. **If you only have 30 percent to give and you give all 30 percent, you gave 100 percent.**

Tip #4: Allow emotions.
If you started a fire in a fireplace but didn't open the vent, you'd likely poison everyone in the room with the smoke. Peace is found by opening your vent to not hurt you or anyone else around you. Feeling sad? Cry. Feeling angry? Go to a boxing class and hit something. Find outlets for releasing the emotions before they smoke up the room and hurt other people or your other characters.

Tip 5: Lean on people.
Remembering that you are not alone in your struggle is key to moving through it and finding peace. My only caution: Do not center relationships on your trauma. My best friend and I were

both going through a divorce at the same time. We would allow a ten-minute vent session, and when the timer went off, we couldn't talk about it anymore. Don't confuse venting and support with trauma bonding.

Tip #6: Celebrate progress.
Acknowledge and celebrate even small victories along the way. Shame depletes energy. Celebration generates it. Got outside today? *Celebrate it.* Showered? *Let's fucking go.* Stayed focused on a project for an hour? *Rock star!* Inner narratives matter so much when searching for peace.

Tip #7: Seek help.
There will be times when the mud gets too thick and you need some professional help getting unstuck. Friends are great, but they usually mirror our own emotions back to us. The best way to find a therapist is to ask others around you for a referral. Need a prompt? Try this: "Hey, I'm feeling a bit stuck lately and realize I could benefit from an independent third party. Do you happen to know a great therapist?"

No matter what you are navigating right now, I hope you know you are not alone and you deserve to go find peace and stability.

Finding Confidence
It's an icky feeling, but we all know it. When you feel an inner voice start to judge yourself, judge others, and pick everything apart. Your

brain starts to close up with a tunnel vision for the worst in people. I name this voice. She's the villain in my story. Low self-esteem Amanda is called "Mandy." I've found the more I scroll on social media, the louder Mandy gets. She's constantly wanting to buy or try new skincare products or techniques to fix the list of my imperfections she keeps tally of in her mind. She compares her social life, love life, and body to everyone she sees. Your inner critic doesn't get to direct the movie of your life. Mandy gets kicked off the bus.

Let's look at the difference between confident and insecure people to help you identify if you lost some confidence along the way.

Confident People	Insecure People
Open-minded	Close-minded
Abundant mindset	Scarcity mindset
Accepts responsibility for mistakes	Blames others
Adaptable	Afraid of change
Proactive	Reactive
Willing to try new things/take risks	Indecisive
Empathetic	Defensive
Always learning and growing	Pretends to know everything
Aware of gaps and flaws	Tries to hide flaws
Self-assured	High need for approval
Resilient	Fears failure

When you start to feel your inner critic take over and you feel yourself losing confidence, it's time for a reality check.

Is your CEO lacking confidence at work? Reality check. Ask your boss for a performance check-in to get proactive feedback on a project.

Is your Socialite lacking confidence? Reality check. Ask a friend who brings out the best in you to go with you.

Is your inner Doctor lacking confidence in her body or worried about her health? Reality check. Get off social and go to the gym or go for a walk. Get your annual physical done. Look at *real* bodies. Find beauty in all the shapes and sizes around you in the real world, not an algorithm.

Is your Partner lacking confidence? Reality check. Recognize your worth and remind yourself of the value you bring to the relationship. I remind myself that if someone wants to leave or cheat or treat me horribly, I can't stop them or control any situation to prevent it. Instead, I trust in my strength to walk away from anyone who doesn't treat me with the value and respect I deserve.

Is your Caregiver lacking confidence? Reality check. I tend to compare myself to a 1950s parent when I worry I'm not supporting my kids' entire emotional, physical, social, and mental well-being. From the 1960s to the 1990s, they literally had a public service announcement that would come on the TV and say, "It's ten o'clock. Do you know where your children are?" as a reminder to make sure your kids are safe. They needed the reminder! So if my kids are safe, loved, healthy, and happy… I must be doing a few things right. Just asking, "Am I a good parent?" puts you in the top 10 percent of parents. Remember that. Caring and intention are self-fulfilling qualities. Because you care that you are a good parent, you are. Because you care that you are a good friend or daughter or sister, you are.

Lost and Found It

Character agency is about knowing you have the power to go find something if you've lost it. Stop waiting for someone else to find it for you. There are so many things that will happen in the movie of your life, and your characters will inevitably stumble or lose their way. Come back to this chapter to help guide them through it and remind them they have everything they need to find what they are looking for.

Throughout the first two sections of this book, we've focused on each of the ten characters who exist within us and how to navigate and honor the imbalance of them in our lives. We've learned how to rightsize the most dominant characters and created a system for incorporating proactive rest to ensure we don't burn any characters out. But life is messy. We may set a vision and plot for each character and realize they keep stepping on top of one another. Our friends or family need us during an intense season of work. Our days and energy become consumed with to-dos and make it impossible for our Goddess or Doctor to show up. We can honor the imbalance of our life, but we must also master the coexistence of our characters: When multiple characters are on screen at the same time with multiple plotlines playing out, we need to know where to point the camera.

Part 3

Master the Multiverse

Chapter 10

Welcome to the Multiverse

The top regret of the dying, as outlined by Bronnie Ware in her book *The Top Five Regrets of the Dying: A Life Transformed by the Dearly Departing*, is "I wish I'd had the courage to live a life true to myself, not the life others expected of me." So much of life is dictated by external events and external relationships deciding which of our characters are on screen: Work taking over your vacation or time with friends. Friend drama when you want to get to the gym. Family needing you when you want to relax or have sexy time. The thing about expectations, as we continue to reinforce throughout this book, is we are in control of how we want the movie of our life to play out. No one gets to the end of their life and says, "I'm so happy I went all in as a (insert singular character here)." We want all of our characters to succeed, whatever that means to each of them.

But navigating the multiple characters inside of us is creating an intense conflict within us. You are not a one-dimensional human. We see your multidimensional characters very clearly now, but until this point in the book, you've met the characters that exist within us independently. It's important to now understand the concept of coexistence and interplay. Each of the ten characters coexists in their own storylines *simultaneously*. In this part of the book, we will develop the skill of building character permanence and prioritization and address how to navigate when multiple characters show up at once or need to quickly flow from one to another.

Before we talk about prioritization, let's discuss character permanence. Object permanence means knowing an object (or, in our case, character) still exists, even if it is out of sight or not in the current plot. A character's plotline is still progressing whether we are embodying and focused on that character or not. Have you ever played peekaboo with a baby, and they startle when your face pops out from behind your hands? It's freaking adorable and also a sign that they have not developed object permanence. The baby doesn't realize you still exist, even though your face has only been hidden for two seconds. So when you pop back out, it's actually a surprise. The same is true for our characters. At any given moment there is a version of you that exists to a group of people, places, and things that may not be in alignment with the character you are embodying in that moment. It may not even be a character that is top of mind for you. But that character very much still exists within you and to others and may pop back out and surprise you, causing stress and overwhelm. This is the reason so many of us feel like we are teetering on our last piece of sanity. We never know when we need to switch characters or try and hold space for multiple at once. We need to be equipped for these situations and learn when to block a character from taking over, throwing our current plotline off script, and when to allow a transition.

Let's talk through a few examples of character permanence to illustrate the ever-present possibility of out-of-sight, out-of-mind characters distracting our leading character.

Scenario 1:

Your Lazy Girl and Socialite exist simultaneously. One group of people knows you as the life of the party, while you are currently chilling and watching Netflix, blissfully unaware of what social gathering is happening right now. Just because you are in your Lazy Girl character doesn't mean your inner Socialite doesn't exist to you or those other people. You need to create intentional boundaries so your Lazy Girl and Socialite don't step on each other. Both exist, but you've made the conscious decision to be in your Lazy Girl character, and her goals are being prioritized. And guess what? She doesn't give AF what is happening outside or on social media. She is three episodes into *Selling Sunset* and just ordered Shake Shack. But at any moment, your friends will begin texting you drama or sending you memes, not fully allowing your Lazy Girl to achieve her goals and needs to satiate your overall desire for rest and decompression.

Scenario 2:

Your entire team sees you in your CEO character, but on the weekends you explore your sexuality, fulfilling the needs of your Goddess character. Just because you are one character in one moment does not detract from another character existing at any other given moment. Your CEO character is presently concerned with finishing this deck, preparing for that meeting, and answering that urgent client call. The idea of being touched is not fathomable at the moment. This doesn't mean that your sex drive is gone—your inner Goddess still exists—it just means you aren't accessing that character at the moment. And that's OK. But transitioning from one character to a drastically different character can cause a lot of friction (OK, that may not have been the best choice of word for this particular scenario). So when your date for the evening or partner starts texting you flirty messages and making an attempt at digital foreplay, your Goddess may love it, but your CEO may find it distracting and possibly even annoying.

Scenario 3:

If you are in Caregiver mode and taking care of a loved one (could be a family member or someone else), your Explorer still exists. The thought of packing a bag and traveling the world may be the last thing on your mind as you are in the thick of caregiving, but your inner Explorer still has their own needs and goals for their plotline. The present existence of your Caregiver does not remove or diminish the role of your Explorer, and there may be an opportunity that pops up for your Explorer. Someone wants to go on a taco crawl around the city or check out a new museum. Even though your Caregiver is on-screen in the movie of your life and has no desire to leave your loved one, your Explorer needs to be able to pop in and make that decision. I watch so many of my friends lock up their Explorer when they become parents and then find themselves feeling uninspired or stuck in routine life without novelty. Your Caregiver loves that routine and took over the script, but navigating this peekaboo character permanence will teach us to allow space for each of these characters to coexist when they pop in and say, "Hey, I know you don't need adventure, but I sure could use one!"

This book is about creating a framework of ANDs not ORs while giving you the systems and tools to create space for all the different characters within you. Character theory is not about bifurcating our identities to appease the world around us and making us more palatable or easily indexed, but rather the opposite. It's about honoring the separate identities within us and learning to flow between them in some scenarios or creating boundaries for them in others. It's about creating space for those roles to coexist in our lives and relieving guilt for not being able to embody multiple characters with competing goals at the same time, all the time.

> *The trick to juggling is determining which balls are made of rubber and which ones are made of glass.*
> —UNKNOWN

Whether we are making space for them or not, all of our different characters exist within us every day at the same time across different groups of people and different dimensions, a.k.a. the multiverse. Our job is to now *master the multiverse*.

Welcome to the Multiverse

If you've never seen *Doctor Strange in the Multiverse of Madness* or *Spider-Man: No Way Home*, then let me give you a brief explanation of the multiverse. The multiverse is a theory that our universe, with all its hundreds of billions of galaxies and stars spanning tens of billions of light-years, may not be the only one. Hollywood movies have used this theory to show parallel universes: the same character living distinctly different lives in parallel to the current one we see. To continue with the Spider-Man multiverse example, you may see one dimension with a main character still living with their parents, never bitten by a radioactive spider, but the world is ridden with unchecked crime. Then you see another dimension where the hero loses their father but becomes a superhero, saving thousands of lives.

All of the different characters who make us who we are exist within us every day, while we switch back and forth between our own parallel universes. Who we are with certain friend groups versus who we are with our partners versus who we are at work versus who we are as caregivers. They are different versions of your own reality. I don't believe in alignment. My CEO and Goddess will never see eye to eye. My Caregiver and Explorer will never want the same things (at least not while my children are so young). Intentional misalignment is what this book is all about. But **burnout comes from having a lawless multiverse.** In this type of multiverse, characters are jumping timelines whenever they want, interrupting a storyline for a character, or just getting lost entirely. We have no systems or tools to decide who gets our attention, for how long, and at what cost.

The concept of a multiverse is a lot easier when the characters never have to travel to the same dimension. They stay in their own universe, living their own storylines, blissfully unaware of the needs of any of the other characters. Spoiler: That's not what it looks like for us. Our multiverse will inevitably get smashed together with multiple storylines playing out all at once on one stage. It's like if Broadway mixed up its bookings and you had to see *Hamilton*, *Wicked*, and *Book of Mormon* all happening at once on the same stage. Why is Alexander Hamilton in Oz, and why is Glinda talking about baptism?

Just imagine a day in your life: You are trying to lead a meeting at work while your friends are texting to plan a night out, and you aren't sure if this is financially smart; you still need to work out; and you forgot to text your date or partner back. You suddenly realize you forgot to pay that parking ticket. Seven different characters on stage at once. We have to learn how to set down the guilt, prioritize, and stop wearing "busy" as a badge of honor.

The New Pandemic

It doesn't help that we, as a society, got through one pandemic only to end up in another: the busyness pandemic. After watching the world freeze in what felt like a suspension of time, the days and nights blurring together, no semblance of who we were or what we were trying to accomplish at a macro level, *we started micro-living.* We focused on the small tasks and stacked them up to make a day with the hope of making ourselves feel productive. What am I eating next? What show am I going to watch next? What Zoom happy hour is happening tonight? What TikTok dance am I learning next? What sourdough starter should I research? Micro-living led the way to the busyness pandemic. We trained ourselves to fill our time in order to attach a sense of purpose to our day. But now, in a post-pandemic world, micro-living and busyness don't lead us to a path of joy; instead, they're the on-ramp to the interstate of burnout. A lot of the next few chapters will be equal parts learning and unlearning to make the appropriate space in our day for our characters to thrive and coexist without burning out.

We trained ourselves to fill our time in order to attach a sense of purpose to our day.

Story time. It was a normal pandemic day (is that an oxymoron?), and I was upstairs working in the master bedroom of my pandemic rental house in Charlotte, North Carolina, building my start-up. Thanks to the ability to trade the astronomical NYC rent costs for a suburban rental house, I was able to hire two young women to help me during the day since I was juggling my start-up as a single mom to three kids under the age of six. I completely recognize my privilege in this scenario and know this was not the reality for many women during COVID. I think back to that time in our lives and truly wonder how women did it. I was struggling upstairs while also having two amazing twenty-three-year-old women downstairs (shout-out to Caitlin and Chessie) homeschooling the kids in our COVID bubble Montessori school of sorts. To anyone who had to do all of this alone, you are a force. You have all of my admiration.

It was almost 5:00 p.m., and I was about to open the door to what felt like a domestic version of a natural disaster: a 95 percent chance of hunger, neediness, and category 4 meltdowns. Chessie and Caitlin were packing up to leave, and I was about to take over the kids and the house after a full day of pitching five VCs, navigating a supply chain issue, doing a podcast, and dealing with lawyers on a new partnership agreement. I was in CEO mode. Super intense and focused. Ready to bark back at you with Shopify percentages. CEO Amanda was operating at 100 percent, and that character doesn't do well with kids, to be honest. So, I needed to figure out how to slowly let Caregiver Amanda take over. The next day I decided to end my day fifteen minutes early so I could take a 4:45 p.m. bath. I scrolled TikTok while playing some Leon Bridges and softened like a piece of pasta in boiling water. CEO Amanda's intensity was noodling nicely into a softer, more maternal character. I emerged from the water ready to be a mom and forever coined the term "commute bath." Since that day, my kids ask if I'm headed to the bathroom to "become a mommy," as if I'm Superman stepping into a phone booth.

And then there were the weeks without childcare because of exposure to COVID and a need to isolate myself and the kids. These were the days when my Caregiver and CEO characters stepped on each other all day. I prioritized the CEO from 10:00 a.m. to 3:00 p.m. while allowing an ungodly amount of Bluey to be watched and then needed the commute bath to allow the CEO to melt away, making way for my softer, less chaotic Caregiver character to come out and take over.

We know being fully in one character doesn't erase the existence of the other, and we've already said character theory is about the AND not OR. But we have to honor the transition between them. **Transitions are key for mastering the multiverse.** Have you ever gone straight from work or family time to a date and realized the idea of being touched is the last thing on your mind and suddenly you can't get there? Suddenly an internal narrator steps in: "Am I not into them? Am I not sexual? Am I just too tired? Am I a bad partner?" I've watched this scenario play out over and over again with new parents. Sex lives get thrown out with the dirty diapers because we were never given the tools to identify these shifts in character seasons while also learning to transition between the characters. Yes, you will be tired. Yes, you will have hormonal shifts. But given the right amount of time and routine, your Goddess character is waiting on the sidelines, eager to jump into the episode of your life because they are horny little devils and would still like to play.

Honor the Transition

At any moment, either a character may jump the multiverse or you'll decide it's time for the movie to transition to developing their storyline. If there isn't a ton of alignment between the current character you are embodying and the one you want to transition into, you need to initiate a transition sequence. A character transition sequence consists of three parts that you can remember with the phrase "juggling characters is an ART":

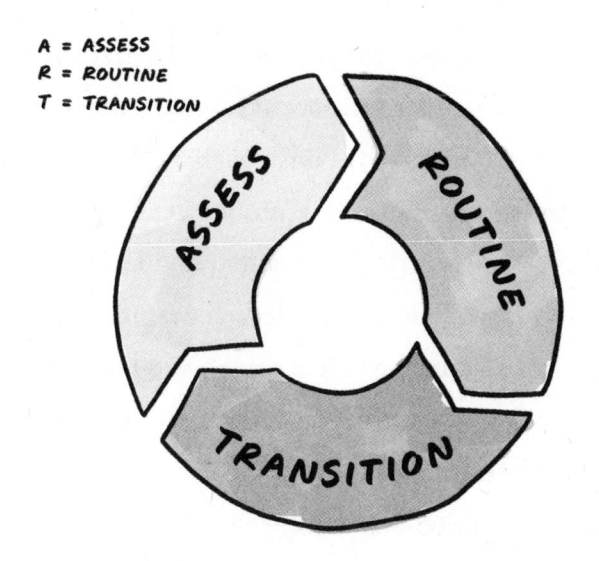

A = ASSESS
R = ROUTINE
T = TRANSITION

Assess

First you must assess which character you want to transition to and how long it might take to transition to them. Some characters are more alike than others. They require less time to transition. Others couldn't be more dichotomous and will need a very intentional and longer sequence. Let's use three scenarios to paint these pictures.

- **Scenario 1:** Your inner Doctor wants to go to the gym, but you are in CEO mode.
- **Scenario 2:** Your inner Goddess wants to get ready for sex, but you are in Caregiver mode.
- **Scenario 3:** Your Socialite has to go to an event, but you are in Soloist mode.

Routine

You need to create a routine to signal to your brain it's time to transition. The routine must be simple, repeatable, and low friction. If the routine is too complex or contains high barriers of entry, you won't adopt it as a regular routine, setting up your characters for transition failure. This is why I push back on the idea of viewing vacations as the time and space for fun and pleasure. It creates such a high barrier to accessing those characters, and then we wonder why we feel stuck or low or not able to have fun in our everyday lives. A transition sequence with a simple and repeatable routine allows you to access more of the characters whose roles are to bring levity and joyful experiences to your life.

Repeating the routine over and over again will create a Pavlovian response in the future. Pavlovian responses, also known as classical conditioning, were discovered by Ivan Pavlov. This learning process involves pairing a neutral stimulus with an unconditioned stimulus to produce a conditioned response. Pavlov demonstrated this with dogs, where the sound of a bell (neutral stimulus) was paired with the presentation of food (unconditioned stimulus), causing the dogs to salivate (unconditioned response). Eventually, the dogs began to salivate (conditioned response) at the sound of the bell alone, even without the food. This illustrates how we can learn to associate two stimuli, leading to a learned or conditioned response. We can literally trick our brains into transitioning characters without a ton of effort. For example, I wake up every morning at 5:00 a.m. and make the same Nespresso iced latte and peanut butter–honey toast. I'm in my Soloist character and sip my coffee while I look out the window. When the clock strikes 5:20, I fill up my water bottle and head to my desk. I turn on the same Post Malone playlist on Spotify and begin my work. My routine: Time + Water + Music = transition from Soloist to CEO.

Some of my favorite routines include:

- Special drink
- Specific snack
- Bath or shower
- Walk
- Song or playlist
- Specific outfit
- Type of movement
- Taking a supplement

Let's continue with our three prior examples:

- **Scenario 1:** Your inner Doctor wants to go to the gym, but you are in CEO mode.
    - → **Routine:** *Before you work out, you always make the same drink and snack.*
- **Scenario 2:** Your inner Goddess wants to get ready for sex, but you are in Caregiver mode.
    - → **Routine:** *Before a date, you always take a bath or shower, listen to the same playlist, and drink a mocktail or glass of wine.*
- **Scenario 3:** Your Socialite has to go to an event, but you are in Soloist mode.
    - → **Routine:** *Before an event, you go for a walk around the block and listen to your favorite podcast to have a topic to break the ice with, or talk to the hosts out loud as if you are on the podcast with them and get ready for the event.*

Transition

The last part of the transition sequence may feel unnecessary, but it's an equally important part of this process: acknowledge the transition. You literally say it to yourself in your head or even out loud: "I'm going into (insert character) mode" or "Time for (insert character)." One of my favorite books, *The Alter Ego Effect*, written by Todd Herman, explores the power of adopting alter egos to enhance performance and overcome personal challenges. The concept of an alter ego is presented as a psychological tool that allows individuals to compartmentalize traits, behaviors, and strengths they may not readily access in their everyday selves. Examples include "Sasha Fierce," Beyoncé's alter ego for when she steps on stage, and Kobe Bryant's "Black Mamba." Beyoncé and Kobe adopted these alter egos to enhance their on-stage and on-court performances. Whether you want to give your various characters an alter ego is up to you, but the point of this last step is to "step in" to the character you've transitioned to, take on their values and goals, and start reading from their script.

- **Scenario 1:** Your inner Doctor wants to go to the gym, but you are in CEO mode.
  - → **Routine:** *Before you work out, you always make the same drink and snack.*
    - » **Transition:** *"OK, it's time to take care of my body and get some energy out. Let's fucking do this."*
- **Scenario 2:** Your inner Goddess wants to get ready for sex, but you're in Caregiver mode.
  - → **Routine:** *Before a date, you always take a bath or shower, listen to the same playlist, and drink a mocktail or glass of wine.*
    - » **Transition:** *"We are sexy and desired. I'm ready to flirt and have some fun."*
- **Scenario 3:** Your Socialite has to go to an event, but you are in Soloist mode.
  - → **Routine:** *Before an event, you go for a walk around the block and listen to your favorite podcast to have a topic to break*

the ice with, or talk to the hosts out loud as if you are on the podcast with them and get ready for the event.

» **Transition:** *"I'm excited to meet some new people or see my friends. I know I will feel happy and proud I went."*

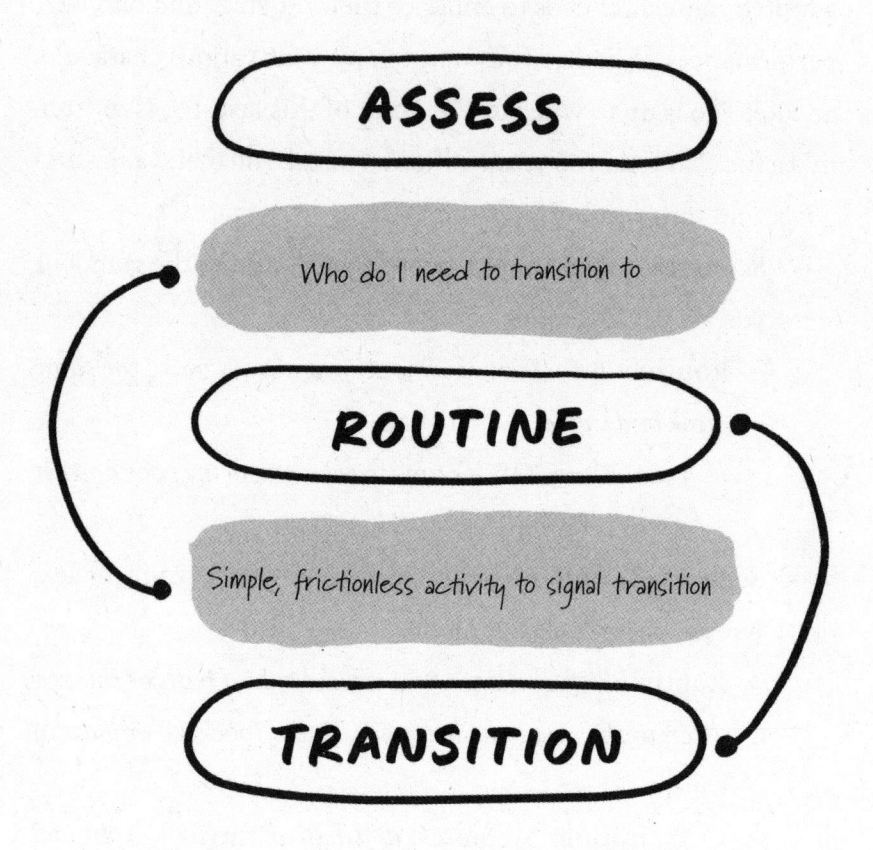

ASSESS

Who do I need to transition to

ROUTINE

Simple, frictionless activity to signal transition

TRANSITION

Let's take a moment to create a simple routine for each of your characters. Come up with a few ideas to test out over the next month to see which cues allow you to signal the transition with the least amount of friction.

Character to become	Routine to use
CEO	
Partner	
Soloist	
Caregiver	
Goddess	
Lazy Girl	
Socialite	
Creative	
Doctor	
Explorer	

There will be times when you are jolted from one character to another. Times where you are not consciously ready to transition to another character but rather forced to acknowledge their needs and existence. Let's look at a few scenes taken from stories I've heard over cocktails with friends.

- **Scene 1:** It's the first month at a new job. You need to bring your A game. You sit down for work, and your roommate comes to inform you the dishwasher is leaking all over the kitchen. Two hours later, your best friend calls to tell you about their incredible date last night.
- **Scene 2:** You are working from home, and your kids' school calls to inform you they are sick and you need to come get them. You have an internal presentation in two hours and still need to finish it, but now also need to run to CVS, pick

up the kids, and care for them in the same environment as your pitch.
- **Scene 3:** You are on a date, and your boss sends you a Slack message with an urgent question and asks to speak to you.

Any of these hitting home for you? This is the madness of the multiverse—full of times where you can't neatly compartmentalize your characters or transition calmly or intentionally between them. Managing multiple roles or characters can lead to role conflict and time pressures that add to daily stress and strain. Character theory is about removing stress, not adding it. We don't want to create a win-loss situation for the various roles, where time spent on one character comes at the expense of time spent on another. Additionally, research indicates that role conflict and spillover can lead to stress, exhaustion, burnout, and lower life satisfaction—not only for those of us experiencing the conflict, but for others in our lives as well. In short, our exhaustion and conflict for one set of characters can spill over to others.

The Lies We've Been Told

I've coached many teams about the fallacy of multitasking. When people try to be more than one thing at a time, they feel like they are one inch away from losing it. And it makes sense based on everything I've studied about the brain. The human brain is not equipped to multitask. In fact, many of you who think you are good at multitasking are actually task-switching rapidly. Studies show that when our brain is constantly switching gears to bounce back and forth between tasks, we become less efficient and more likely to make a mistake. This might not be as big of a deal when we're scrolling while watching TV or walking and talking on the phone, but attempting to create a deck for work while listening to a friend's latest dating drama could lead to more serious consequences: losing a job or a friend.

So how do you handle the times when characters must coexist? I want to first put the word "coexist" under a microscope. Are we actually juggling two characters at once, or do we struggle with boundaries and managing expectations? Let's walk through the common traps we fall into, understand why we fall in the first place, and start giving you the tools to build a ladder to grab when you find yourself falling into one.

The Traps to Avoid
Trap #1: The Urgency Trap
When everything is urgent, nothing is. Oftentimes when multiple characters are pulling for our attention and energy, we fall for the trap that everything needs us right now or else we are a bad friend, colleague, parent, or partner. That's just people-pleasing in disguise. **People-pleasing** is a behavior I know all too well, where we are constantly seeking approval, validation, and acceptance from others at the expense of our own needs. People-pleasers go out of their way to accommodate others before their own current characters' goals and needs. While we are here, I think

it's important to touch on people-pleasing a bit further and look at where it comes from. People-pleasers may have grown up in environments where they received conditional love or approval based on meeting others' expectations. This can create a strong desire to seek external validation to feel accepted. "I must earn their love. I must work for their attention and approval." This conditional programming tells us if we don't respond quickly, we may lose their approval, which then leads to a fear of rejection or abandonment. We are scared to set boundaries out of fear of losing someone's love and attention. When characters collide, it's important to slow down, analyze, and prioritize, knowing you won't lose someone's love or attention if you don't respond immediately.

The 10-10-10 Rule

When placed in a situation where two characters need attention at once, ask yourself: *Can it wait for ten minutes? Can it wait for ten hours? Can it wait for ten days? Can it wait for ten weeks?* In our first scene presented earlier, you can take one minute to call and book a plumber now (that can't wait), but you can wait a day to text your friend back. Both situations felt urgent, but only one truly is. In scene 2, you pick up your child and ask to push the internal presentation back a day. One truly is urgent, even though you may think both are. In scene 3, you finish your date and then text your boss back. Is it urgent, or are you scared of losing their love or attention? Yeah, that one stings for me as well.

Trap #2: The Significance Trap

When everything is important, nothing is. I've worked alongside billionaires and some of the most successful people in the world, and my most shocking discovery: They aren't busy. They aren't sprinting around running errands while replying to every single text and email. They speak slowly, with intent. It's a world of quality, not quantity. Before you say it out loud, yes, they hire people to do many things. But there is a way to mimic this and achieve the same ease and slowness of life. I have studied these people and become a master of the 80/20 rule: to focus on the 20 percent of the work that gets 80 percent of the results. A tech company discovered that if it fixed 20 percent of its most-reported bugs, 80 percent of the errors and crashes would be solved. When multiple characters need you, focus on the 20 percent of their needs that will get them 80 percent of the satisfaction and results. If people-pleasing prevents us from setting boundaries with our time when something feels falsely urgent, **guilt** is the culprit in setting boundaries with our energy when something feels falsely significant. We feel guilty not doing *everything* required as that character. Answering *every* email or Slack. Making *every* meal perfect for our family. Doing a full sixty-minute workout.

But ask yourself this:

Do you feel connected with your friends when they reply to every text or after a good phone call or dinner date? Do you feel more connected with your kids or parents sitting next to them on your phone scrolling for three hours or sitting across from them talking or playing a game for an hour? Do promotions come from cleaning out your inbox or completing a big project? Do you feel healthier after a ten-minute walk versus staying on the couch because you don't have the full hour to go to the gym?

Quality > Quantity

To combat the significance trap, you have to fill a character's jar. My first job after college was at Ernst & Young. This small-town country girl was now commuting every day to work at the Willis Tower (it was called the Sears Tower back then) in the Chicago Loop. In my first year we got to participate in a weeklong training on the book *The 7 Habits of Highly Effective People*. The following exercise stuck with me and quite possibly had the biggest impact on how I approach my days and characters and reinforced the 80/20 rule.

Imagine you have a jar, and your goal is to maximize its capacity by strategically filling it with pebbles, rocks, and sand. The jar represents your life and the way you prioritize. If you start with the sand (smallest tasks), there will not be enough room for the pebbles and big rocks. If you start with the pebbles (medium tasks), you'll still run out of room for the big rocks. The key to this exercise is putting the biggest rocks (the biggest tasks) in first and then the medium pebbles to fill up around the rocks, and lastly, the sand will settle in and fill the cracks and crevices. So many people focus on their characters' sand and then don't have any energy or time left for the pebbles and rocks. We need to start with the big rocks, or the 20 percent of tasks that fill up 80 percent of the jar.

Welcome to the Multiverse

EMPTY JAR   **SAND**   **PEBBLES**   **ROCKS**

I'd rather be a present mom, phone away, for two hours a day than a distracted mom for four. If my CEO and Caregiver characters are at odds, I determine which part of my work is the 20 percent and get that done while the kids watch a movie or play by themselves so I can come to them with a clear head and tech-free hands to play with them. If my Partner and Socialite characters are at odds, I ask to go for a coffee walk with my partner and schedule a dinner with my friend for next week. This is the two-do list we discussed earlier. Your two-dos are the rocks: the 20 percent that gets your character 80 percent of the way to their goal.

The Two-Do Matrix: Example

	CEO	Partner	Caregiver
Two-do #1	Finish deck for client	Coffee walk	Make dinner together
Two-do #2	Write newsletter	No phone cuddle session before bed	Pre-bedtime talks

Your turn: Create your two-do Matrix.

	Character	Character	Character
Two-do #1			
Two-do #2			

When your characters collide in the multiverse, look for the rocks and pebbles and notice which tasks or distractions are getting you a little sandy.

Trap #3: The Spotlight Trap

The third and possibly deepest trap we all fall into is called the spotlight trap. This is our tendency to believe we are being noticed, observed, or scrutinized by others more than we actually are. Filing for divorce at the age of thirty-two, with three young children, while leading marketing for the largest wedding brand in the world, as someone who was raised Catholic, felt like an insanely bright spotlight. What would my family say and think? What would my colleagues think? What would my social media followers think? I work for a wedding brand, for fuck's sake. The reality was, the more I felt my life falling apart, the more I tried to project an image of a Hallmark greeting card on Instagram. Well, guess what? After I filed, nothing really happened. Or at least the people who were talking about me behind my back didn't actually matter. My core friends didn't change. My work didn't change. My family didn't change. Sure, there were some tough convos, but the main thing I realized is that everyone was so wrapped up in their own stuff, they barely noticed or cared. Or at least, I never knew what they said or thought beyond what was shown to me at face value. The most comforting piece of wisdom I can share from going through that difficult season: Nobody cares as much as we think. You can say that with a sad, melancholy Eeyore-like tone ("Nobody cares about me."), *or* you can say it with the excitement and realization that our life is not as magnified or scrutinized as we tend to think, and say it with freedom ("Nobody cares about me!"). We talked about people-pleasing and guilt as the puppeteers forcing us to fall into the first two traps. This trap is all about **perfectionism**. We believe we have to act perfect despite the fact that perfection is a moving and elusive target. When we feel our characters colliding in the multiverse, watch for this trap. Are you really stressed about not finishing that deck by EOD, or do you actually believe people will think you can't handle all the work on your plate? That you aren't the perfect worker you wanted them to think you are?

Ninety-Year Spotlight

The fastest way to combat the spotlight effect is to ask for someone else's opinion. My favorite opinion is from ninety-year-old me. We've referenced this before, but the visual is so powerful. Whenever you feel the spotlight effect affecting your ability to move through your day and set boundaries for your characters, ask the ninety-year-old version of yourself. She misses and wishes she still had all the time ahead of her to live this life again and soak everything up. She is the only spotlight I want you to shine on your life when deciding between characters. Ninety-year-old me kept showing me the possibility of a life full of deep love, respect, and friendship. Let's use an example of your Socialite and Soloist characters at odds. You have a dinner planned with your friends but want to cancel and stay home. Two competing characters. You are worried your friends will be mad. What would ninety-year-old you want? I can assure you the ninety-year-old version of you looks at life with a lens of fragility, beauty, and nostalgia—something that is a lot harder to access at your current age. She wishes she could see her friends right now and get dolled up for a dinner. This exercise helps me to reframe a lot of the collision moments of my day and reframe my actions around making *her* proud, not performing for anyone else.

When characters begin to collide, be careful they don't fall into the urgency, significance, or spotlight traps. Each of these traps was set up by subconscious programming and leads us to make poor decisions that aren't in alignment with the vision and plot for our life. Knowing the traps is the first step; now we must learn about how and when to prioritize and set boundaries when our characters eventually collide.

Chapter 11

Character Collision

The multiverse is messy. There will be times when your new puppy keeps interrupting your book writing (just me?). Or times when a friend, partner, or child keeps distracting you from accomplishing what your CEO set out to accomplish for the day. Or, you finally get to the gym only to find yourself distracted by social media, and you can't stay focused on your workout. Or, you go on a date and your CEO's plotline keeps affecting your ability to be present and advance your Partner character. Or, your Goddess character keeps being rudely interrupted by your inner Caregiver, reciting a list of to-dos for the house, grocery lists, and Amazon orders to place.

Character collision is defined by the existence of two or more competing characters at once. Your ART (assess, routine, transition) sequences will be preoccupied or completely sidetracked despite your best efforts. If transitions are the first step in mastering the multiverse, prioritization is the second. You can't do it all at once. Conflicting priorities arise when there are changing needs, shifting deadlines, or unclear expectations, resulting in confusion and difficulty understanding which character should be leading and why. Lack of clarity is the result of unclear goals, so if you feel an increase of character collision in your life, it's a clear sign you need to go back to part 1 of this book and reset your stovetop. Characters will inevitably collide despite your best efforts to master the multiverse, but ultimately, and as a recurring theme of this book, you are in control. You set the boundaries and determine which thing gets your attention at any given moment. Unclear goals, expectations, or communication can make it challenging to prioritize tasks and their associated characters. Mastering the multiverse requires you to analyze priorities, set boundaries, and communicate clearly. I call this the ABCs of the multiverse.

The ABCs of the Multiverse

Like most things, there is a scientific explanation for the feeling of overwhelm. When we look at the brain (one of my favorite activities) of someone who is overwhelmed, you will usually find overburdened and overworked "executive function" (EF) capacities. EFs, sometimes referred to as "the conductor" of the brain, are the high-level cognitive processes that enable people to quickly process and retain information. These processes take place mainly in the prefrontal part of the frontal lobe. EFs receive incoming sensory input and information from other parts of the brain, so, like an orchestra, the brain combines the functions to play a symphony. EFs allow us to organize and manage our daily lives, make decisions, and focus on important things, as well as self-monitor our thoughts and regulate our emotions and behaviors. Have you ever stared at a task on your to-do list, knowing it needs attention, but felt paralyzed? Has even the smallest item on the to-do list felt like too much? Ever thought, *Why can't I get it together?* This is a sign that your EFs are overworked and unable to process all that's coming in. Executive dysfunction is a breakdown in the ability to organize inputs, focus, and make decisions. Executive dysfunction can lead to overwhelm. Most commonly, we see this as a symptom of disorders, including ADHD, but it can also occur when we get overwhelmed due to the following four impacts:

1. **Time** overwhelm: *I don't have enough time.*
2. **Emotional** overwhelm: *This feels like it's too much.*
3. **Information** overwhelm: *I can't process all of this info.*
4. **Decision** overwhelm: *Too many decisions to make. What if I make the wrong one?*

The ABCs of the multiverse are a protocol to mitigate character collision and overwhelm. When characters keep stepping on top of one another, you will experience irritability, exhaustion, and apathy about *gestures hands in the air* everything. We need to have a tool in our toolkit for navigating these times of overwhelm and character collision.

A = **A**nalyze importance and urgency
B = Set **B**oundary
C = **C**ommunicate expectations

A Is for Analyze

Let's recap the common traps of urgency and significance. The urgency trap is the false thinking that everything vying for our attention and energy is of equal urgency. We need to act on this thing right now, or else we are a bad friend, colleague, parent, or partner. We know this is just people-pleasing in disguise. The significance trap is giving equal importance to everything, and we feel guilty when we place something as less significant out of those same guilt and people-pleasing tendencies.

A reminder: Being busy is not the same as being productive.

Character Collision

The first step in navigating character collision is to pause and acknowledge what is truly urgent and what is truly significant. Some use the Eisenhower Matrix, also known as the Urgent-Important Matrix, a decision-making principle and productivity tool that helps prioritize your many tasks. A reminder: Being busy is not the same as being productive. You could spend hours putting out work fires and, at the end of the day, be no closer to reaching your long-term goals. The Eisenhower Matrix came from the well-known quote by President Dwight D. Eisenhower: "I have two kinds of problems: the urgent and the important. The urgent are not important, and the important are never urgent."

The Eisenhower Matrix is divided into four parts:

	URGENT	NOT URGENT
IMPORTANT	**DO** — Do it now	**DECIDE** — Schedule a time to do it
NOT IMPORTANT	**DELEGATE** — Who can do it for you?	**DELETE** — Eliminate it

Quadrant 1: Important and Urgent: Do

Urgent and important tasks are crises with due dates. Do these tasks first. They require your immediate attention.

Let's look at a few examples:
- You have a client deadline today.
- You have to make food for your kid.
- Your car breaks down.

Quadrant 2: Important but Not Urgent: Schedule

Not urgent but important tasks are the things most likely in alignment with your long-term goals. Successful people spend most of their time here. They schedule the time to make these important tasks happen. Overwhelmed people struggle to make these a priority, thus finding their characters struggling to develop their plotlines.
- You need to go to the doctor.
- You want to update your website or build a new product.
- You want to plan a vacation.

Quadrant 3: Urgent but Not Important: Delegate or Designate*

*This is not a part of the Eisenhower Matrix, but I'm adding it.

If something is urgent but not important, ask yourself if it's something you can delegate. Eisenhower likely had a lot of people to delegate to, but you may not. If you can't delegate to a partner, colleague, or friend, you need to designate a time in which you will attack this task in a controlled window of time so it doesn't bleed into more hours than necessary. Most people spend the majority of their time in this quadrant. They believe they're working on urgent tasks that are important to them when, in reality, completing these tasks does nothing to inch them closer to their long-term goals.

Some examples of this:

- Your CEO character is constantly in Slack and email. These messages may feel urgent, but they may not be as important as the deck or strategy you need to be working on.
- Your Socialite character is constantly DMing and texting friends when you could schedule a one-hour phone call or FaceTime during the week to catch up.
- Your Caregiver character is always running around the home trying to pick up and organize. Instead, you designate a two-hour window on the weekends to clean up the house.

Let me ask you, when you lie down at night, does this sound like your brain?

→ *When was my last dentist visit?*
→ *Did I pay that medical bill?*
→ *I need to call and cancel that subscription.*
→ *Do we need more paper towels?*
→ *Is my friend mad at me?*

I call these "mosquito tasks" that buzz around my brain and add to my distracted context switching throughout the day. So, I created a concept called "Power Hour." I keep a Power Hour list in my phone notes app. Every time a mosquito task flies into my brain, I write it down and go right back to what I was doing. Every week I have a block of time on Friday afternoon when my brain is headed into weekend mode. I knock out as many tasks as possible. (It feels almost like a game at this point.) Batching these tasks together reduces the cognitive load we feel when we just keep pushing them off, "hoping" we remember to do them later.

Quadrant 4: Not Important and Not Urgent: Delete

These tasks aren't pressing, nor do they help you reach your long-term goals. They're simply distractions from what matters most. Delete these tasks from your list.

Some examples of tasks that have caused me stress but, in the end, were not as urgent or important as they felt in the moment:

- Instead of Pinterest perfect birthday parties, I take each kid on a Yes day.
- Instead of baby books, I have a notes app for each kid with milestones.
- Instead of written and mailed thank-you cards, I send thank-you texts with photos.
- Scrolling social media without intention: If I'm not in "creator" mode, I log off.
- I don't take on a lot of "pick your brain" meetings.

We don't always have the time to assess a moment of character collision with the Eisenhower Matrix. In these moments I use another method to analyze if the thing vying for my attention is important or urgent. I use the same 10-10-10 framework as we discussed in the last chapter, but now with the lens of importance and urgency:

- → *Will this matter in ten minutes?*
- → *Will this matter in ten days?*
- → *Will this matter in ten weeks?*
- → *Will this matter in ten months?*
- → *Will this matter in ten years?*

Now that we've T-shirt sized the collision without the noise of our people-pleasing and guilt, you can prioritize the things you are going to do. Let's look at the scenarios from the last chapter again through the lens of these new tools:

Using the Eisenhower Matrix or 10-10-10 tool, you can help avoid the collision with the following:

- **Scene 1:** It's the first month at a new job. You need to bring your A game. You sit down for work. Two hours later, your best friend calls to tell you about their incredible date last night.
  - → **10-10-10 Tool:** *Your friend can wait ten hours while you stay focused on work.*
- **Scene 2:** You are working from home, and your kids' school calls to inform you they are sick and you need to come get them. You have an internal presentation in two hours and still need to finish it, but now you also need to run to CVS, pick up the kids, and care for them in the same environment as your pitch.

→ **10-10-10 Tool:** *The presentation can get moved to tomorrow while you focus on your sick kids.*

- **Scene 3:** You are on a date, and your boss sends you a Slack message with an urgent question and asks to speak to you.

  → **10-10-10 Tool:** *Your boss can wait forty-five more minutes while you stay locked in to your date.*

When we go to communicate these boundaries, we may experience pushback. The ABCs of the multiverse also include two vital supplements to treat character collision: boundaries and communication. If you struggle with knowing what's important and what's urgent, the following are more examples for some of your characters.

Character: The CEO

Quadrant	Task
1: Important and Urgent	• Time-sensitive email • Meeting a project deadline • Handling a financial emergency
2: Important but Not Urgent	• Long-term financial planning • New strategy/business plan development • Setting career goals and networking for your next career move
3: Urgent but Not Important	• Attending a noncritical meeting • Responding to most emails and Slacks
4: Not Important and Not Urgent	• Browsing social media for industry news • Casual conversations with colleagues

Character: The Partner

Quadrant	Task
1: Important and Urgent	• Resolving a conflict with a partner • Creating space when an issue arises for a partner
2: Important but Not Urgent	• Planning quality time with a partner • Proactively planning your week • Participating in couples counseling • Creating future plans together
3: Urgent but Not Important	• Attending a social event out of obligation • Responding to a partner's nonurgent request
4: Not Important and Not Urgent	• Watching TV with a partner • Social media browsing

Character: The Caregiver

Quadrant	Task
1: Important and Urgent	• Taking care of a sick family member • Helping a friend in crisis • Managing a household emergency • Meals and day-to-day needs • The house is almost out of toilet paper
2: Important but Not Urgent	• Planning quality time with a family member • Planning birthday parties or vacations • Discussing future plans
3: Urgent but Not Important	• Errands • Laundry • School requests
4: Not Important and Not Urgent	• Anything you would feel comfortable delegating (laundry, deep cleaning, yard work) or that ninety-year-old you would say, "Eh, didn't need it." Things like perfect birthday parties, scrapbooks, etc.

One of my favorite books about navigating the hundreds of tasks of a Caregiver is *Fair Play* by Eve Rodsky. In her book she outlines one hundred tasks every caregiver has on their plate and how there are three phases to each: conception, planning, and execution. She has turned each of these tasks into one hundred playing cards, and you literally "deal the cards" to help you divvy them up. The TL;DR (too long, didn't read) of all of this is knowing you can't do it all and accepting that some cards have to be dealt out. Not everything carries the same significance and urgency, and it's on our Caregiver to know their limits, ask for help, delegate accordingly, and stop treating everything as equal.

B Is for Boundaries

My son was eight weeks old when I finally booked my first therapy appointment. I was in a dark place, knowing I wanted to end my marriage, raise three babies, and build my career. Note to readers: Don't wait until you can't brush your teeth, shower, or stay up past 7:00 p.m. before seeking help. I remember during my first few months of therapy, I kept hearing my therapist say the word "boundary," and I would shake my head as the omnipotent patient that I was pretending to be. But I only really knew what a boundary was on paper and had no clue what this meant emotionally. So, if you are like me and need a bit more clarification on how to set and hold boundaries to avoid overwhelm, keep reading.

Setting limits in your day involves recognizing what you're

comfortable with, what aligns with your priorities, and what contributes to your overall success and long-term vision for your life. Here are just a few examples of limits you may identify based on your perfect day and main characters' goals.

- → Setting limits on the number of hours you dedicate to work each day.
- → Setting limits on the amount of time spent socializing or attending social events, either with the goal of seeing friends more or preventing burnout.
- → Setting limits on the time spent scrolling to prevent you from skipping workouts or losing sleep.
- → Setting limits on the amount of news you ingest to avoid the emotional overwhelm of the dark things happening in the world that feel out of your control.
- → Setting limits on personal space and privacy—how much information you plan to share about your different characters to different groups.
- → Setting limits on how much support you can provide to others to avoid overextending yourself and not taking care of yourself.

This is a great moment to pause and journal. What limits do you want to bring into your life based on what you've defined as the most important characters and goals for this season and the category of overwhelm (time, emotional, information, decision) you currently experience most?

C Is for Communicate

Setting boundaries and limits can help to ensure all your characters are working toward the same goal, even though the minutiae of the day may lead to collision and competition. But you have to communicate these boundaries not only to yourself but also to others—reminding everyone of them over and over again.

A study on accountability was done by the Association for Talent Development. The researchers found that individuals have the following probabilities of completing a goal by taking these actions:

- Having an idea or goal: *10 percent likely to complete the goal*
- Consciously deciding that you will do it: *25 percent*
- Deciding when you will do it: *40 percent*
- Planning how to do it: *50 percent*
- Committing to someone that you will do it: *65 percent*
- Having a specific accountability appointment with someone you've committed to: *95 percent*

That's a 45 percent jump in likeliness to achieve a goal just by adding accountability! You *need* to communicate and commit to others that you are setting these goals and boundaries and prioritizing your metaverse accordingly. It is your path to almost guaranteed success. But you also need to communicate with yourself about where your priorities are going to lie. Picture a meeting with all ten of your characters. You call it to order and reveal the perfect day to them, along with the grand announcement of who is on the stovetop for this current season to get us closer to the perfect day. Everyone cheers and then spends the rest of the meeting deciding what boundaries we all need to adhere to so we can hit the macro goals. Everyone agrees and signs on the dotted line. This is what mastering the multiverse looks like: All your characters know there is a season for some and a season for others and journey through life with respect for the intentional imbalance. We can't give 100 percent to each character at every moment.

After selling my second start-up, I analyzed and shuffled my stovetop. CEO Amanda was not there for the first time since I started my career, as I took a new role as a VP of marketing to get health insurance and have a job (aka a spin cycle). I needed to focus on my kids, my mental and physical health, myself, and my friends. All my characters attended that board meeting. They knew what was going on. But I also needed to communicate it to my new boss and colleagues. I was thankfully part of a very flexible work culture, so after a few months I felt empowered and able to make that decision. After a 1:1 with my boss sharing the need to have a month where my workload was a bit lighter, I wrote an email to my team communicating that for the next month I needed to focus on my kids and my health. I said that I will be logging in at 10:30 and logging off at 4:30 for the next few weeks, but I will be checking my email and Slack after my kids go to bed to ensure I am staying on top of urgent tasks. I want to acknowledge that this is a privileged position to be in. I had quickly built enough trust with my boss and organization to be able to communicate this need.

So for the next month, at 4:30 p.m. every day, I left work to go be with my kids. I worked out every morning. And because I communicated it with those around me, I held myself accountable and was given the space I needed to get me closer to my perfect day. Most people just want to feel a part of the process and abreast of changes. They want to feel important and considered. Communicating your boundaries will prevent you from having to backpedal or experience an awkward postmortem explanation when you prioritize one character's needs over another's. I've done this with friends and partners as well. "Going heads down for the next month to get this project done." Now they know what to expect, and I won't feel guilty taking a bit longer to reply to texts or schedule a next dinner date. In the absence of information, people will make up their own. And most people make up the worst-case scenario. Had I not communicated my need for some mental health time and focus on my kids and health, most people would think I was interviewing for new jobs and planning my departure. Or my friends would think I'm retreating from the friendship when I'm just trying to launch a new project. Communication is the third and final key in mastering the multiverse and avoiding character collision.

The Highly Ambitious Couple

It's common and painful when the CEO and Partner characters collide. Two wrongs don't make a right, and two ambitious people don't make for easy prioritization without resentment. Is one career less important because someone makes less money? How do we prioritize one's ambition over another's? I used to think the answer to these questions was simply that two highly ambitious people can't be in a relationship together. I thought I would need to have someone who valued their career less or valued mine more. But that's just not the case. Thanks to spin cycles and the tools in this book, I've been able to navigate the intensity of my and my partner's careers. We have weekly and monthly check-ins to discuss whose career is going to require more focus and presence and who has more flexibility. We have a rule: We both can't be pushing at the same intensity in the same week, month, or defined season. We make intentional trade-offs because of this, and it helps us analyze the importance and significance for each of our characters. If I'm pushing that week to get something done for work and the school calls to pick up a sick kid, he is placing that urgent task above his other tasks. And vice versa. If he has a deadline to ship something for a game he's working on, I will answer the door, get the packages, feed the dogs, and handle the dinners so he can squeeze out those extra hours of work in the day. We plan our work accordingly. If he has a massive event coming up for work, I will decline that extra consulting work so I can be more physically and emotionally present at home. He has blocked out months for this book launch so he can be more present at home and for the kids while I further my mission to end hustle culture.

Steal the following weekly check-in if you are navigating a relationship with two highly ambitious people. Remember: Two people can't be pushing at the same intensity at the same time, and there has to be a macro balance amid the intentional micro imbalance.

The Sunday 6: Six Questions We Ask Every Week

1. What's the work schedule for the week?
2. What's the family schedule for the week?
3. What does everyone need to feel supported?
4. Is date night confirmed?
5. Is family time blocked?
6. Is workout time blocked?

Your toolbox is really starting to fill up. You now can assess when characters are in conflict and how to make conscious prioritization decisions rather than letting your people-pleasing, guilty subconscious decide and ultimately watch your characters crash before your eyes.

Chapter 12

Supporting Cast

Your characters don't exist in a vacuum. There are many external variables that will affect their various plotlines, including your movie's rotating cast of supporting characters. At this point in the book, you will now embrace your inner Reese Witherspoon and add the roles of director and producer to your resume. You not only write the script, but you also produce the whole fucking movie.

> *You can design and create and build the most wonderful place in the world. But it takes* **people** *to make the dream a reality.*
>
> —Walt Disney

As producer, you'll need to evaluate if someone is right for parts of your movie, if they are adding or detracting from the plot, or if someone needs to be written off the script. The focus of part 2 of this book was to separate your characters, giving them each their own plotlines and space in your day to achieve their goals for a season of life. But many of us are keeping a cast around from our pilot episode without evaluating if they are lifting us up or pulling us down as the plot develops.

Knowing who is lifting your characters up or pulling them down is the first evaluation you must make as a producer. Imagine two people standing on the same platform. One starts climbing and progressing up to the next platform. The other stays put, not pushing themselves or attempting the climb to the next level, so you end up with two people on different platforms.

Now let's imagine you are the one standing on the higher platform. You really want the other person to be at your level, so you lean down to help pull them up. But guess who has the leverage? The other person. Physics tells us that they are way more likely to pull you down than you are to pull them up. Gravity is in their favor.

Relationships are a lot like this scenario. You can't want someone's growth more than they do. As much as you try to pull them up, they are more likely to pull you down.

When I was first contemplating my divorce, I asked my ex to go to therapy with me, but he didn't want to go. I was in a pretty dark place emotionally after having three babies in the span of five years with no family or support. It had reached a point where my life depended on me seeking help. I ended up going to therapy for six months before I actually filed for divorce. I learned a common thing that happens when a woman finally decides to leave: It is at that moment when their partner begs to do the work. To try and save the marriage. But when a woman finally makes a decision to end it, it means she has spent months or even years attempting to save the relationship, and it would take the entire U.S. Navy to turn that ship around. She has already tried everything to fix or save it and exhausted all options. She has already fought all her feelings and then eventually accepted them before taking this step, so by the time she makes the decision, the decision is usually final. "Where's the girl I married?" That question blindsided me in one of our final conversations. "The girl you married? You mean the twenty-one-year-old college student? She's *long* gone." I had changed so much in eleven years, a career, three babies, and six months of therapy, I didn't even know who that girl was. When you grow, you are no longer in the place they left you. You moved, you expanded. Partners in the most successful relationships grow together, but once I chose to go to therapy and he didn't, we would never be at the same starting block again. We would always be starting from two different spots. And the longer you widen that growth gap, the harder it is to close.

If you are growing, you will also be *outgrowing*. The more work you do on yourself, the more likely it is that you will outgrow friendships, colleagues, jobs, family members, and even partners. And that's OK.

The pandemic was a dark and weird time for most people, myself included. I found that some of the friendships that formed when I was in low spots in my life didn't continue when I came out of the darkness. Low vibrations tend to attract other low vibrations. But when you start doing the work to break patterns and become aware of who is driving your emotional bus, you will start to vibrate at a higher frequency. You will climb out of the darkness. If the other person isn't doing their own work, eventually you will be on that platform again, trying to pull them up to your level. Ending a friendship doesn't have to be a canon event or even something that requires finality or a long text wishing them well. But you do need to protect yourself and your growth, making sure those who were down in the valley with you and navigating a dark time are doing their own work to climb out versus clinging to you in hopes that you will pull them with you. You are not responsible for other people's growth, and you can't want it more than they do. Simply focus on your growth and path ahead and surround yourself with those who are doing the same.

What Cookies Do They Have?

But how do you know if you've outgrown someone? Imagine someone made you a plate of oatmeal raisin cookies. They have always made oatmeal raisin cookies; they are their favorite cookies, and they are always going to be prone to making them. But you *really* want chocolate chip cookies. They can't give you chocolate chip cookies. They only have the ingredients, recipe, know-how, and passion to make oatmeal raisin cookies. You have three choices: accept their oatmeal raisin cookies, make your own cookies, or go find someone else who has the cookies you want.

In any relationship, you may find yourself wanting something different from someone and have to evaluate if that person has the ingredients to give you what you want. You need to either accept what they can give you because every time you ask for chocolate chip you, will be disappointed, or you need to go to a different bakery to find the cookies you want.

I know this is a silly analogy, but it's one that helped me a ton with my relationship with my family. My parents had a very different and difficult upbringing. My dad was left by his parents when he was young and raised by his grandparents. He even lived out of his car for a period of time in high school. My mom was one of eleven children raised on a farm, competing with her ten other siblings for love and attention. There was a time in my adult life I kept repeating a pattern of seeking things from them that I was not able to get, and I had to realize that, based on their upbringing, they didn't have the ingredients to make the cookies I wanted. They supported me the way they knew how, but I wanted and needed something different. So I accepted the cookies they could give me and stopped getting frustrated that they didn't have the other ingredients. I made the decision to go elsewhere to find the cookies I needed to satiate my cravings and needs—a.k.a. therapy.

To be clear, this is not a knock on them. My parents love and support me in their way, and those cookies are good in their way too. This is about taking control over my reactions and knowing what I need. Instead of being frustrated and wishing for something different, I chose acceptance. Are there any relationships in your life where you are asking for something from someone who may not be able to provide it? Are you willing to accept what they can give you, or do you need to find a way to fulfill that need from somewhere else? Or is it time to find a new bakery?

Mirror or Telescope

The hardest part of growth and self-discovery is learning which people, places, and opportunities create an environment conducive for positive change versus those who benefit from you staying exactly as you are. As someone who went through a three-year heated divorce battle, I can easily say that my personal tortured poet department is ripe with friendship breakup haiku and lyrics. Losing friends can be one of the most devastating moments in your life, and oftentimes we are left with more questions than answers. We spend years wondering what we did, but the biggest learning of my life is that it's usually not about us. Well, not us *exactly*. To some people we are mirrors, and to others we are telescopes. Those who see us as mirrors will eventually depart from our lives. We hold up a reflection of who the person is or is not. Our growth and success can reflect their stagnancy. Our brightness casts a shadow on them. The brighter we grow, the more they squint and try to dim us. These are the people you want to create boundaries with in your life. Anyone trying to tear you down to bring you back to their level is living in a fun house full of mirrors that you cannot remove them from. They will likely never be able to hold space for you and your success due to their inability to see past themselves.

Other people see you as a telescope. You expand their horizon. As you grow and expand, you display the infinite nature of power and life. They want to be an additive to your life and are grateful to be in your orbit. Look for people who see you as a telescope, not a mirror. And vice versa. You want people who show you what could be. Who look at the world and see opportunities and are excited to be on this journey with you.

And lastly, there is my favorite phrase, "right person, wrong time." There will be people you need to remove from your script solely because the scene is changing. It's not about their cookies, mirrors, or pace of growth. You are just moving on to a new scene in the movie.

Finding Your Third Place

As the director and producer of the movie of your life, you have the power to decide who gets VIP access to your characters, who is influencing the plot, and who is sitting in the audience. Character theory's eight circles of influence will help you better understand and appreciate the nuance of the various supporting roles.

Many of you have heard of Dunbar's number, a concept proposed by British anthropologist Robin Dunbar suggesting there is a cognitive limit to the number of individuals with whom we can maintain stable social relationships. While the exact figure varies slightly depending on context and individual differences, Dunbar proposed an average value of around 150, spanning from 5 close friends to 150 in your tribe (the number of people you can maintain somewhat of a meaningful relationship with).

Dunbar's number was observed and created in 1992, almost twenty years before Instagram, Snapchat, and TikTok changed the way we interact with friends. I have hundreds of thousands of followers on social media, but social media is a curated view of our lives. One that we control. Someone watching your life on social media is getting served the exact storyline you curated for them. It's not the full reality, yet so many people view this trailer and think they understand the entire movie. Dunbar didn't account for the social media parasocial spectator sport of life. He also didn't account for a global pandemic to take place about thirty years later, isolating our worlds and shifting work from a second place in our daily lives to (for many of us who work from home) two steps away from where we eat and sleep.

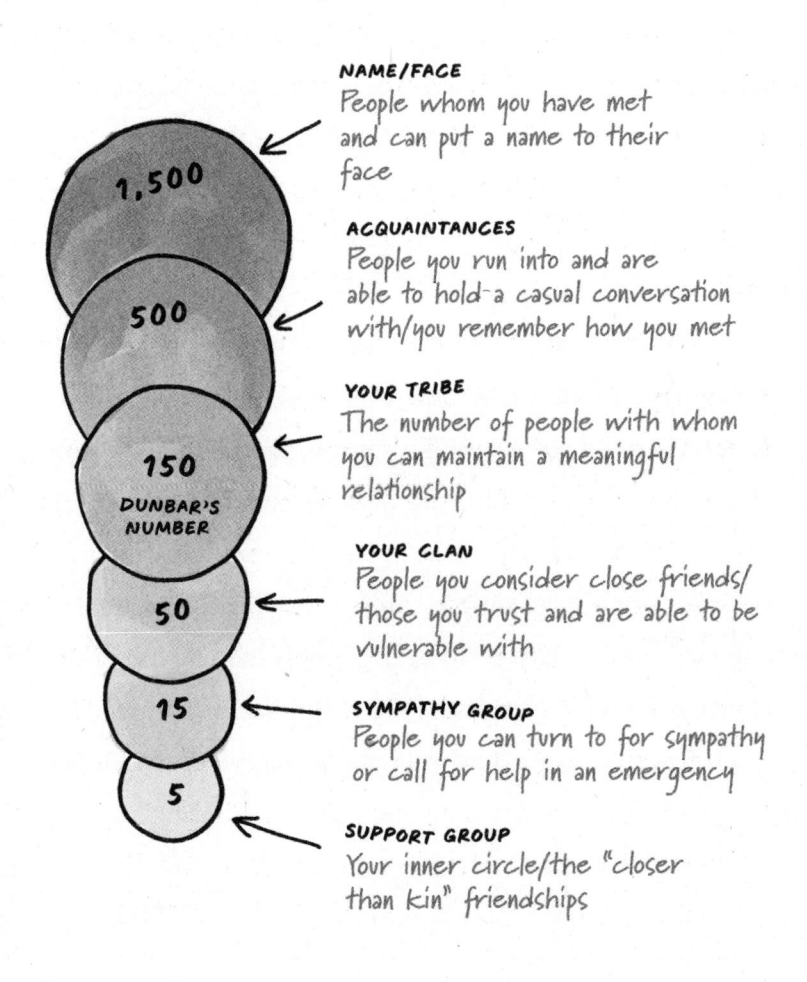

1,500 — NAME/FACE
People whom you have met and can put a name to their face

500 — ACQUAINTANCES
People you run into and are able to hold a casual conversation with/you remember how you met

150 DUNBAR'S NUMBER — YOUR TRIBE
The number of people with whom you can maintain a meaningful relationship

50 — YOUR CLAN
People you consider close friends/ those you trust and are able to be vulnerable with

15 — SYMPATHY GROUP
People you can turn to for sympathy or call for help in an emergency

5 — SUPPORT GROUP
Your inner circle/the "closer than kin" friendships

Energy and relationships are experienced differently in today's modern world. Dunbar's number may even cause anxiety at the thought of having fifty close friends. Some studies show that over 60 percent of people in the United States report feeling lonely on a pretty regular basis. Let's dissect this. We spend more time at work than ever before, but many of us work from home. So when the clock strikes 5:00 p.m., we shut our medium screens and walk over to our big screens so we can scroll our small screens while ignoring the big screens until it's time to go to bed. We have to swim against the technological stream pushing us to stay at home, swapping daytime sweatpants for nighttime sweatpants.

Enter the 5 to 9 routine you already created as well as the concept of the third place. For many of us, our first place (home) and our second place (work) have merged. So we need to think more intentionally about our third place. A "third place" is a familiar public spot where you regularly connect with others over a shared interest or activity. The term was coined by Ray Oldenburg in the early 1990s, as increasing work hours and more heavily siloed communities (think: suburbs) became the norm. When you have access to everything you could possibly want or need at home (or online), leaving the house becomes optional. Third places were most commonly thought of as a local bar, a country club, or a religious location. People gain a sense of psychological ownership over a third place, that feeling where you walk in and know you belong—where someone knows your face or name.

As an adult woman with kids, a career, and a move that took me away from my closest friends, I think a lot about friendships and third places. Friendships take two things to form a bond: time + consistency. That's why third places are important—they become the vehicle for repeated interactions with the same people to create the soil for a friendship to blossom. The rule of thumb in advertising is you need to see an ad seven times before you consider purchasing the item, so let's girl math this and assume you need to see someone at least four to five times to establish a strong enough bond to form an emotional connection. DMs or texts don't count. We've all ridden the "let's grab coffee sometime" merry-go-round. You see someone on social media and say, "Hey! Let's grab a coffee!" and they say, "Yes! Let's do it. I'm traveling or busy for a few weeks, but let's connect when I'm back!" And that cycle continues until you just stop trying. Filling your friendship cup requires an exchange of energy in person and over multiple times. Virtual communities have been tied to positive psychological benefits, but they do not match the positive impact on well-being and social health of an in-person connection.

Making friends has to be an active goal for your Socialite character and something you need to put on your stovetop for it to happen. I'm bullish on the growth and evolution of third places to combat technology that enables us to never have to leave our couch.

Struggling to make connections? Here are some examples of third places for you to consider:

- Working from the same coffee shop a few times a week
- Hanging at the same bar every Friday after work
- Joining a weekly running or pickleball club
- Gyms (bonus points if there is a place to sit and hang)

- Dog parks
- Volunteer groups
- Social clubs
- Theater clubs

Or creating your own! Offer to host a weekly book club, meetup, or monthly game night.

Unlike Dunbar, I'm not going to assign numbers to the following categories because every person's capacity to hold space for a group of people is different. Your movie may have scenes with a ton of extras, like a Marvel action film, or be an intimate rom-com with just a few main characters. The goal of the eight circles of character influence is to help you assess and bucket your relationships accordingly and assign a cast member the right access to your life. The following circles of influence will decide who we let guide us, inspire us, and affect our characters.

A few things to remember about your supporting cast:

→ *You are in control of the access level. You can upgrade or revoke access at any time.*

→ *Compartison is the thief of joy. Make sure to look ahead for inspiration, behind for gratitude, and around for motivation. Stop comparing your day one to someone else's day 1,000.*

→ *Intention is everything. If you leave an interaction full of energy, seek more interactions. If you leave an interaction drained of energy, seek fewer interactions.*

→ *A bad friend is never a good idea. Great friends talk about ideas. Bad friends talk about other people.*

Supporting Cast

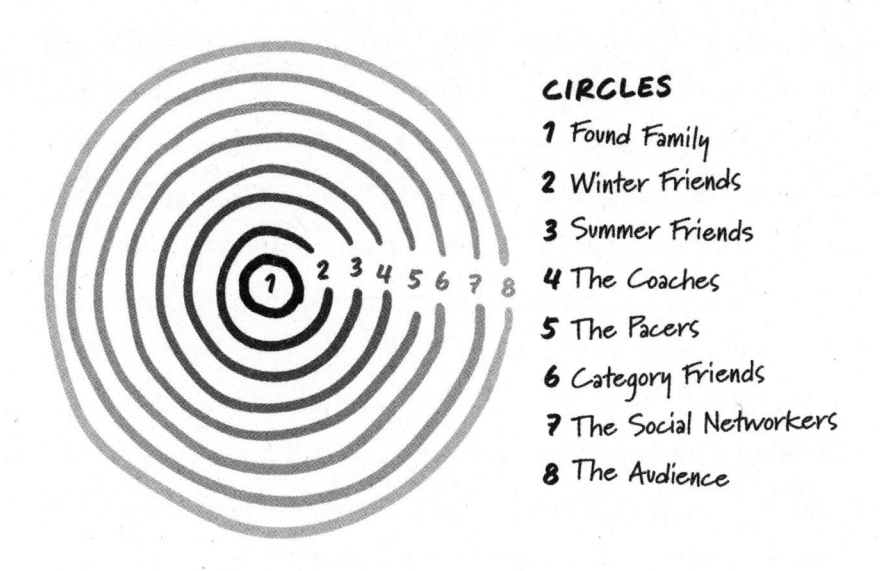

CIRCLES
1 Found Family
2 Winter Friends
3 Summer Friends
4 The Coaches
5 The Pacers
6 Category Friends
7 The Social Networkers
8 The Audience

The Eight Circles of Character Influence
Level 1: Found Family

You will notice we won't immediately assume family means blood relatives. For many it does, but for some the word "family" is a source of pain and trauma. Found family is the group of people you let into the deepest part of your life. Who do you call when your world implodes? Who will sit with you in a hospital room during the scary, real-life shit that can be thrown at us? Your partner and perhaps a few close friends or family members gain this VIP access to your life.

If you want to grow, it's important to assess your environment. You cannot fully embody a new version of a character when your brain is triggered to regress into old habits and ways of behaving. Family can be an environment that holds us back from growth. If you notice yourself revisiting past behaviors, habits, or thought processes when around a family member, you might have outgrown that younger version of you. It may feel awkward or uncomfortable, but this is a sign of growth. You don't have to shut out people from your past life, but it will be important to audit these regressive loops and identify the appropriate boundaries to keep your characters moving forward.

Level 2: Winter Friends

Author George R. R. Martin, famously known for his fantasy novels that later were turned into HBO's *Game of Thrones*, once wrote, "Summer friends will melt away like summer snows, but winter friends are friends forever." Florida winters are also hurricane season, and in my first year living in Miami after eleven years in NYC, I learned about hurricane parties. When anything under a category 4 is coming, people get together for the day and eat a bunch of food and hang out until the storm passes. It allows people to be together in case of an emergency while also bringing a bit of levity to a somewhat stressful situation.

Winter friends are there with you when you weather a storm. They love and care for you through the good times and the bad. Winter friends are the people you want to prioritize when life gets busy, but they tend to be the friends we most easily deprioritize because we know they will always be there. Be careful of that trap. These are the friends you want to have fun with in the summer even though you know they will also be there in the winter.

Level 3: Summer Friends

I toyed with the phrase "7-Eleven friends" because a lot of these friendships are based on convenience. You just need a loaf of bread and milk? Run to the closest store. Want some social interaction? Neighbors, colleagues, or parents of your kid's friends are easily accessible. They are in close proximity and usually have a lot lower friction point than winter friends. But what happens when seasons change? These people are nowhere to be found. Summer friends fulfill a surface-level need of social interaction, but when you peel back the layers, you realize these people have their winter friends with whom they are doing life.

The three characteristics of summer friends:
1. They're around when things are good.
2. If you stop putting in the effort, they likely will as well.
3. If the convenience factor changes, you likely wouldn't hang out.

Summer friends are great for your Socialite. They give us a feeling of familiarity and belonging within our communities or work. Some may even turn into winter friends when the seasons change. Just make sure you are aware of who is there for a long time, not just a good time.

Level 4: The Coaches

Coaches are the people who are a few steps ahead of one of your characters. They impart wisdom and remind you where you want to be. They push you a little further on your journey. Whenever you are around them, you are inspired to be the best version of yourself in whatever character they embody. They are your telescopes.

Coaches are important to identify and cultivate relationships with. You may find that each of your main characters for a season of life needs a coach. For example: I need someone who has raised junior high kids in my life to prepare me for what's coming for my Caregiver role, I want to be around a happy and successful couple to learn from as my partner and I grow together, and I want to meet regularly with someone who has navigated this new chapter of my career to show me what I need to exercise to get better and stronger. Coaches are a critical part of growth for your characters.

Level 5: The Pacers

Unlike coaches, pacers are the people your characters are running alongside in the same race. They are right next to you, complaining about how hard it is but making sure neither of you give up. Coaches are meant to prepare you for the race, but pacers are the people you actually run with. They started at the same starting line. Know the difference and stop running a marathon with no pacers or with people who started the race way before you.

Level 6: Category Friends

It's not healthy to make someone an everything-bagel-friend, meaning we can't expect one person to match up in all our unique passions and goals. Category friends are crucial to advancing your various characters, specifically your inner Creative and Explorer and Doctor. You may not see these friends as much, but when you do, they fulfill a need that perhaps your found family or winter friends aren't able to fulfill.

Level 7: The Social Networkers

A lot of Level 1–6 friends start as Level 7: the social networkers. It's a feature, not a bug. Today it's a lot easier to see avatars six to seven times over a period than it is IRL faces. These are the people there to cheer you on, support your content, and connect in the DMs. Some of my closest winter friends started as social media acquaintances that led to a dinner, workout, or business partner. The trick for this level of cast member is to get them to audition for a bigger role as quickly as possible. Online connections paired with offline interactions will be ten times more powerful and likely to move up the levels of access in the movie of your life.

Level 8: The Audience

Not everyone wants to support you. Some want to watch you. And you have to know the difference. I had a group of friends I only saw about once a year, and when I saw them, I felt like a zoo animal. They wanted all the juicy details of my life: whom I had slept with and what parties I had been to. I realized they were not in my movie; they were the audience. And here's the thing about audiences: You can't let them get too loud, or it will ruin the movie.

You have to understand this on social media as well. Not every social follower wants the best for you. Yes, there are trolls who want to tear you down behind anonymous accounts, but there are also people who are there watching and waiting for you to stumble and fall so they can point and laugh.

Theodore Roosevelt once said in his famous "man in the arena" speech:

> *It is not the critic who counts; not the man who points out how the strong man stumbles or where the doer of deeds could have done them better. The credit belongs to the man who is actually in the arena, whose face is marred by dust and sweat and blood; who strives valiantly; who errs, who comes short again and again, because there is no effort without error and shortcoming; but who does actually strive to do the deeds; who knows great enthusiasms, the great devotions; who spends himself in a worthy cause; who at the best knows in the end the triumph of high achievement, and who at the worst, if he fails, at least fails while daring greatly, so that his place shall never be with those cold and timid souls who neither know victory nor defeat.*

Don't let the people in the audience be the critics. Make sure you only take advice from people who are in the arena with you.

Casting Calls

Now that you've assessed the cast and assigned them roles in your life, it's time to create intentionality. Life gets busy, and months

Supporting Cast

can go when you haven't spoken to your winter friends. Your other characters need time with their category friends. You're feeling a bit lost and need time with a coach. You hit a wall, and all of sudden you realize you lost your pacers.

Go through the eight layers of influence and think through the people you've cast in those roles. Let's ensure we create space to nurture the relationships. I approach my yearly planning the same way I approach building a marketing calendar as a CMO. We will slice the calendar in four ways:

1. Annual
2. Quarterly
3. Monthly
4. Weekly non-negotiables

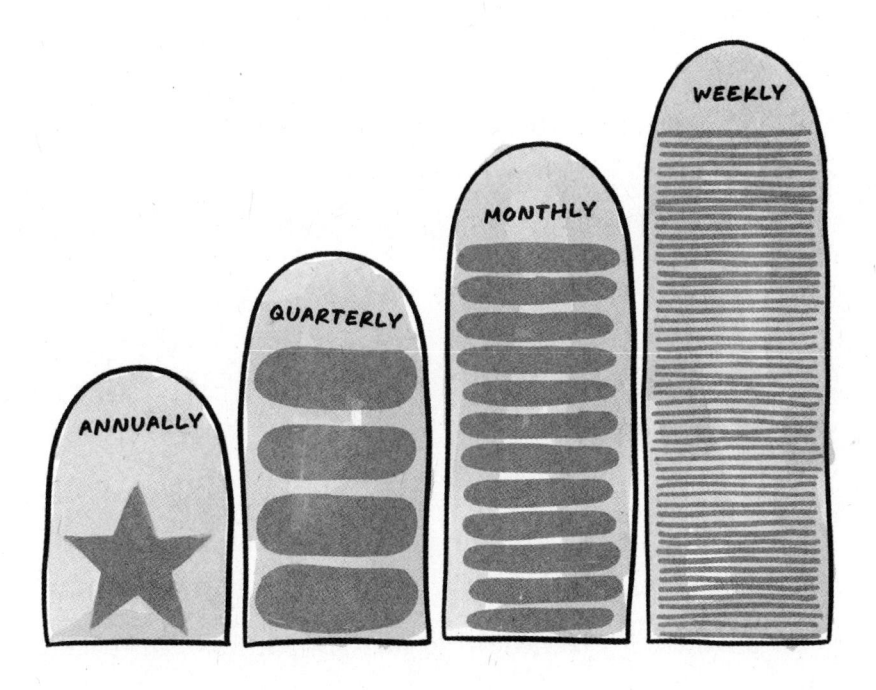

First look at the year as a full calendar year and identify your tentpole moments: things that require you to step away from your life and do something new, exciting, and different.

Examples may include:
- Vacations with winter friends and found family
- Competitions
- Conferences/trainings to meet coaches and pacers
- Sporting events

For example, my tentpoles every year include:
- Solo long weekend at the start of summer
- Family trip during summer
- Couples trip
- October birthday trip with winter friends
- One weekend with my winter + some summer friends
- Two conferences to see coaches and pacers

Next, add other annual moments to connect with those important people in your life:
- Birthdays
- Anniversaries
- Holiday gatherings

Now look at the year as four quarters and add your quarterly goals. What do you hope to do in the upcoming year? Let's break those into quarterly launches and goals. By putting each goal on a calendar, you now have something to plan toward and hold you accountable instead of punting it into the obscure "this year I want to achieve X" verbiage. The quarterly planning usually lines up with your character stovetop.

You may say things like:
- The quarter I launch something for work
- The quarter I run a half marathon
- The quarter I build community
- The quarter I move to a new apartment/home
- The quarter I prioritize dating

I have a few things that I want to happen every single quarter that I make sure to put on my calendar ahead of time, so the quarter doesn't pass by without these happening.
- Overnight staycation with my partner
- 1:1 dates with each kid
- One industry event (virtual or in person)
- One coaching dinner

Now look at the year as twelve individual months and add your monthly non-negotiables with your supporting cast. Every month it's important to create the things you know your movie needs and then schedule them into your calendar.

Here are my three monthly staples:
1. At least one dinner with winter or "spring" friend.
2. One planned, fun outing with my kids (found family)

3. One deep-dive check-in with my partner (found family)

Lastly, you will want to look at your calendar as fifty-two weeks. Every week has a rhythm. Without planning ahead, it can become easy to let it just slip by.

Here are my non-negotiables in a week with regards to my supporting cast:

- **Kids:** Three family dinners together
- **Partner:** One date night
- **Winter friends:** One call a week to a friend in my winter friend list

Don't let life just pass you by with a series of "we should catch up soon." You are writing the script. You are producing the movie. If you start to feel lonely, take control of your calendar and use this planning process to book time with people in your various circles of influence.

Chapter 13

Going Off Script

Y ou have the power to find things when you lose them. You also have the power to change the set design for your characters. If you don't like how something looks or feels, change it. As we've discussed several times throughout this book, the set was designed by another group of people with ideas for your movie loooooong before you were cast as the main characters, director, and writer.

Every rule in this life was created by another human playing in their own multiverse with their own goals and rules. And most are BS. (And many were created by a white man with a stay-at-home wife and a financial safety net.) The quicker you realize it was all made up somewhere along the way, the quicker you start to calibrate your BS radar...and let your characters go off script.

Your time is limited, so don't waste it living someone else's life. Don't be trapped by dogma—which is living with the results of other people's thinking. Don't let the noise of others' opinions drown out your own inner voice. And most importantly, have the courage to follow your heart and intuition.

—Steve Jobs

For each character within you to exist and succeed (in the storylines and goals we outlined in previous chapters), you must begin questioning and transcending the rules that have been laid before you. This is not an anarchist cry for retaliation, but rather permission to look more closely at "why" something exists in its current format and to become more acutely aware when your BS radar goes off so you can go off script.

Meet Your Heroes

Going off script requires another look at impostor syndrome and limiting beliefs. The cure for impostor syndrome is proximity to those you look up to and admire. This proximity demystifies the stories we are telling ourselves and brings more facts to the surface. Like a Paul Signac pointillism painting, the farther away you are, the more beautiful, cohesive, and clear the picture looks. But the closer you move to the painting, the more you see the small dots of colors and the more chaotic it begins to appear.

I think the person who said, "Don't meet your heroes," was

someone's hero. They didn't want people to see their tiny dots of humanness that inevitably shine through with proximity and exposure. My first job out of college was running the Ernst & Young Entrepreneur of the Year program, where I got to spend time with founders of America's fastest-growing companies. My second job, shortly after I moved to NYC, was planning NBA, NFL, NASCAR, and celebrity weddings. You have to remember, I came from a rural town in central Illinois and had never been on an airplane until I was sixteen, so seeing and meeting these people was a bit of a shock...until it wasn't. Repeated exposure helped me to analyze and understand the biggest lesson of my life...

People Are Just People

The human experience guarantees headwinds, insecurity, and comparison traps no matter your pedigree, bank account, or LinkedIn profile. Every adult was once a child seeking attention, validation, and love from their parents. Every adult has their own emotional bus with past versions of themselves attempting to drive them to spiral city. Every adult has a group of people they admire and want to emulate. Every adult wants to look better, achieve more, and be seen as something they feel they are not. And every time I find myself assuming, albeit self-hatingly, that a person in my presence has it all figured out, I get closer. My goal is always to disarm them like a bomb so I can start to see the human behind the title or status, peeling back the layers of defenses until I get to something that feels raw and real.

Going Off Script Requires Reading People

Connecting to someone is knowing someone, even if it's perceived knowledge and not reality. The easiest way to take down someone's guard is to find a connection point. A lot of my "off script" time happened when I connected to people more deeply than the script called for. Start working for this person? Go deeper. They later recommended me to a divorce attorney. Make a friend on Twitter? Go deeper. They later introduced me to my book agent. Go to a fitness class? Go deeper. The teacher later became my friend and trainer. Met a person at a tech networking event? Go deeper. They later introduced me to my therapist. Saw a person sitting on the park bench with a cute dog that you had to pet? Go deeper. They later became my husband.

The common propensity for people to be drawn to those similar to themselves is known as the "similarity-attraction effect." Meeting people who share our attitudes and values makes us feel more confident in our own view of the world. When you initially meet someone, if you can find the connection point quickly, it increases the perceived similarity: They assume there must be way more in common. Your CEO character does this in networking, your Socialite does it in social situations, and your Partner character does it in dating, so understanding this will allow you to get closer to those you admire. Understanding this concept will also simultaneously help you avoid a toxic situationship or friendship because the similarity-attraction effect is leading you to believe you met your soulmate or BFF just because you both like the same music or love the same TV shows. Vulnerability and out-loudness are key parts of going off script. You can't go deeper with someone unless you share what you want and need. Sharing that I was going through a divorce led my colleague to talk about theirs and recommend an attorney. Telling my friend over coffee that I was thinking of writing a book led me to getting a meeting with my agent. Asking the fitness instructor in NYC if he would do Zoom private training led to being his first private client. To find connection points, you must be vulnerable and share your goals out loud. No one can read your mind. The movie of your life doesn't have subtitles.

The Three Qualities of Successful People

Studying the most "successful people" in my career allowed me to see a pattern. Despite what your TikTok or Twitter feeds may lead you to believe, the most successful people don't all get up at 5:00 a.m. Some stay up late. The most successful women aren't all neglecting their kids. Some are quite involved mothers. The most successful people aren't working seventy-hour weeks. Some have a lot of free time. These are just more of the BS narratives we are told to get us to conform to a certain lifestyle, like a '90s commercial jingle: "Grind. Neglect. Push. The award-winning secret to success. Get yours now." And my characters are not buying it.

What I *have* found is that the most successful people (as defined by career and financial success) in the world all share three qualities.

1. They feel there is something greater for them.
2. They believe they can achieve it.

3. They fear they won't live up to their potential or will be "found out" as an impostor.

These qualities are likely ones you resonate with. I do as well. I believe I am meant to do big things with my life and believe I can achieve them. But there is an undercurrent of fear, constantly reminding me of where I come from and how different I look from others who have achieved financial and career success before me. These are the messy dots of someone's humanness that, from far away, come together to form a beautiful picture and story.

When you get closer to someone, you will likely see that they have achieved success in some of their characters but other characters are a huge mess. Our society has placed so much weight on the scale of financial and career success. TechCrunch is infamous for headlines of big fundraises and valuation numbers, but less headlines of bootstrapped, profitable companies. What is seen as sexy isn't actually putting money in anyone's pockets. We've been sold a mirage of success that feeds egos, not mouths. I wish there was a podcast that talked to the partners and children of the most successful-on-paper founders and execs. We will likely find that as they got closer and closer to monetary success, they grew further and further from their hobbies, passion, and relationships. According to Morgan Housel, partner at Collaborative Fund and author of the book *The Psychology of Money*, there are thirteen divorces among the ten richest men in the world. Seven of the top ten have been divorced at least once. The new definition of success, the one we are talking about in this book, is about feeling you are meant for something greater, believing you can achieve it, being nervous that you won't live up to your potential, and understanding you have different characters with different goals and measurements of success. We are creating space for each of them to move to the next level of the game of life. You are creating a painting of your life that looks a little less pointillism and a little more realism.

Putting the BS in Bias

Once you understand and internalize that people are just people chasing this moving target of "more," it's time for lesson #2 in going off script: **They are making it up as they go along.** Ninety-nine percent of business case studies and podcasts will lead you to believe the successful founder and CEO had this magic map they followed perfectly, picking up piles of gold coins at every red X along the way. And if you follow the same map, you too will acquire piles of gold coins. Every parent of a thirty-year-old talks blissfully and whimsically about the toddler days, making it sound like they had some step-by-step IKEA guide they followed to be the perfect parent. Every happily married person is ready to give their single friends advice on how to find the perfect partner. It's all BS. I bet if we got closer, we'd learn: Those founders almost shut down their company at some point. Those parents had many nights where they cried and had no clue what they were doing. Those married people stumbled through heartbreak and loneliness while dating and had times in their marriage where they had to really put in the work when times got tough. When everyone is in the mud, they're all getting dirty and frustrated and wondering how the hell they will ever get clean.

Everyone is a genius in a bull market.

This common financial phrase reminds us that when things are good, most people fail to separate their skill at the task from the outcomes. Just because they achieved the result you want doesn't mean they were an expert at the skills needed for you to achieve the same thing. In short, just because it happened doesn't mean they were good at it. Let's look at the common biases around us influencing the advice we receive and the script we were given.

Selection bias is most commonly seen when asking someone for a recommendation. They are biased to recommend or cheer for the thing they chose. Because if you choose it, it further validates their knowledge and expertise. Try this on your friends or social media audience. Put out a poll for the best places to live and see just how many say the city they currently live in. You choosing that will help validate their choices and confirm their expertise.

Hindsight bias, also known as the "I-knew-it-all-along" effect, is the inclination to perceive events as more predictable after they have occurred. Most people ascribe more inevitability to an event than there actually was. When going off script, assure your inner CEO that most people would never have been able to predict that outcome because they couldn't predict the macro landscape, team, or timing. When going off script, assure your inner Goddess or Partner that you need two things: "the right person, right time," when it comes to dating with intention. And no amount of dating advice can ever predict when you will meet someone who is ready and able to jump into a relationship.

Bandwagon bias is the strong tendency to speak, act, or believe things simply because everyone else is doing it—even if those things don't feel right for us. Evolution brought us from primates to social creatures that survived by sticking together. We may not be mindless monkeys anymore, but it still feels uncomfortable to go against the groupthink around us. Going off script means you allow your characters to zoom out and look around at the masses. And if you feel uncomfortable but still find yourself wanting to do something a little different? Celebrate it! You are jumping off the overcrowded bandwagon. I remember having a long talk with my therapist about this when I met my partner at the age of thirty-seven. I had already done the big wedding when I was twenty-one and remember it consuming all my thoughts and energy. I wanted it to be perfect. The irony was I spent more time thinking about flowers and chocolate fountains than the marriage itself. My therapist reminded me that there are no rules to follow. I can create whatever second wedding I want. I can go big or small. The wonderful thing about getting older is that the bandwagon gets less and less comfortable and you are ready to drive your own vehicle down whatever path you want. Allow your characters to jump off the bandwagon and see what actually works for their goals.

Lastly, ever notice that something you just learned or thought of seems to pop up everywhere around you? When you are thinking about buying a new white car, all of a sudden everyone has a white car. How have I never noticed how many white cars are on the road? Or when you see 11:11 on the clock almost every day (for me it's 10:23, and I have no clue why). This is called the *Baader-Meinhof phenomenon* (also called the "frequency illusion"), which states that an increased awareness of something creates the illusion that it is appearing more often.

In summary, there are four biases you must be aware of when helping your characters go off script:

1. Selection bias
2. Hindsight bias
3. Bandwagon bias
4. Frequency illusion

The more you are aware of the biases around you, the more equipped you are to navigate the world for your characters, and the more discretion you will use in allowing others to give advice or alter the script. The trick for navigating all of these biases is to gather enough information to form your own opinion. See which pieces of advice give you energy and which give you pause. Because indecision is an awful mud to get stuck in.

The Seven Common Types of BS We Live In

As you become more aware of the BS set design our characters are being thrust into, you will also become more aware of how many people fall into a binary thinking framework. Binary thinking is a cognitive framework that simplifies complex situations or concepts by reducing them to only two opposing categories or perspectives, often resulting in dualistic thinking or polarization. Something is simplified as either good or bad, true or false, in a category or not. But life most often exists in the gray, and your characters will thrive when you start building more permission to live in the gray area of their script.

When I first took over brand marketing at The Knot, the leading brand and magazine in weddings, I studied the next generation of people getting married. I asked people in their twenties to come in and answer questions about their future wedding. The more I spoke to them, the more I realized that rules and traditions were mostly seen as suggestions, mere guidelines for them to put their own personal spin on. Cake cuttings were being replaced with cheese cuttings. Flower girls were replaced with flower men. Big ceremonies were replaced with private moments followed by a celebration. With this knowledge, we repositioned the brand payoff to be "make tradition" and rewrote any article that came from an editor. We took every "How to do X" with more choose-your-own-adventure "20 Ideas for X." Twenty new ideas to walk down the aisle. Twenty new ideas to cut the cake. Weddings were no longer a formulaic, one-size-fits-all script to follow. And neither is the movie of your life. The irony that I led this brand repositioning and *still* needed to be reminded of this from my therapist when I started thinking about a second wedding is not lost on me.

Nuance has been lost alongside the art of conversation on social media. I could tweet out "The weather is so beautiful today!" and

I will have trolls yell at me about how I'm not acknowledging global warming or I'm diminishing someone's storm experience in another part of the world. As you read through the most common BS we exist within, I ask that you start pumping nuance back into the world like the oxygen all our characters need to breathe.

BS #1: Working More = Success

Movement is not the same as progress. I've watched many people work hours upon hours and not get to where they want to go. Output doesn't equal outcomes.

Back in 2019, pre-COVID, Caregiver Amanda wanted to leave work at 4:00 p.m. After a thirty-minute subway commute, she knew she'd only have two hours with her babies before the warm little sleep sacks would be set inside a crib for the night. (Yes, my babies went to bed at 6:30). I was already separated, so I didn't get to see my babies every night, which was (and still is) a struggle for me.

So, I blocked my calendar from 4:00 to 6:00 p.m. every day I had the kids, got my work done, and headed out. Two months into this, my manager called me in for a 1:1. "People are talking. They think you aren't working as hard as them because you leave at 4:00 p.m. and it's not seen as fair." *Fair?* I thought to myself. The only thing not fair about this scenario is the idea that I wouldn't see my babies because Sara in Editorial wanted me to sit and answer emails from a desk instead of my phone.

"Am I hitting my goals and meeting expectations in my role?" I asked politely. "If I am, it is important to me to have this limited time with my children." After a discussion about supporting women and working mothers, I used this opportunity to share thoughts about how a more flexible work environment would help people feel more agency in their jobs and would likely lead to greater retention. My manager agreed and officially approved my schedule. Sara went on to talk about me behind my back, my manager continued to have my back, and I went on to cuddle my babies and answer emails from the subway. My learning: proactive conversations are the key to breaking through the BS.

The corporate world is full of BS rules that were handed to us, not created with us. If you find yourself navigating one of these BS moments, you have two paths: you can use it as a catalyst for change in the organization or use it as a signal that your values no longer align with the company's. I also see a future where more and more roles are fractional and people have multiple income streams, but that's a different topic for a different book.

Working more does not equal more success. It usually means more filler activities. When I was at work, I was laser-focused on the projects and goals. When I was training to be an ACE-certified fitness trainer, I had a coach tell me that no one should have to be at the gym for more than fifty minutes. With good programming, you can build strength, cardiovascular endurance, and mobility in under an hour. Most people who spend two-plus hours at the gym spend at least thirty minutes looking at themselves in the mirror or walking back and forth to a water fountain.

More time does not equal more success. Optimization and a focus on outcomes does.

BS #2: Relationships Are Hard

Don't take advice from someone you wouldn't want to switch places with. When I first told a lot of my extended family I was getting a divorce, I heard, "Marriage is supposed to be hard" from several people. And yes, their marriages did look hard. For many years I believed this was the norm because I didn't see a lot of people putting in the proactive work to make something easy. Running a marathon without any training is a lot harder than running one when you've diligently prepared and put in the miles. When I was dating post-divorce, I experienced many relationships that rode the volatility roller coaster: intense passion followed by intense anxiety and avoidance.

Then I met my current partner and realized my Partner character had been living off a script that was full of BS. *All* relationships have ups and downs. Life is hard, and doing life with other people is hard. But a relationship rooted in respect, growth, kindness, and proactive work will always lead to faster repair cycles when you experience a rupture. Everyone fights, but the best couples figure out how to fight fairly, kindly, and with the goal of resolution. Relationships are complicated, but they don't have to be hard.

BS #3: Traditions = To-Dos

Similar to the wedding industry, something seen as traditional in your family or culture or by society should be looked at as a starting point, not a prescription. You can honor your family and culture in your own ways. Traditions feel like little loopholes that are immune to time and change and inherently carry the weight of obligation and guilt. Our characters are not allowing others to introduce guilt into their script.

Think of the "traditions" that inspired the phrases "It's always been this way," "That's just how it is," and "Boys will be boys." If we never stopped to challenge traditions, then the world would never change for the better and never become safer.

My Partner character struggled with challenging traditions in my twenties. I saw my mom take on the "traditional" roles of a wife: the cooking, cleaning, and child-rearing (can we all agree that's such a weird phrase?). But as I became a wife myself, I found myself struggling to take on all of those while also now taking on the role of my father: the breadwinner and weekend fun parent. So, I bucked tradition and started thinking like a "1950s dad." I'm sure there were many amazing dads in the 1950s, but when I was getting a divorce, my lawyer called it the "1950s dad schedule": dads show up one night a week and every other weekend. They weren't classroom parents. They weren't aware of every homework assignment, playdate, or after-school activity. I want to acknowledge that there are many amazing men out there changing these stereotypes and taking on the roles that work best for the family dynamic and relationship they are in, my current partner included. He does the majority of the cleaning up, and we share the cooking duties. He shuts down his computer to help the kids with homework if I need to keep working. But before meeting him, I had to go off script. My mom/Caregiver character had to think like a 1950s dad. I wasn't going to volunteer for every classroom activity. I wasn't going to have the perfect lunch packed every day. I was going to forgo a clean house for a fun weekend. This was difficult at first. It felt like I was slacking in my "traditional" gender norm and expectations of what a "good mom" looked like. Redefining what a good mom looked like for me and my children and not what it looked like for others helped me to not only survive my six years as a single mom but also enjoy the moments I had with my kids.

Going off script will mean challenging what "traditions" you've been exposed to by society, culture, or family and deciding what parts honor your characters and what parts force your characters into a script they don't want to act out. Traditions are suggestions, not directions.

BS #4: Positions of Power = Respect

Hierarchy does not deem respect. Respect begets respect. I will respect a person if they display the ability to also respect others, no matter their position. Growing up with a dad who was a plumber/electrician, I learned quickly how people could treat him. When we'd go to the "fancy" part of Peoria, Illinois, I'd watch some people ask him to use the back door, not offer him any water when he was working for hours in a crawl space, and just not see him as a full human. My grandpa figure growing up was also my elementary school janitor. I remember on "bring-your-grandparent-to-school day" having Don pause his shift to come sit with me only to get made fun of by kids in my class. "Your grandpa cleans the toilets!" "Your grandpa cleans up vomit!" Kids are cruel. But both of these experiences as a child taught me that power does not warrant respect. Humanness does. Be careful who you allow your characters to put on pedestals until you get closer to their humanness dots. Then decide if that's a painting you want to bring into your home.

BS #5: There Is a "Right Way" to Do This

We've all seen it: "Five Steps to Better Parenting, Relationships, Career Satisfaction, Skin, Workout." Our entire social feed and algorithms lead us to believe someone out there has figured out the path to success. But no one has the exact same situation as you. Your childhood. Your skills. Your trauma. Your timing. Your goals. Your DNA. Whenever you feel stuck in making a decision for a character on how to achieve their goal, remember there is no right or wrong decision. You gather enough data to make the most informed decision you can by a deadline you choose. Then you make that decision. The rest of the work and energy is spent making it the right one for you. Not sure whether to move to a new place, leave a company, or end a relationship or friendship? Set a timeline to make the decision, gather as much information as you can, make the decision, and then spend all your energy confirming it was the best one for you. Keep your characters looking forward. There is no right way; there is your way.

BS #6: There Is a Deadline

Society leads women to believe we walk off a cliff at age thirty. That we have to have it all figured out by the end of our third decade on this earth.

Netflix was created by Reed Hastings when he was forty-two. Vera Wang started her business at age forty after two incredible careers at Condé Nast and Ralph Lauren. Kerry Washington talks openly about how she feels her career is just getting started in her forties. Before Toni Morrison became a Nobel and Pulitzer Prize–winning novelist, she was a single mom working as an editor for Random House. Morrison's own first novel, *The Bluest Eye*, didn't get published until the author was forty years old. Julia Child didn't even learn to cook until she was thirty-six.

Stop treating your life like there is a plank walk at your next birthday milestone. When you treat life like a check-the-box, you will seek the most accessible thing to sufficiently fulfill the checkbox instead of questioning if that is the right outcome you want. I did this. I thought I needed the husband, the career, and the kids by thirty. So, I got them. But in filling out the checkboxes, I forget to question if those were the right boxes. **Question the box.**

I found my life partner and best friend in my late thirties.

I started two companies in my thirties.

I left my career at thirty-seven to start a new career.

I'm in my forties and publishing my first book.

You own your timeline.

BS #7: Be a "Good Girl"

Good-girl narratives keep women in subservient positions. Period. Self-care for good girls is baths and manis and pedis. It's seen as not polite or "good" to want money, power, or fame. Yet men can prescribe themselves a dose of all of it without anyone batting an eye. Good-girl brainwashing is to care for ourselves in soft ways. We can empower and care for ourselves by wanting hard things, difficult goals that reward us in joyful ways. You may not have heard the term "good-girl brainwashing" before, but you can probably decipher what it means—and you may even relate to the concept.

The phrase was coined by my friend and former Olympic gymnast Lisa Carmen Wang, the founder and CEO of Bad Bitch Empire and author of *The Bad Bitch Bible*. Lisa defines good-girl brainwashing as "a set of subconscious messages that are perpetuated by society and media that train women to stay silent, small, and subordinate." These messages encourage certain traits and behaviors and discourage others. "Good-girl habits are things that may have served us early on as girls...obedience, politeness, self-effacing modesty, perfectionism, and people-pleasing." By releasing your characters of these habits and narratives, you allow them to seek out scenarios, environments, identities, and experiences that spark energy, curiosity, and joy. If you are feeling like your characters are stuck, ask yourself if they've been brainwashed to stay a "good girl." What would it look like to release yourself of those narratives?

When You Play with BS, People Start to Stink

When you start questioning things that have never been questioned, people get agitated. They start "should-ing" all over you. "You should be doing this. You should have achieved this by now. You should be friends with these kinds of people. You should date these kinds of people. You should look like this." Questioning norms requires a should-shield.

When you start to feel your choices are activating and agitating someone, grab your should-shield. Remember that your characters are reading off their own script, not someone else's. This shield will allow you to stand more freely in what you believe is right for your characters. In order to do things differently, you have to be willing and able to be different and march to the beat of your own drum.

Know your values.

Make your decisions.

Go off script.

Grab your shield.

Watch out for the shoulds.

Character Agency

Once upon a time, an old scholar was asked to wean a boy from his bad habits. The wise old man took the child for a walk through a garden. As they approached a vegetable patch, he asked the boy to pull out a tiny plant growing there. The boy held the plant between his fingers and easily pulled it out. The old man then asked the boy to pull out a slightly larger plant. The child pulled hard, and the plant came out, roots and all. Then the wise old man pointed to a bush and asked the youth to pull it out of the ground. The boy pulled and pulled using all his strength and finally yanked it from the ground. The old man then pointed to a tree and asked the young boy to bring it to him. The boy grasped the trunk and tried with all his might to remove it. But the tree would not budge. "I can't do it. It is impossible," said the boy, huffing and puffing from the effort. The wise old man said, "So it is with bad habits and choices and taking responsibility for your actions. When habits are initially formed, it is easy to stop them from growing, but when they become entrenched, they are harder to uproot." The boy learned a valuable lesson from the old man: Take responsibility for your bad habits and choices while you have control over them before they start to control you.

This last section is for all the people-pleasers and those shrinking to fit in the space others have created for them. My script ultimately changed when I stopped expecting anyone to fix something, change my circumstances, or advocate for me. We are in charge of our habits, choices, and decisions. We are the writers of our script. Life is happening for us, not to us.

Life is happening for us, not to us.

"Agency" is a word that gets thrown around a lot in business and coaching. Agency is the sense of control that you feel in your life, your capacity to influence your own thoughts and behaviors, and having faith in your ability to handle a wide range of tasks and situations. Your sense of agency helps you to be psychologically stable yet flexible in the face of conflict or change. We've spent a lot of time preparing characters to set and achieve their goals within the movie of your life, but character development is also about preparing them for the external world—ensuring your characters feel agency over their storylines and plots.

In my first job out of college, my boss sat me down and told me a harsh fact: no one is ever going to look out for my career—that's my job. "My work will speak for itself." "If I just work harder, they will notice me." That's more BS. No one can read your mind, and no one can see all the work you are doing. I created several tools in my career and personal life to advance me and keep me in the spotlight and set boundaries. The first is called "Managing Up Mondays," where I send an email every Monday to the people who are in charge of my fate within my company or career: my boss, other leaders impacted by my work, mentors, etc. Managers only see a fraction of your work due to the breadth they cover. This is a great way to prevent "seagull management," where someone gets anxious because they feel out of the loop and swoops in, causing chaos. Steal my format below:

Hey (Manager)!

Wanted to start a weekly "what's on my plate" email to help with three things.

1. Give line of sight into my priorities.
2. Get ahead of misalignment/strategy shifts.
3. Share any roadblocks or answers I may need from you to move faster.

I also wanted to highlight a few wins from the week prior. (insert wins)

Look forward to a great week.

All the best,

Me

When you take your career into your own hands, you will notice how much "luckier" you become. The same goes for other characters. I learned in my first marriage that if I didn't set the baseline expectation for what I deserved out of the relationship, I'd get loaves of bread, then muffins, then doughnut holes, and eventually just breadcrumbs. Use this formula to share your needs and give your partner the playbook for exactly how to love and learn you as a partner:

I feel X when you do Y. In the future I need Z.

No one is going to stop you from spending more than you are making. No one is going to stop you from jumping into yet another relationship too quickly and not learning who the person is before you give your entire heart and energy to them. No one is going to put in the work to make friends for you. No one is going to stop you from eating those unhealthy meals despite you wanting to eat healthier. This is the difference between internal agency and external agency.

- **Internal agency:** You make things happen.
  - → *Look at what I can do!*
  - → *I can make things happen.*
  - → *I can determine my future.*

- **External agency:** Things happen to you.
  - → *Why bother?*
  - → *There is nothing I can do about my future.*
  - → *Why does this keep happening to me?*

Let's look at a few examples of the difference between looking at a situation through the lens of internal agency versus external agency.

Character: Partner

Agency: External	Agency: Internal
You've been casually seeing someone for a few months, and it's not progressing in the direction you want. You keep waiting for them to take the relationship to the next step. You start feeling like you will never find someone. Everyone is emotionally unavailable.	You've been casually seeing someone and are ready to take it to the next level. You ask to talk. You share that in order for you to continue investing time and energy, you need exclusivity. You share that you require more emotional safety at this stage of the relationship and ask if that is something the person can give you. If not, you are prepared to walk away and find someone who is.

Character: CEO

Agency: External	Agency: Internal
You've been working hard on a project for months, giving more and more hours of your life to it as the launch approaches. It's finally time for the project to launch, and everything goes smoothly. No one says anything to you. You start to think your boss doesn't like you. Your colleagues are trying to sabotage your career. No one in this company appreciates you. There is no way you are getting a promotion because they don't even acknowledge your hard work.	You've been working hard on a project for months, giving more and more hours of your life to it as the launch approaches. As someone who takes their success into their own hands, you begin sharing a weekly update with your boss and their counterparts with the milestones and updates. You share that you will be working through the weekends to ensure the project's success. In your 1:1s, you share your goal of working toward a promotion and ask for constructive feedback on how to get there. After the launch, you share all the success metrics with the leadership team. You make it impossible to not be recognized in the next promotion cycle.

Character: Socialite

Agency: External	Agency: Internal
You've been scrolling social a lot more lately and are starting to feel like everyone has a full social life but you. You feel left out. All of a sudden, the stories start playing. "No one wants to hang with me." "I'm boring." "I struggle to make friends." "I'm not lovable."	You've been scrolling social media and see your friends doing a lot of cool things. You say, "That looks like fun!" and text a few friends, asking what's happening next weekend. You make plans. You get excited.

The script for the movie of your life is exactly that. **Your** script. No one else is coming to rewrite it, and you can either choose to keep getting stuck in the bias and BS rules that were given to us or break your characters free and start living in the gray, the beautiful and undefined middle. This is the final step in character theory. Giving your characters the freedom to develop beyond what you can see and to realize everyone else's beautiful picture of their life is actually just a bunch of messy dots that happen to look pretty good from far away. Character theory allows you to stop focusing on the picture you want to portray to the outside world and take agency over each dot and decision that is being added to the canvas. What a beautiful picture you are creating, messy dots and all.

Conclusion:

Seven Steps to Master the Middle

Growing up on a farm, I intensely desired to leave the vast cornfields behind to live in a big city. So after college among the farmlands of Illinois, I moved to Chicago, then New York City, and, eventually, Miami. Twenty years later I find myself daydreaming of owning a lot of land with a chicken coop (with those super-fluffy white chickens) and Nigerian dwarf goats with my calendar as free as the chickens themselves. The reality is, I know that would be a welcome change to my busy life, but within months or possibly even weeks, I'd be filling my days with projects to optimize the farm life or creating "how to" content while I stoke the sparks of ambition once again. This is what an entire generation of women feels today. The push to have more, do more, and be more, with a whiplashed, dichotomous desire to soften and to pull back, cautiously aware that our ambition will never really go away. We've found ourselves in the messy middle, smack between the Girlboss–Lazy Girl Venn diagram. For years I've watched friends, colleagues, and clients vacillate between hardening enough to achieve their career goals and break glass ceilings and softening enough to find love, be present with their friends and family, and frolic around the world. It was an **OR** statement. If you are **this**, you cannot be **that**. Pick a lane and brand your entire life and social media feed around it. But life is about the **ANDs**. To be hard and soft. To be sexual and maternal. To crave solitude and a vibrant community of people to do life with. This book is the antidote to the binary prescriptions society would like us to follow. We are breaking free of the paint-by-number scripts that have been given to us by generations before us and swapping them for a script that is created by us, for us.

So many people talk about being our "authentic self," showing up exactly as we are in every scenario. Authenticity has felt like a buzzword designated for my marketing presentations and not something actually achievable in my life. For many years, I couldn't understand if that was because I didn't know who I was or something bigger. **Turns out it was both.** I didn't know *all* of myself. I needed to understand the ten distinct selves within me. It's not possible to be each of my ten characters, in their authentic selves, at the same time. That's why I created the character theory multiverse to learn how to ebb and flow between these characters both in the days and then the years of our lives. **Authenticity and balance**

Seven Steps to Master the Middle

happen in the macro, not the micro. Attempting to get CEO Amanda and Caregiver Amanda to show up with continuity and authenticity in the same moment was not feasible, and it's what led me to feel guilty, shamed, out of alignment, and disconnected. Character theory is crucial to our ability to understand ourselves, *all* of ourselves. If a woman from the 1930s time traveled to our current lives, she'd be shocked and overwhelmed at how many choices women have in front of them. And it is my belief that if someone from the 3030s could travel back in time to our present day, they'd be shocked and overwhelmed at how few systems and frameworks were created to support women in navigating this insurmountable number of choices. And that's what led me to writing this book.

One of my favorite phrases I use in coaching is "the key to juggling is knowing which balls are glass and which are rubber." Glass balls are likely to shatter if dropped, while rubber balls can usually be recovered easily. You are juggling a lot right now, and the following synthesized seven steps of character theory will help you rethink how you juggle and maybe give you permission to set a few of the balls down entirely and avoid the painful byproducts of toxic grit. You've learned a lot over the last thirteen chapters, and the following is the TL;DR of the book.

Step 1: Your Perfect Day

It all starts with the end. You have to know where you are going before you attempt to go faster or add more people to the car. The perfect day exercise illuminates which characters are ready for more screen time in your life and if your daily actions are in alignment with the end destination. This exercise also reminds you of your agency in life. You get to decide how much attention you give to the various characters of your life. No one else gets to decide that for you. Not society. Not your culture. Not your family. You. This is your multiverse.

- **Reminder:** Destination first, route second.

Step 2: Set the Plot

Now that you know which characters are taking up some more screen time based on your perfect day, it's time to arrange them on your stovetop for the next month and set some goals. The reason we, as women, are facing extreme burnout is no one has given us permission to say "not right now" or "not as much right now." Setting the plot determines who is getting more time and who is getting less, guilt-free.

- **Reminder:** Plot = Vision + Season + Values + Goals

Step 3: Rightsize Your Characters

Some characters start taking up more space than they need, and it's important to rightsize the characters before they become toxic. We looked at the Big 3 characters who tend to take over someone's entire movie script and learned how to take back your 5 to 9 for the other supporting characters in your season of life. Mastering the middle is making sure one character doesn't get left on the front burner too long and starts to burn(out).

- **Reminder:** Give 100 percent of your focus a fraction of the time.

Step 4: Honor the Transition

As you navigate the multiverse, the three key success levers are prioritization (know which character needs your focus and presence in this moment), boundaries, and the ART of transition. Being aware that it is not a simple task to bounce from character to character, so we need to create space for the transition so we can show up in those characters fully...for ourselves and for those around us.

- **Reminder:** Juggling characters is an ART (Assess > Routine > Transition)

Step 5: Plan a Spin Cycle

Life will inevitably get intense. Even with the intentional planning, goal setting, and rightsizing of your characters, you will find yourself pushing hard and getting dangerously close to your limits. Before you hit those limits, you will proactively plan a spin cycle. These spin cycles may take place throughout a day, a week, or even a larger season of life after a major event. The average human lifespan is terrifyingly short, and if we keep our heads down too long, we may miss it. Spin cycles are proactive moments in our day to take in all that is happening around us. Every character will be able to climb multiple mountains with time in the valleys between. Spin cycles will be your opportunity to come up for air, see where you are, and make sure you are using your time on this earth how you want.

- **Reminder:** When you've only been driving at 100 miles per hour, even the speed limit will feel slow.

Step 6: Assess Your Supporting Cast

Much advice on success and happiness is dependent on the people you surround yourself with. Show me a person's circle, and I'll tell you if they will be successful or not. When you are growing, you are also outgrowing, and assessing your circles of influence is important to ensure your characters can continue developing in the way you've outlined in the script for your life. Your CEO can't keep growing if your toxic boss won't allow you to. Your Partner can't keep growing if you stay in situationships with emotionally unavailable people. Your Socialite can't keep growing if you don't audit the health of the relationships and understand who is a summer versus a winter friend and allocate your time accordingly. We are in control of our movie, casting included. Stop allowing others to take up space and energy without furthering the plotline in the direction you've deemed important.

- **Reminder:** To some people you are a mirror, and to others you are a telescope.

Step 7: Own Your Script

Perhaps the most recurring theme of this book and the first law of character theory: You write the script. Life is not happening to us; it's happening because of us. The faster your characters adopt an internal locus of control and start moving through their days with agency and empowerment, the faster you will see doors open, relationships blossom, creativity sparked, and newfound momentum in your life. A perk of coaching people is pattern recognition. When someone keeps finding themselves in similar situations over and over again, it's a sign of a recurring pattern they have weaved for their life. That web will catch their characters over and over again until they realize they have the power to tear it down and create new responses and patterns. You own the script. You own the boundaries. You own the outcomes.

- **Reminder:** A new set can't change a bad actor. But a director can change both.

Take a moment to pause here and imagine you have taken everything in this book and implemented it into your life. You've carefully separated the parts of yourself that have been competing and stumbling over one another for years, and now, instead, intentionally transition between them and honor their various needs and goals. You no longer have a one-dimensional life but rather live in the multiverse of multiple storylines for each of your characters, who all make up the movie of your life. You've finally thrown balance out the window and embraced intentional imbalance. You no longer subscribe to hustle culture and toxic grit. How would that feel? What would that look like? It looks a lot like the beginning of having it all while actually loving what you have.

A Letter to the Reader

Dear Reader,

I'm so thankful for you.

I wrote this book as an antidote to hustle culture and the binary pendulums we, as women, face every day. I wrote this book for my daughters, to help them learn the things I wish I'd known sooner. Life is full of contradictions. To be hard and soft. To be assertive and receptive. To be consistent and free-spirited. When the world is pushing for us to be "in alignment," the happiest people I know have created separation to allow for the contradictions of life, which is what led me to create character theory: the antidote to hustle culture and toxic grit.

I thought of my daughters when creating the ten unique characters that every woman has within her—already foreshadowing the tug-of-war they will face, even at a young age. To go to college or take a gap year? To push their career forward or soak up their twenties? To date casually or go all-in on one person? Using the frameworks in this book, I hope all of you can now create intentionality around which characters are getting more space in a season of life and which are getting less, without losing any characters along the way.

Guilt is a manipulative emotion and one that seems to be injected into every societally approved standard thrown our way. But this book gives you a new guilt-free standard: The first law of character theory, **you write the script.** You are creating and directing the cast, plotlines, and scene changes. You are the only person writing and living your script; thus, no one else can shame you for the choices you make.

To change, we must become aware. Throughout this book, we paused often to look more closely at your characters' programming and identified some necessary software updates. Your characters can now be in the driver's seat, not sitting back allowing others' realities to dictate the direction of your life. No matter where you are in the cycle of ambition, I hope you take away from this book that it's OK (and necessary) to pause and look around. To stop and ask yourself if the path you are on is, in fact, getting you closer to your perfect day.

Your movie is going to happen whether you take over the script or not. Everything will change when you realize life isn't happening to you; it's unfolding based on your decisions. Step into your agency. Cast your characters. Go after the life you want even if it means going off script.

I can't wait to watch your movie unfold and your characters step into the spotlight.

Love,

Amanda Hoelz

Acknowledgments

The most incredible part of the human experience is being able to accomplish great things together. Writing this book was a test for many of my characters. I had to place my CEO on the front burner for many months, and I'm incredibly grateful for the understanding and support of my friends and family.

First of all, this book wouldn't be in your hands without my friend and bestselling author Amy Shoenthal, who believed in my proposal and graciously introduced me to her agent, Courtney Paganelli from Levine | Greenberg | Rostan Literary Agency. Courtney spent months working with me to refine my idea on how to help women avoid burnout and helped me articulate it into character theory. I'm so thankful for her holding my hand and calming my nerves whenever my characters were lacking confidence.

A huge thank you to another woman juggling multiple characters in her life, my incredible editor Meg Gibbons at Sourcebooks, a publisher focused on books that will change lives, and that is exactly what we set out to do together. We gave ourselves permission to think bigger and create a book that will give women a guide to live a life that works for them, not anyone else.

Thanks to the thousands of women I've met, managed, mentored, and traded DMs with throughout the past two decades. You've been on this journey with me through my fertility struggles, divorce, dating as a single mom, building and selling House of Wise, and now this new season of life. Every message, conversation, and interaction is woven into this book. I hope you all see yourself in it.

Thank you to my winter friends. The people who have been with me through the dark times, the wild times, and the happy/stable times. Thank you for loving each of my characters, no matter where they were in their plotline.

Thank you to my parents. I know I was not easy to raise as someone who was constantly asking "why" and pushing the boundaries of what boxes were being given to me. You both gave me the space and support to keep growing and have supported me every step of the way. I love and appreciate you both so much.

To my partner, Dan. I can't believe I found you after years of thinking my Partner character had been written off my script. You were worth the wait, and I'm so thankful for all your support, love, and reminding me to take my spin cycles. Thank you for allowing my CEO character to stay on the front burner and showing me what true partnership looks like.

Acknowledgments

And last but not least, to the people most directly affected by me placing this goal and CEO character on the front burner, thank you to my children. Hadley, Lincoln, and Greyson—you are my reason I push so hard to change the narratives of the world. I want the world to be better for each of you. You deserve it. I love you more than you will ever know.

Notes

1 "Rihanna's Tips for Confidence #shorts," E! News, August 27, 2021, YouTube Video, 0:17, https://www.youtube.com/watch?v=d3kp3eMcBco.
2 Melinda Wenner Moyer, "Your Body Knows You're Burned Out," *The New York Times*, updated June 22, 2023, https://www.nytimes.com/2022/02/15/well/live/burnout-work-stress.html.

About the Author

Amanda Goetz is a two-time founder, four-time chief marketing officer, and was a single mom to three small children before finding love again. She spent two decades building and growing consumer-facing brands before shifting to writing, teaching, and coaching ambitious working parents on how to balance success and life. She graduated summa cum laude from the University of Illinois and, after hustling the streets of New York City for over a decade, is now testing out every sunscreen in the world on her children in Miami.